HUDDY

The Official Biography of Alan Hudson

HUDDY

The Official Biography of Alan Hudson

Jason Pettigrove

St David's Press
Cardiff

Published in Wales by St. David's Press, an imprint of

Ashley Drake Publishing Ltd
PO Box 733
Cardiff
CF14 7ZY

www.st-davids-press.wales

First Impression – 2017
ISBN
Paperback: 978-1-902719-57-3
eBook: 978-1-902719-58-0

© Ashley Drake Publishing Ltd 2017
Text © Jason Pettigrove 2017

The right of Jason Pettigrove to be identified as the author of this work has been asserted in accordance with the Copyright Design and Patents Act of 1988.

All rights reserved. No part of this publication may be reproduced, stored in a retrieval system, or transmitted, in any form or by any means without the prior permission of the publishers.

Every effort has been made to contact copyright holders. However, the publishers will be glad to rectify in future editions any inadvertent omissions brought to their attention.

Ashley Drake Publishing Ltd hereby exclude all liability to the extent permitted by law for any errors or omissions in this book and for any loss, damage or expense (whether direct or indirect) suffered by a third party relying on any information contained in this book.

British Library Cataloguing-in-Publication Data.
A CIP catalogue for this book is available from the British Library.

Typeset by Replika Press Pvt Ltd, India
Printed by Akcent Media, Czech Republic

Contents

Acknowledgements   vii
Foreword by Jeff Powell   xi

1. Childhood   1
2. Chelsea   19
3. Marriage and the 'Good Life' Don't Mix   38
4. Mr Waddington   56
5. Stoke   76
6. England   94
7. Arsenal   113
8. Seattle Sounders   138
9. Chelsea and Stoke ... Again   159
10. The Accident   180
11. A Third Life   199
12. Keep Moving Forward   218

For Celine, Callum, Alice and Elliott xx

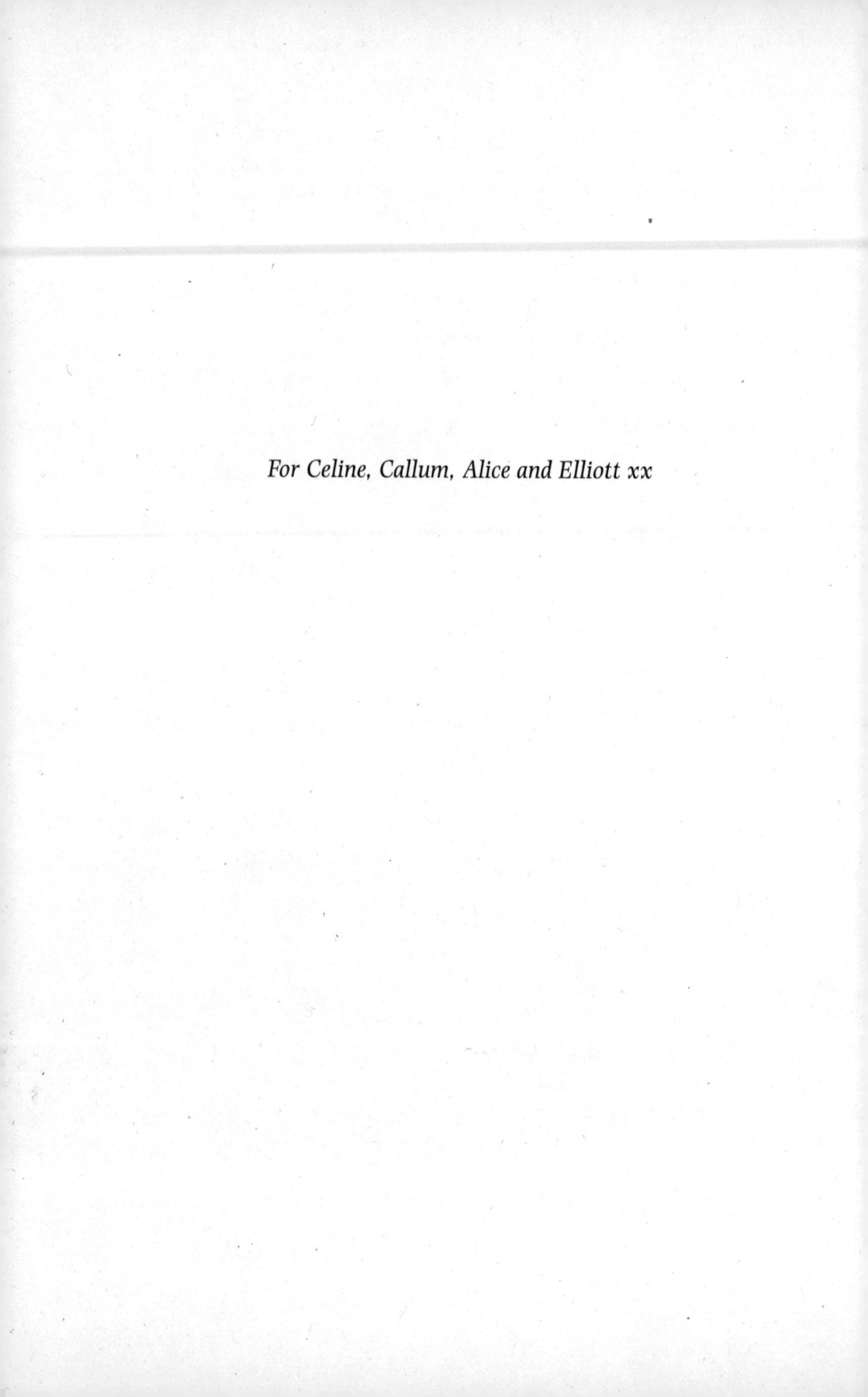

Acknowledgements

When I first started my career in journalism, it was always an aim of mine that one day I would be able to have a book published. That my dream has now been realised is down to a handful of people who I would like to sincerely thank over the course of the next few paragraphs.

I hope that those of you that think you know Alan Hudson will get to the end of this book and have changed your perceptions about him. Huddy has been exemplary in all of our dealings and what has particularly stood out for me is his insistence at not sugar-coating any part of his life story. Far too often nowadays, sports people in particular are frightened to say anything even mildly controversial, for fear of it harming their careers, popularity and earning potential.

I'd been told certain things by him before the book had even been discussed. Private matters that were not in the public domain but which I knew would be interesting and engaging for an audience. When I first floated the idea of an authorised biography with Huddy, I did so with a caveat that it needed to be an honest recollection.

His story is an incredibly interesting and multi-faceted one which hopefully comes across in the following pages, but I wasn't going to attempt to tell it if some parts were going to be held back. What that meant of course is that Huddy would have to go to places he'd not been for some time mentally, and probably thought he wouldn't need to go to again. Yet he agreed without a moment's hesitation.

To his absolute credit, he was as good as his word during the entire process and I'll be forever grateful that he let me see a side of him that not many have. Above all else, his friendship is something that I truly treasure.

So, I now had the subject matter and basis for what I wanted to write but before actually going ahead to spend time on the computer and telephone crafting the manuscript, I had to convince a publisher to commission the work.

Ashley Drake of St. David's Press was interested but given that I was a first-time author, he was out on a limb initially. My enthusiasm for the job in hand sold the pitch to him and as each chapter was finished, Ashley provided me with fantastic, to-the-point advice, and a helping hand whenever I needed it. That has been absolutely invaluable in getting the right tone throughout the book, whilst taking nothing away from the rawness of certain parts, which is, in my opinion, necessary.

It's been my pleasure to have worked with someone so helpful and knowledgeable, who has been willing to answer every question, and pick apart the tiniest detail, to ensure the end product is worthy of the subject. Thank you Ashley, here's to book number two!

As an editor myself, I understand that a second pair of eyes is essential for proof reading work. Andy Moore answered my clarion call and was excellent when providing notes on grammatical errors and structure, and also critique which, as any good writer knows, is essential. Andy did this in his spare time, and at the expense of spending those hours with his family. I cannot thank him enough.

To everyone else who has contributed in some way: to Jeff Powell for the Foreword; to Alan's family; his friends; the PFA; his old playing colleagues; and the medical staff who saved his life, you have provided the alternative voices needed to make this – I hope – a well-rounded biography. From the bottom of my heart, thank you.

I can't finish before speaking about the sacrifices my own

ACKNOWLEDGEMENTS

family have had to make in order for me to get the book completed. Although I tried to stop this project from taking over our lives, on many days that was inevitable and they suffered as a result. Despite a drain on almost every aspect of daily life for the six months it took to write the book, I hope they'll be proud of what I've achieved.

Finally to you. Thank you for purchasing this book. I very much hope that you enjoy reading it as much as I did writing it.

Jason Pettigrove
September 2017

Foreword

When Alan Hudson was mowed down by a car which mounted a pavement on a London street, the official report described it as a 'hit and run' incident. In this context the word 'hit' could have been drawn from a Mafia lexicon.

It was some weeks before the old-time maestro of Stamford Bridge could be restored to full consciousness, but from the moment he became vaguely lucid he began to voice concerns, which he has articulated to his day, that the incident was no accident and may well have been an attempt to end his life. Almost all the bones in his slender body were broken, most of his vital organs ruptured and he lost enough blood to have filled the donor bank at the hospital where a dozen surgeons – who performed more than 70 operations upon him – admitted that had needed the help of a miracle to save his life.

Since that dark day in 1997, the languid movement of one of the most elegant midfield footballers of his generation has been replaced by a hobbling defiance of the constant pain and financial privation which invade and threaten his very existence. The creative maverick of those giddy seasons in the sun with Chelsea, Stoke City and Arsenal has been displaced by the gritty fighter who claims each new year as triumph of survival.

Hudson always has been a prickly as well as an engaging companion and he still nurses a profound disbelief of the two-cap brevity of what might have been a majestic England career, as well as resentment at what he perceives as indifference by Chelsea since his trauma. That anger now serves a valuable purpose, fuelling as it does his rage against the dying of the light, without which he would have been a lost soul long ago. *Huddy*, Jason Pettigrove's well-crafted biography which Alan has willingly authorised, describes the valiant ethos of a man who refuses to feel sorry for himself. Yet without its nostalgic recall of the free spirit which infused that dazzling young Chelsea team in which he kept beautiful company with such other unique talents as Peter Osgood and Charlie Cooke, it would be impossible to connect the two very opposite halves of Hudson's life, to reconcile the '60s darling of the King's Road with the 60-something warrior against adversity.

During the interval between those two extremes came the lovely cameos with Stoke and Arsenal, Indian summers in North America and fleeting returns to the Bridge and the old Victoria Ground. Then came the hit from that unidentified car, the driver of which was never found.

Never one to suffer fools, or inferiors, gladly, Hudson accepts that he has made enemies as easily as friends. Such, however, is the uncompromising character of genius.

The Alan Hudson story is one of dizzying highs and desperate troughs. As such, it is not only fascinating of itself but also a graphic parable of our sporting lives and times. He could ask for no more faithful chronicler of his saga, because its telling is a labour of love for Jason.

Read this book from the start and remember Huddy, the magician. Read it to the end and pray for Alan, my friend.

Jeff Powell
September 2017

1

Childhood

"We won every trophy there was because of one outstanding player – me."

London in 1951 was still desperately trying to get back on its feet again after the ravages of the Second World War. Although the devastation of the war was now only a memory, England's capital still had plenty of ruins. Manufacturing businesses that had kept the country ticking along for decades had upped and left as the Luftwaffe dropped its bombs, never to return. The shells of buildings bombed years earlier, but still to be rebuilt, gave an eerily ghost-like feel to parts of the city.

Elsewhere, the thick smoke billowing from the capital's chimneys stained buildings a dirty soot-black as smog enveloped the city. A couple of miles from the grandeur of Buckingham Palace, the heart of Chelsea was, in the main, decrepit and somewhat tired looking. A built-up area full of prefabricated houses and, at the time, certainly not associated with the glamour of its residents today. Indeed, it was a world away from the pomp and circumstance of the Palace that *Pathe News* would have had everyone believe was the real face of post-war London.

Just across the Thames, Battersea at least had its park and that beautiful expanse of green was heaven when compared to some of its surroundings. George VI reigned, Clement Attlee and Winston Churchill swapped prime ministerial duties at Downing Street, *The Archers* began its incredible run on the BBC's *Light Programme*, and *The Goon Show* also had its first airing. Pea-souper fogs were caused by the excessive amount of coal that London's homes were burning and it had become a dull, dreary and pretty depressing place to live. However, spirits remained remarkably high.

The Festival of Britain was helping all parts of the British Isles recover some of its lost glory. The King and Queen's tour to promote it would also be the last time that they would be seen together in public. Battersea showcased the Festival Pleasure Gardens and South Kensington promoted the British contribution to science, meaning that at least some corners of London were a little more sanguine than elsewhere, its inhabitants doing their level best to afford everyone a warm welcome. Nothing was going to take the shine off William and Barbara Hudson's happy day either – a hot summer afternoon when they would become proud parents again.

Alan Anthony Hudson's arrival on June 21, 1951, went exactly as planned and without any complications, meaning John – born two years and a month previously – was no longer his parents' only child. Already a toddler, John would take an immediate shine to this new bundle of joy without a hint of the animosity that would later completely destroy the relationship with his sibling. Delivered at 75 Elm Park Gardens in Chelsea, a home birth wasn't entirely uncommon at the time but nor could it be regarded as a popular choice. It was, however, what Barbara – or Bub as she liked to be called – wanted, and it afforded her a great deal more privacy than the three hospitals which were only a stone's throw away. But it was hot on that Thursday, boy was it hot.

To make matters worse, every window in this compact prefab

CHILDHOOD

was shut in order to make it as soundproof as possible. Bub's blood-curdling screams during a prolonged labour didn't stop a few curtains twitching, suggesting that their efforts to keep the peace in the neighbourhood had failed dismally. Thankfully however, it was soon over and the breeze that flowed once the doors and windows had let the summer back in was more than welcome. Once all of the routine checks had been completed, Bub was left alone to nurse her newborn, and he latched onto her breast with the accuracy that would later define his professional career – this healthy, bonny chap certainly knew where the goal was!

Being only a short walk from the King's Road, Bill would've been forgiven if he were to take full advantage of the plentiful amount of public houses to wet the baby's head, but it wasn't his style, preferring to be at the beck and call of his wife and helping out as required. Alan's arrival had given everyone a lift. It was some good news that helped take minds off the day-to-day post-war difficulties, the daily grind to earn a living and the drab exteriors in the neighbourhood. In an area that was predominantly working class, with little money to go around, the sense of community was nevertheless unmistakable. Friendships were easily made in this part of the world and people looked out for each other, always leaving their front doors open and allowing their kids to play in the street until dark.

The corner shop at the end of Elm Park Gardens, adjacent to Elm Park Road, remained a hive of activity and the comings and goings were always peppered with brisk conversation. If you wanted to find out anything about the neighbours, a weekly trip there would put you right. How else do you explain that everyone knew of Alan's arrival before Bub had finished her brief convalescence indoors?! News travelled almost as fast then as it does now in the age of electronic communications.

Bub loved the local 'grapevine' and the accompanying fuss that people would make of Alan. A short shopping trip for day-to-day essentials often turned into an escapade of an hour or more and it was precisely that friendly and welcome tittle-tattle that was needed to keep spirits up. After all, there wasn't an awful lot else for her to look forward to.

The two-bedroom prefab that Alan called home included a shared bedroom with John and, in keeping with the needs of the area at the time, was hardly the most salubrious of dwellings. Built as a result of the bomb damage inflicted on the district, it was more than a little cramped at times – but it was home, and a loving one at that. Alan had certainly hit the jackpot in that sense, for two more loving and dedicated parents you couldn't wish to find. Bill was a grafter. He had to be. In order to keep a roof over his family's head, he would turn his hand to anything he could and was known for being a dab hand on the tarmac run. He was a proud man who always lived by the 'honest day's work for an honest day's pay' mantra.

A window cleaning round meant Bill got to know just about everyone in his immediate vicinity, and he was a reliable and cheerful man who enjoyed his work. If the need arose, Bill would turn his hand to painting and decorating and other odd jobs to keep the finances ticking over. The family's unforgiving financial situation dictated that, no matter what the temperature or the weather, Bill would have to be up with the capital's dawn chorus and ready to take on the world. If he disliked it, he never showed it, and continued setting a fine example to both of his boys. At home, Bub ensured a hearty meal was on the table for her man, and the children never wanted for anything including some undivided attention, even if Alan was hard work in the early days. He would certainly play up in his formative years and, with Bill working his fingers to the bone, Bub was often weighed down with the stresses of caring for two wee nippers – a situation that almost every mother can identify with.

"The problem was she never knew what time he was getting back to our prefab," Alan recalled. "If he was a drinker or womaniser, like so many blokes in the area at that time, there might have been problems, but he was working. Always working, to pay the family's bills for the groceries, for football boots: you name it, Bill funded it. I've truly never known someone to be so family-orientated. Without him, we had nothing!"

Neither parent relied on booze to get them through the day – they rarely had the time – but on occasional Saturday nights they'd let their hair down at home with a few friends – a close-knit group of genuine, salt-of-the-earth people – who in essence became the Hudsons' very own extended family. Those *soirées* also helped to lift the mood after the drudgery of their relentless and punishing schedules. Aside from the parties, Bill would also use football as a vehicle to rid himself of any anger and angst that had built up over the working week. He played for Chelsea Boys Club, as Alan would do years later but, as a Fulham boy living in Chelsea and as fearless on the pitch as he was in his daily life, even his own teammates were a little wary of him.

The nickname 'Bullock' accurately described his approach to any opponent that came within touching distance, his sheer physicality and the enjoyment he derived from 'putting himself about' ensured that scars of battle were a regular occurrence at the end of each 90 minutes. Although she accepted it was part of the game, Bub wasn't overly enthusiastic about seeing him come home looking like he'd gone a few rounds with Cassius Clay. Young Alan was, however, already learning a valuable lesson about the school of hard knocks, because Bill's own unique way of dealing with matters on the pitch certainly rubbed off on him in later life.

"I saw him come back home after a Sunday match with plasters all over his face, broken nose, the lot. It wasn't pretty but it was probably necessary," Alan recalled. Elm Park Gardens was, and still is, set in a square around a small plot of green space and it was here, when Bill had the time and energy, he would take John and Alan to kick a ball about. Both boys enjoyed a love of football even before they were able to walk. Holding onto a chair leg or another piece of furniture, Alan would try to balance himself in order to throw out a leg and kick the ball back to his dad or to his brother. That enjoyment was clearly inherited from the old man, and the time the three Hudson males spent together remains a special memory for Alan. If Bill had one regret, it was that such tender moments were rare because of the need for him to earn a living.

Even as schoolboys, the Hudson brothers would race home from class and head straight out for a kickabout. Nothing else mattered. As Alan remembers: "For me, that was the best time of my life. I loved living there and being with my mates Bobby Eyre, Chris Maughan and Keith Davidson. About a quarter of a mile up the road lived my best mate Leslie May, who sadly died so terribly young. We would play for hours on end and enjoy every minute. I really wouldn't have swapped my upbringing in Chelsea with any other, and it goes to show that having no money meant nothing to me – because I was surrounded by everything I needed; the love of my family and friends."

Back in those days, when a PlayStation, GameBoy or other electronic gadgetry weren't yet even a thought in the mind of some technical genius, it was the love of the game played with the leather ball that was the all-consuming obsession of Alan, John and their pals. The trials and tribulations of *Tiger* comic's hugely popular *Roy of the Rovers* cartoon strip were played out

CHILDHOOD

in parks everywhere. If you weren't Roy, then Blackie Gray was your man and Alan and John would routinely take turns to be one or the other. Unlike today, where there is so much choice to occupy a young mind, football was king. If the lads weren't to be found in the immediate vicinity, they'd be a few streets away having a kick-about.

They would spend literally hours kicking a ball, often aimlessly, at just about anything that tested their ability and improved their skills: trees, brick walls, garage doors, even windows and unsuspecting passers-by. You name it, Alan was kicking a ball at it, which would often get him into trouble, but it didn't bother Bill, who recognised early on that his son had 'something'. What that 'something' was, at that point, was undefinable, but Bill just had a feeling that Alan had a natural talent above that of the other boys of the same age. Maybe it was the way he controlled the ball, or positioned himself perfectly, or the ferocity with which he could belt it further, faster and with more accuracy than the others. Whatever 'it' was, Bill knew Alan had 'it' and found it impossible to contain his excitement. Alan recalls, however, that his father's praise and encouragement didn't make him popular amongst his peers.

"Professional football was a long way off and simply something I never thought would happen anyway, but that was where Bill came in. He insisted I would be the best and told everyone of his belief in me. They thought he was biased and knew nothing beyond a dad pushing his own son, but he knew a real player when he saw one, and it just happened to be me." By the time Alan was 10 years old, even he knew, as did everyone else, that he was a cut above the competition. Those hours of practice and dedication, combined with the necessary cajoling from Bill, were beginning to pay off. Park Walk's primary school team was the first that Alan would play for and, even at this stage of his personal and football development, he gave this group of rag-tag ruffian street kids something extra.

Only the strongest survived and if you didn't have fists to fight your battles, then you sure as hell needed to be able to talk-the-talk or walk-the-walk. Luckily for Alan, who abhorred violence – and still does – he always had magic in his boots and that was more than enough to keep the bullies out of harm's way. Even then, although his young teammates wouldn't necessarily identify with it, the reflected glory of being in the same team as this brilliant young player was evident – even if some would not acknowledge it.

Bill had learned enough about the game to know that if Alan wanted it badly enough and had a continued thirst for learning, then the football world was his oyster.

He'd take the knocks just like his old man did, but they were few and far between because opponents just couldn't get near him when he had the ball at his feet. His movement on the football field, even at such a remarkably young age, can best be described as silky. As the boots – and often fists – came flying in, this 10-year-old was able to expertly shift his body weight, and the ball if necessary, out of harm's way. His skill set was already jaw-dropping in its execution, and those who bore witness to it in its infancy would know what they had just seen was real enough. But it was so other-worldly that some kind of explanation was required.

Was his birth certificate wrong? Perhaps he was behind in his studies so he'd dropped back a couple of years to get a more rounded education. How could such a waif of a lad be *that* good? It wasn't an illusion of course, but the uninitiated would always ask the same questions or make certain assumptions.

"Park Walk primary school didn't have much competition," Alan recalls fondly, "We won every trophy because of one

CHILDHOOD

outstanding player: me! My mum would wash my kit and she once said to me that, 'There's no reason to wash them really because they were as clean as when you put them on.' It was a common occurrence, to be fair. We had videos – that have sadly gone astray now – where I would beat players and, whilst getting the ball on the other side of them, would jump over the puddles on the asphalt pitches. I genuinely cannot remember us losing a game, but all those matches and kickabouts on the school playground, rock hard pitches and pavements near our prefab took their toll on me. Even 'the cage' on Upcerne Road – a fully enclosed area we used as a pitch – did me no good. In fact, it eventually saw me diagnosed with Osgood-Schlatter disease."

An affliction of those more active youngsters, OSD – as it's more commonly known – is an inflammation of the area just below the knee where the tendon from the kneecap (the patellar tendon) attaches to the shinbone (the tibia). Alan was, at times, in terrible pain but hated to miss out on any form of football-related activity. Even when the pain was at its worst, he would grit his teeth and get on with it, but the symptoms persisted because he wouldn't allow his injury to recover. This would annoy the hell out of Bill and the family doctor who, on more than one occasion, prescribed absolute rest from all forms of physical activity.

One person, and one person alone, ignored the medical and parental advice and, as later in life, Alan Hudson was sometimes Alan Hudson's worst enemy. There's every reason to believe that if he'd taken the advice from those who knew best, he could have been an even better footballer. Taking advice, however, wasn't – and still isn't – Alan's *forte*. "I was a shy kid, whose rebellious side was quite something, and I've always rebelled against those in authority. Deep inside, both on and off the pitch, I was as cool as ice. I was very aware of how good a player I was and enjoyed showing everyone what I could do, so I always – quite naturally – wanted to play whenever I had the opportunity. Being self-confident can sometimes be mistaken as 'cockiness', and although I was overflowing with self-belief, I never thought I was being cocky. Others may see it differently of course."

As primary school became a distant memory, Kingsley Secondary Modern became Alan's new stage. It was a big change from Park Walk and a different way of life for Alan and his pals to quickly adapt to. Victorian in its grandeur, it was enormous, imposing and bigger than Park Walk, itself a behemoth of a primary. It was as if the entire youth population of Chelsea had descended on this school of some 1,500 pupils and, metaphorically speaking, it was a whole new ball game. The PE teachers knew of Alan's prowess before he joined the school, so he was a shoo-in for the school team without even kicking a ball. It gave him instant kudos and *cachet*, particularly with the opposite sex who would soon play a big part in his life. Even the adolescent Huddy was partial to a beautiful girl or two.

Frustrated by the petty antagonism towards Alan, which he regarded as simple jealousy that had developed amongst some teammates' parents at Park Walk, Bill could see it was clearly weighing heavily on Alan's young shoulders and advised his son to just ignore it and get on with his schoolwork. Bill was certainly vociferous in support of his son whilst standing on the touchline, but his support was always within the bounds of acceptability. However, it soon turned nasty. "Kingsley was different as we played schools from the other side of London. We had a decent team, made up of good players from the Chelsea/Fulham area, but I remember one evening a player pulled a knife out of his sock and threatened our centre-half. This was certainly not a situation a youngster wanted to find

CHILDHOOD

himself in. It wasn't long before Bill stopped me playing for the school and decided to coach me himself. He always played me with kids two years my senior so when 'I grew into myself' my outstanding ability, as he always said, would come to the fore."

Regular school days weren't necessarily boring to Alan but he was a loose cannon at times, even then he revelled in seeing just how far he could push the teaching establishment. He was an articulate, confident and courteous young man whose obsessive desire and constant need to play football had already hindered his education.

"They wouldn't accept me at Chelsea Secondary School, on the corner of the road where our prefab stood, because they said my mind would always be in the playground not the classroom. All because – in my interview when asked about ambition – I told them I wanted to be a footballer first, or a journalist second. I was the only one of 14 children who'd passed the 11+ who wasn't given a place. There'd be a plaque on the wall now if they'd have let me in! Sometimes honesty isn't always the best policy, but that was me then – and still is me now."

Not willing to allow that disappointment to affect him, and despite Bub's fear that he was throwing his education away in pursuit of a pipe dream, Alan did what he did best; tearing opposing teams apart on the pitch. He must've been doing something right, because it wasn't long before West London schoolboy honours were bestowed upon him and now an even wider audience would marvel at the talents of this lithe, athletic and gifted young man. Tommy Tranter was the coach for West London, and it was under him that Alan and his colleagues took on Charlie George and Islington boys in the early 1960s at Highbury – a ground later to be synonymous with both of them.

Chelsea Boys Club also had a helping hand in Alan's football development, with Bill again instrumental in guiding his streetwise know-it-all son down the right path. "We played against all other under-14 teams from London's Boys' Clubs and had one other outstanding player in Rodney Udall, who was like a grown man compared to little old me. I was a late developer who had to train hard with cross country runs to build up my strength and stamina. Don't forget that at this stage I was only 12, and playing in an under-14 side was hard work. A team called Manor House were rated as the best in London and we turned them over 4-2, winning the National Association of Boys' Clubs trophy at Craven Cottage in the process. It was under the management of my father Bill, with the great Johnny Haynes – my hero – presenting the trophy. Well, you can imagine how proud I was. If I didn't know it before, that was precisely the moment when I decided I was going to become a professional footballer."

Away from the pitch, there was another addition to the family. At the third time of trying, Bill and Bub had a daughter, Julie. She would, as might be expected, complete the family unit and her birth came at just the right time. Even as a baby, Julie was a bright and bubbly character and her sweet-hearted innocence brought smiles to the faces of her parents. Almost overnight Alan and John became her guardian angels, ensuring that no harm would come to their 'little princess'.

Born on September 14, 1963, Julie was the daughter Bub had always craved. Taking nothing away from her sons, whom she loved dearly, this was different, a chance for Bub to do all of the feminine things she'd been dreaming of for the past decade or so: dressing Julie up to the nines, taking her to dancing classes, and teaching her to put on make-up. There'd be no more traipsing across London in all weathers to watch football either, even if she'd grown to like the sport which always dominated the family landscape.

CHILDHOOD

Julie's arrival gave the whole family a lift, with Bill beginning to experience the very special bond between a father and his daughter. Julie's birth, in many respects, softened him a little. Still very much a man's man, however, he couldn't do enough for this little lady. The long days that he worked quickly became a bind, more so than before. Not getting in until late meant that, in the week at least, there was less time than he would've liked to be able to learn how to be a father again. It's somewhat ironic that as Julie became a toddler, she would go out and join the boys kicking balls around. Despite being 12 and 14 years her senior, Alan and John loved it.

Chelsea, and London as a whole, was swinging by now, but Julie was far too young to appreciate the impact her hometown was having globally. One thing she did understand, however, was that by the end of the decade Alan was making a lot of people happy. Very happy. Perhaps it would still take years for her to fully grasp the impact that her brother had made in the world of professional football, but it was clear to her, even as a youngster, that Alan was different. Why would all these people want to talk to him and have photos with him otherwise?

More so than ever, Bill and Bub would need to throw that protective arm around their daughter as she, along with the rest of the family, was caught up in the whirlwind of Alan's burgeoning popularity. However, while Alan's fledging career was on an upwards trajectory his brother John was allowing his focus to slip, something that Bill wouldn't tolerate.

"I grew up in John's shadow and looked up to him. Sharing the same room meant we were very close as young kids. Bill worked tirelessly for us, and John was the first to sign for Chelsea, whilst I was still at Kingsley Secondary Modern. I took it that he would go 'all the way' and admired him as he swanned around in his flash Chelsea FC club blazer with his two mates Barry Lloyd and Roger Wosahlo. I remember when it all began going wrong though. My father packed John's bags and threatened to throw him out of our prefab after a match at Charlton in the FA Youth Cup. 'He swans round up the King's Road in that blazer and when it comes to having a great opportunity to show he can play he goes missing', Bill would say. He was livid and John went downhill with Chelsea from there on. I was shocked by it all to tell you the truth but I was still naïve at that stage in terms of how things worked."

It was no surprise to anyone that, once Bill began focusing on bringing Alan through to the level from which he'd propel himself further forward, his and Alan's relationship with John soured. Girls, fags and booze were John's weaknesses. Like many young men of that age, his huge potential was never realised because of a love of extra-curricular activity. Not for him the regimented training regime which would keep him out of harm's way. As his fitness quickly fell away, so did his application on the pitch and eventually his confidence. It was hardly fair on a father who had worked day and night, and often for weeks on end to afford his family the opportunities that he'd never had. "He and my mother never got a penny for bringing us up the right way. Paying for our boots, football strips, travel and, more importantly, the football education given to us by Bill. That was precious!" Not precious enough, apparently, for the elder Hudson son, who thought he knew it all.

Alan would eventually join Chelsea after being rejected by Fulham. "I was seen playing for the school team and invited to a trial. However, when the coaching staff at Fulham looked at me they said, 'He's too small.' Bill told them, 'He's only young. He'll grow,' but they weren't interested." As Fulham fans the club's decision was tough to take for the Hudson family but in 1966 Bill walked a 15-year-old Alan through the gates at Stamford Bridge, accompanying him as he signed his first apprentice contract. It was a short, quarter-mile stroll from

CHILDHOOD

the prefab, but the most significant walk of Alan's life at that point. This was the real deal, and more important on a personal level than what the England team achieved in the same year.

Luckily for Bill, the magnitude of the moment wasn't lost on a young man who remains to this day the most locally-born player to have made the grade at Chelsea. First team honours were still some way off, of course, but now Bill really had his work cut out. What if another gifted young Hudson was to also throw it all away, after every sacrifice that had been made? After countless reassurances to Bub down the years that, "It would all be worth it in the end"; what if Alan – like his brother – couldn't be bothered to see this through?

Fortunately, lack of application or indifference was never a concern with Alan. The fearlessness that characterised Bill's own playing style was evident in Alan from the very beginning and, being far better than his contemporaries of the same age, Alan was again played a year or two above his age grade to see how he would cope with the battering at the top end. John, meanwhile, had been hanging onto his own career by the tips of his fingernails. "Bill just wanted us to give it our all, but John seemed not to take the game as serious as me," said Alan. "As I got closer to signing as a professional, we became distant as his disinterest in football and playing at that level became more apparent. He seemed to drift away from the Chelsea crowd and spent it with people from a different world. I was totally confused."

The straw that finally broke the camel's back came when manager Tommy Docherty, reneged on handing him his first professional contract. A *melee* in Blackpool in 1967, involving a number of Chelsea players, ended with the hard-line Scot sending eight players home. Although John wasn't directly involved, he had been in the vicinity and, judged guilty by association, was sent packing.

"John was his own worst enemy at the time" recalls Alan, "but Bill still chased 'Tommy the Tyke' – as he was called – round his office. He told Docherty, 'I'm taking Alan away from here', to which Docherty replied, 'If you do, I'll see he'll never kick another ball.' That was the harsh reality of professional football back then."

If a close family was being ripped apart because of Bill's undying commitment to turning at least one of his boys into a star, there was always a feeling that the situation was only temporary and that any ill-feeling would be explained away in good time. After all, Bill loved his children equally. It was never the same after that though. How could it be? Your own father tying his hopes to the mast of one son in preference to the other; a recipe for disaster. Bill would've been hurting at the time, really hurting, but being the sort of man he was, he wouldn't have shown it. The archetypal breadwinner, the whole family looked to him for guidance and it wouldn't do for him to drop that manly exterior, to show weakness or even a more human side.

Rightly or wrongly, he had made a decision, stuck by it and the family were forced to accept it. It was hard on them and him because, after all, he'd only ever done right by his family. Generous to a fault, now was the time he had to be selfish. For himself, for his younger son and for the rest of his family, which included John of course.

Bill knew exactly what it would take to ensure that both his sons had the best opportunity to make it as professional footballers, and he also knew he would have to go to his own limits mentally, emotionally and financially to make it happen. After investing so much into the 'project', it was blindingly obvious that if the opportunities arose – whatever the cost to family relationships – he would have to take that risk. He was too far in to give up now. If John wanted to pass up the

CHILDHOOD

opportunity because he couldn't be bothered then, frankly, that was his problem and Alan quickly had to accept that no passengers were allowed *en route* to the top.

Sadly, for such a tight-knit bunch, John's feeling of resentment never really went away. In 2017, some 50 years later, the wounds are still so deep that Alan and John are not on speaking terms. "After John was best man at my wedding in 1971," Alan commented, "we seemed to drift apart at a rare old speed of knots, something I never truly did understand. I simply adored him but he seemed to think differently about me and for some unknown reason attacked me verbally about my way of life. We hardly talked in the end and he left for Italy. The last time I recall him kicking a ball was whilst I was playing at Stoke. He visited me, and Tony Waddington allowed him to train with us. After that we drifted further apart and it's been so bad between us that I don't even know the place where he's been living for the past 30-odd years."

Whether or not it's the case, Alan believes that his brother may have resented the success his younger sibling had enjoyed and, unable to reach the same footballing heights whilst seeing his own chance at the big time go down the pan, it was easier to take pot shots at someone who, by John's own admission, had done nothing wrong. If being a revelation on the football pitch was a crime, then Alan Hudson was guilty as charged. Even in his earliest days, there was no getting away from that fact. But why that should lead to resentment and feelings of bitterness from someone who Alan held in the highest esteem, only John knows. Those personal feelings cut so deep that he would end up driving a stake through the heart of the family, alienating himself in the process.

"I wouldn't absolutely swear it was because of my success but it coincided with him changing dramatically," says Alan. "What's worse, and frankly unforgiveable, was that later on he would send our mother terrible letters complaining about his upbringing. I truly believe that we had the greatest childhood and I thought that was out of order and disrespectful."

Clearly, the issue was very black and white for John and the beginning of the end of that particular relationship started almost as soon as it became clear that Alan, unlike his brother, was going to make something of himself at Chelsea.

2

Chelsea

"There was talk about Stevie Perryman being the most outstanding prospect in London and I stuck it through his legs twice in the first 15 minutes to let him know that he had better think again."

There couldn't have been anyone prouder than Bill when he strolled through the gates at Stamford Bridge, arm in arm with the second of his sons to be courted by Chelsea Football Club. This was a big deal, and the confirmation of everything that he had believed for a number of years. No more raised eyebrows from family or friends who were too polite to tell Bill to his face that his dreams were only ever destined to end in disappointment. He knew enough about the game and the characters within it to understand that Chelsea were keen on Alan. Very keen, as it turned out.

Unlike the present day, where the Academy structure is God and professional clubs hoover up young players from six years and upwards – some of whom can do a little bit more than kick a ball in a straight line – in the 1960s, clubs were a little more selective. Only the very best young players even got so much as a sniff at parading their wares on such a stage. It wasn't enough to be the best player at your school, even if Huddy was obviously that. Nor was it enough to hold your own at district level. You had to have, to coin a well-worn phrase, the 'X-Factor.'

The Blues had, unknown to the Hudsons, been tracking Alan for a while before making their move. By the time they were ready to approach the family, Chelsea were certain of their decision and knew what young Huddy could bring to the club if he was willing to knuckle down and learn. Despite his youth, Alan immediately understood the gravitas of the situation.

"When Bill first walked me through those gates I was in total awe, dumbstruck. As a cheeky teenager I wasn't normally lost for words, but I was that day. This was it, I thought. The big time. I initially trained on Tuesday and Thursday evenings and it was like nothing I'd been used to before. Even as a youngster at the club, training sessions were structured and serious and I recall that there was an immediate expectation that you got your head down and worked. This wasn't Sunday League with your mates anymore. A whole new football world was opening up for me."

Bill would accompany Alan as often as his long hours would allow, because it was as much in his interests as Chelsea's that his son's development was managed in the proper way. Given young Huddy's general dislike of authority, there was always the worry in the back of Bill's mind that a wrong word here or there could be the catalyst for that short fuse to blow. In the event it was never an issue, because Alan had to recognise that his own dreams of success would be up in smoke if he put one foot out of line.

Even if respect wasn't his strongest attribute, how could he not fail to be impressed by the CVs of the men who held his career in their hands. "I first came across my soon-to-be coaches as an apprentice: Tommy Harmer, a great Spurs inside-forward, and Frank Blunstone from Crewe, who was in the first ever league-winning team in 1955 at the Bridge."

Although both father and son dreamt that one day Alan would run out onto the pitch in the iconic royal blue strip – not yet besmirched by a sponsor's logo – with the white lion standing proudly upon the chest, neither could have envisaged that it would be less than three years between signing apprentice forms, aged 15, and his official debut against Southampton in February 1969. In the intervening period, Huddy literally lived for football. If he wasn't going to crack the big time, it wouldn't be for the want of trying.

Both Bill and Bub noticed a change in him, and a positive one at that. Unlike John, who'd got to a certain point before deciding it was all too much, Alan was more single-minded. His friends could either be pleased for him, knowing that he was going all out to give himself the best chance of success, or they simply wouldn't be his friends anymore. There was no middle ground. It wasn't as if he was completely isolated, though. Aside from his regular sessions down at the Bridge, Huddy was still honing his skills in 'the cage' at Upcerne Road.

"I cannot stress enough how fantastic it was. We were all like one big happy family with Bobby, Keith Davison and Chris Maughan. When the ball bounced, the sound would bring boys running from all around. It was the centre of the universe for me. Although I dedicated myself to the pursuit of glory, if you want to call it that, what I had there was why I wasn't too bothered about going to Chelsea as a schoolboy. I simply wanted to play with my mates in 'the cage' where we had great teams – 5-a-side and 7-a-side – run by Bill. He made me go to the Bridge though, because he didn't want me to miss out like he'd done when playing for Wimbledon and Wealdstone in the Southern League. He was considered good enough to make it but was never discovered. I owed it to him to take it seriously."

HUDDY

If Bub had thought that football couldn't possibly play any bigger a part in her life than it already had, she couldn't have been more wrong. The boys were regularly taken to Highbury and White Hart Lane as well as to Craven Cottage, with Bill explaining the different elements of the game to them and picking out the performances of one or two individuals. "That's the level you need to be at," Bill would say.

This was another psychological masterstroke because it meant that, even in the earliest days of training with Chelsea, Alan had the fullest appreciation of both the rudimentary and more advanced elements of play. There were players – just like those at Kingsley – who'd clatter you, given half the chance, and those who allowed the ball to do the work. Those players were always finding space and time, even in the tightest and most congested spaces. Alan was definitely in the latter camp and quickly got to know what the tricks of the defensive trade were. A little tug here, a raking of the calf there. Avoiding the tricks of defenders was something that he added to his repertoire at Chelsea, and his growing maturity in a football sense hadn't gone unnoticed.

"I was still playing for my father, my school, and captain of West London Boys, but after showing what I could do on a Tuesday and Thursday evening, it was obvious Chelsea were going to offer me apprenticeship forms for the two years leading up to my 17th birthday, when you could sign professionally. I knew that other London clubs had good players too. Trevor Brooking was at West Ham, Gerry Francis at QPR, Charlie George at Arsenal and Stevie Perryman at Spurs. I'd already played against Charlie before, of course, but I'll never forget a match against Stevie at Chelsea's training ground, The Welsh Harp, in Hendon. There was talk about Stevie Perryman being the most outstanding prospect in London and I stuck it through his legs twice in the first 15 minutes to let him know that he had better think again."

Alan was certainly announcing himself in the manner only he could. Once he'd graduated to play in Chelsea's youth team, his was the name on everyone's lips. That he was still able to express himself fully in such exalted company meant that more and more people began to sit up and take notice. And Bill, as usual, wasn't backwards in coming forwards when espousing the virtues of his son.

"My father was born in Walham Green, Fulham," says Alan. "And although he was not a mad keen fan, he was Fulham 'rooted' until Chelsea Old Boys FC headhunted him for their terrific team.

"He didn't really take me to the Cottage, he took me to Arsenal to watch George Eastham, and Spurs to watch John White and the first Double-winning team. That was if he could get home in time – from his work on the asphalt – to take me and my brother.

"But I would go to Fulham every Saturday, even after playing for Chelsea's youth team – at Barn Elms – which was opposite Craven Cottage. I'd finish playing, report back to Stamford Bridge and then slip away to meet Bill Boyce – my close friend from school – and we'd go together.

"Johnny Haynes was coming to the end of his career at that time, but he was a hero to me and everyone else.

"I loved my youth team days at The Welsh Harp, with the likes of Ian 'Chico' Hamilton, who scored at Spurs – on his debut – as a 16-year-old. He was bigger and stronger than me but Bill would tell the coaching staff, 'Don't you worry, Alan will go a lot farther in the game than him.' He wasn't being deliberately nasty of course, simply reminding the coaches who was the boss on the pitch when they kept singing other players' praises. I played with youngsters like Dave Bibby and

Alan Cox at that time; great lads but who were never going to make it. They were good times, really good times."

One of Huddy's recollections that still brings a broad smile to his face is of a strong Chelsea side playing Crystal Palace in Banstead, near Epsom. The pitch was located near a psychiatric hospital, and the consequences were entirely predictable.

"It was one of the funniest things I ever saw! We were attacking their goal and when they got the ball, I turned to get back to defend, and saw this couple, ballroom dancing in the centre circle, oblivious to the game going on around them. I think it was a waltz but whatever it was supposed to be, it was hilarious!"

Alan would go on to captain his Chelsea side to an FA Youth Cup final which they lost to West Brom, but by now everyone knew what he was capable of. Tommy Docherty was still Chelsea's first-team manager, and his son Michael also played in Alan's youth team. It was another stroke of luck as, whilst watching his own son's progress, Docherty's eye was caught by Alan's on-field exploits.

"I was enjoying playing with Michael and we struck up a good partnership in midfield but, just when I thought he would make it at Chelsea, 'The Doc' sent him off to Burnley, which bewildered me a little. I liked Michael as both a player and young man. He played in the first team for the Clarets but disappeared and went into management an early age."

Despite impressing everyone with his natural talent, Alan's recurrent OSD problems threatened to curtail his progress and potentially end his career. He couldn't face that, because he'd given everything he had to the game already. There was simply no way he was going to allow the condition to get the better of him.

"When I was about to turn 16 I was playing in the reserves but, hearing a doctor formally diagnose the pains I'd been having as OSD, and say, 'It might take up to your 21st birthday before the knee properly knits together' crushed me. It would have ended my career before it had really started. I couldn't take five years off and hope to pick up again with Chelsea. I was totally gutted. Luckily for me, I did have treatment and the knee was playable again within six months."

Injury would shape his career later on, but the OSD had denied him the chance to become Chelsea's youngest-ever first-team player at 16: the first of many career disappointments. Docherty began to lose control of the senior squad around this time too. His hard-line approach was well-documented and, although appreciated by his paymasters, it was never particularly liked by those under his supervision. The players wanted to be treated as adults, not five-year-olds, and it was only a matter of time before such a tight grip would have consequences.

As it turned out, Docherty would resign after being suspended by the FA for 28 days following incidents on the club's tour to Bermuda. Dave Sexton took over, just as he would years later when 'The Doc' was sacked by Manchester United. Post-OSD, Huddy just happened to be in the right place at the right time.

"He [Sexton] had never seen me play but had read the youth team coach's glowing reports, and selected me to play in a testimonial at QPR. It was my 'D-Day'. The pitch at Shepherds Bush was a quagmire and I can't remember anything of the match, but Dave obviously saw enough and signed me up as a professional as fast as he could get the paperwork together. Shortly afterwards I was flying out to Mozambique with the first-team where I found out just what the lads were all about.

"I knew the players because, whilst out injured with the OSD, I'd been in the dressing room cleaning their boots, the toilets, the baths and showers. Anything that was dirty, I cleaned it. I already knew who I liked, who I could trust and who to be wary of, but luckily they all knew that I could play and I was more or less accepted straight away, even by the senior pros in the squad. Eddie McCreadie was one of those I respected and loved, and then I soon struck up relationships with Peter Osgood and Ian Hutchinson. My father was actually the person who discovered Hutch after seeing him play against my brother at Burton Albion in the Southern League. He recommended him to Chelsea and once Ron Suart, one of the coaches, had run the rule over him at a game in Cambridge, he was snapped up."

It wouldn't be long before Huddy's first-team debut, under well-remembered circumstances, and if it hadn't been for the misdemeanours of a few teammates, Alan's dream of playing for Chelsea may have taken a bit longer. Having said that, Sexton was in no doubt that Alan's big moment had arrived. As Rick Glanvill wrote in his *Chelsea Who's Who*, Sexton insisted that Alan, "Isn't in on sentiment, but because he is a fine young player. The way he organises things in midfield is first-class."

Being thrown in at the deep end was probably the best thing that could've happened, because it didn't allow Alan the time to worry about the game.

"Peter Osgood, Tommy Baldwin, Charlie Cooke and Johnny Boyle were the culprits. Instead of reporting for training, the four thought they'd enjoy a 'liquid lunch' instead, not realising that someone had tipped off Dave Sexton that they were 'rather the worse for wear'. Sexton called the treatment room and asked, 'Is Alan Hudson fit for tomorrow?' When Harry the physio asked me if I was fit – I was lying on the treatment table at the time – I said I didn't know until I practised and saw how my injury reacted.

"I thought that he was talking about playing in the reserves, then all of a sudden Harry said, 'If you're fit you'll be playing for the first team at Southampton.' I was completely stunned because I thought that I wasn't playing that well but after training – and rather stupidly and instinctively – I told everyone that I was fit. I'd said it knowing that had I been in the reserves I'd have cried off because of the injury. It wasn't until I got home that I heard on the news that four Chelsea players were dropped for breaking club rules and, in the papers the following day, I was headline news after a 'snapper' came to our prefab and took a shot of me and my dog, 'Ossie', named after Chelsea's great centre-forward and one of the disciplined players. We lost the match 5-0 and I was left out until the following season.

Just imagine the impact that the occasion had on Bill Hudson in particular, but also on the wider Hudson family. It was a poor result and Alan's performance on the day wasn't much to write home about either but, just as Bill always believed he would, Alan had made his professional debut and the bizarre circumstances via which it had come about were incidental. A chink of light had emerged, the door that was slightly left ajar had now been wedged wide open and in through the gap marched Huddy, taking the unexpected opportunity. He'd spend the remaining three months of the season keeping his head down and working as hard as his body would allow, given that his injury hadn't properly healed at the time of his debut.

Off the pitch, Alan was well liked, and he was becoming increasingly known amongst his peers for his flamboyance. The youngest player in the first-team squad was fair game for the banter that fuelled the egos of this tight-knit bunch, but he could give as good as he received. His sharp wit and abundance of skill were an intoxicating mix and he was therefore quickly accepted, even by the top players in the side, as one of their own. The fearlessness that had characterised his playing days as a youth hadn't deserted him on the pitch either.

"I thought that after such a beating [against Southampton], I would never get another opportunity but right out of the blue, after Chelsea had a quite average start to the following season, I was thrown in at my all-time favourite ground, White Hart Lane. In front of 50-odd thousand and against a few of my heroes, one being the great Jimmy Greaves whose famous number 8 Chelsea shirt I was wearing. I loved it and just soaked it up. We drew 1-1 after leading by a David Webb goal, before Jimmy Pearce scored a brilliant 30-yarder. Dave Sexton blamed me for passing a ball square instead of 'down the line', which was what coaching was all about then. He'd rather I'd knocked it into space for no one in particular, instead of square to a team-mate asking for the ball. It did put a dampener on things, being blamed for that."

Alan couldn't afford to allow the criticism to get to him. In this man's world, if you were a shrinking violet you were found out immediately. Luckily, his body language as well as his skill set meant that he could take care of himself with or without the ball, and once the Tottenham match had been forgotten, an 18-year-old Huddy was in for a nice surprise.

"I retained my place! I was slowly finding my stride in the team, we were drawing consistently and I was outstanding in a match at Derby County where I scored my first goal, a fantastic volley from thirty yards in a 2-2 draw. Again, we led but got pegged back in the last ten minutes in a pulsating game. It had me thinking that I was now ready to make my mark. We went on an amazing FA Cup run, which took us all the way to Wembley, scoring a record amount of goals along the way: 2-2 and 3-0 v Birmingham, 2-2 and 3-1 against Burnley after looking like going out with about 15 minutes left, before Peter Houseman equalised for us with time running out.

"In fact, that was the nearest we came to losing until reaching Wembley to play Leeds United. We hit Palace for five and QPR for four on their grounds and after that hammering at Loftus Road, Alf Ramsey, the England manager, was asked by the press about me and what claims I might have for a place in the England senior side. I was thrilled when he said, 'There is no limit to what this player can achieve, he could become one of the greats,' considering it was in the same match where Osgood booked his place to Mexico with a brilliant hat-trick."

Alan was handed his England under-23 debut just two weeks later against Scotland at Sunderland. That he was being noticed was vindication enough that he should carry on doing exactly as he had been, up to that point. A consistently high level of output meant that the calls for his inclusion at full international level couldn't be ignored and, not long after the Scotland game, he was listed in Ramsey's initial party of 40 players under consideration for the World Cup. There was still club business to take care of but subconsciously, Huddy's thoughts were turning to Mexico and starring for his country.

By now, his age wasn't even a topic for discussion, he had deftly slotted in to the Chelsea midfield as though he had played there for years. On quagmires of pitches, he beat his opponents at will and his natural gifts when on the ball were a joy to behold. That he could do all this as a teenager in England's top flight hinted at just how good a player he was becoming.

"My two outstanding moments of that 1969-70 season were two identical goals. At Coventry, I picked a ball up in the middle of our half and ran 70 yards to beat Bill Glazier by flicking it over him. It was so good that after scoring, Ossie ran up to me and said, 'Brilliant son, let's go and celebrate,' taking my hand and running behind the goal in triumph. On the way back to the half-way line he said, 'That was nearly as good as the one I scored at Burnley,' which had us falling about.

"About ten days later I did exactly the same thing against Sheffield Wednesday, this time beating Peter Grummitt. Matthew Harding [at that time just a supporter but someone who would go on to be inextricably linked to the club], said it was his favourite goal because he was sitting in the North Stand, just above where I'd scored.

There was no inkling at this stage of the drama that would unfold later in the season, and for the time being Bill wanted to concentrate on keeping Alan's feet firmly on the ground. By this time, the prefab was attracting regular visitors: school kids now waited for him after training and young women hung around hoping for a glimpse of the new Chelsea star. By now everyone wanted a piece of England's bright young thing. The reality of such a scenario wasn't lost on Alan but fortunately, despite his penchant for a pretty girl, work came first. It had to if he really wanted to achieve all that he had set out to do.

Albert Sewell noted in the *Chelsea Football Book* of the time: 'His size in hats, metaphorically speaking because he doesn't wear one, did not increase a fraction amid the headlines and adulation. It's just that he is a supremely assured and self-confident young man who has set his mind on reaching the top of his profession. Footballers, like artists and musicians, have to be born with talent. How high they climb in their profession is up to the individual. Alan Hudson is the sort of dedicated and determined young man who could play football eight days a week and twenty-five hours a day.

'In 1969-70, his first season at the top level, he has brought a touch of genius to the Chelsea midfield, cohesion to the whole side. David Webb forecast: "This Hud is going to be some player." Well, he already is, isn't he? If ever I saw a boy who's got it all set up for him, he has with his talent. What a future he should have.'

Chelsea were a real joy to watch during this period. Free-flowing, attacking football at its very best, but with a core of 'generals' who'd look after the more technically skilled in the squad. By the middle of the campaign, Alan was being seriously considered for the England World Cup squad.

CHELSEA

In the February 2001 issue of *Chelsea FC* magazine, Alan commented: 'To be shortlisted at 18 was ... fantastic. I later found out that Alf Ramsey told Ken Jones of the *Daily Mirror* that I would have been in the final squad and more likely than not in the first eleven.'

But injury would strike at the worst possible moment. The Blues had already secured their place in the FA Cup final, and Leeds were lying in wait. With dreams of Wembley perhaps already on their minds, Chelsea were ripped apart at Goodison Park by eventual First Division champions Everton. 5-0 up on the hour, it could have been 10, and it was a stark and timely reminder that, no matter how well they were shaping up, on any given day it was still just 11 v 11.

Sexton was having none of it and laid into each and every member of the team, Huddy included, and not long after that came what remains the most heartbreaking moment of Alan's entire career.

"It was Easter 1970, we were at West Bromwich Albion and I collected an innocent-looking ball from John Hollins on my thigh, with nobody near me. In fact, Asa Hartford was the closest and he was about 10 yards away. As I turned to move away I 'fell down a hole' and as soon as I hit the ground I knew something was badly wrong. My worst fears immediately flashed through my mind – 'No Wembley for you my son' – and that was just the way it turned out.

"This was the same ground where I'd had my England Youth trial the previous year, but never had a look-in. At that time Bill had said, 'Don't worry in the next year you'll get stronger and leave them behind,' which is what happened. But it was of little comfort at that moment. The pain was unbearable, the like of which I'd never experienced before."

Although Alan's omission from the FA Cup final wouldn't be officially confirmed until two days before the game, he knew from the moment he had winced in pain that there wasn't a chance of him strolling out at Wembley. Even having an ultrasonic machine installed in the treatment room in order to help try and speed up his recovery didn't have the desired effect. In one of the better decisions he'd make in his life, Alan ruled himself out of the final, knowing that had he played, he'd be denying a fully fit teammate his chance of glory. Dave Sexton would later say that had Alan played, Chelsea would not have struggled as much as they did.

In 2010, Alan once again recalled his agony on missing the FA Cup final with *Chelsea FC* magazine: 'When the game at Wembley ended in a draw, we tried everything to get me fit for the replay. Bill was on the phone non-stop, I saw doctors in Harley Street – including one who treated all of the top boxers – acupuncture specialists, a faith healer in Victoria and just about anyone else. Sadly it wasn't to be.'

Although Chelsea would go on to win the replay in an epic war of attrition in Manchester, the whole experience left Alan feeling numb. He was a teenager with the world at his feet, denied the opportunity of performing on the biggest stage. It's little wonder that the mental anguish from this exact period still haunts him even now.

"On the night of that glorious FA Cup final replay at Old Trafford – the first since 1912 – although I was dragged onto the pitch for the lap of honour, I was sick, as if my whole world had fallen apart. And it took me a long time to get over the experience. I actually caught the last train – the 'sleeper' – back to London rather than face the celebrations in Manchester. I drank all the way back home, and headed straight for the London Sporting Club casino for another drink.

"The whole place was going berserk because of this incredible comeback – they were all Chelsea supporters – so I left. I was that upset. The following day, I watched on as the open top bus parade passed by my local pub, The Stanley Arms. I then headed back to the prefab for a party, but it felt more like a wake to me. The last thing I can remember doing was lying in a bath, washing my hair with lager and sobbing. It was the most sickening feeling of my life."

The disappointment for the whole family was palpable. Around this time, it was also becoming more and more noticeable that Alan liked a drink. In order to enjoy the company of his teammates and peers, there was an expectation that you had to be 'one of the lads' and for someone so lithe, Alan could certainly knock them back.

Prior to the FA Cup final, alcohol had never really been a problem as such for Huddy. He enjoyed drinking because he enjoyed life. The fact that he was living the dream he'd strived for so many years to achieve meant a deserved celebratory existence. However, the change when it came was dramatic, quick and unpleasant. The Cup disappointment sent him spiraling downwards, to the point where the family feared for his mental state as much as his physical.

"That summer I went to Spain with my best friend Leslie May and our girlfriends, but came back about two stone overweight. I thought that I would be okay after going through pre-season but my injury meant that I couldn't train to my usual high standards. I struggled with my weight and so, for all the wrong reasons, I began drinking more and more. It was already out of control."

It would take a stern talking to from Dave Sexton, which unsurprisingly Alan didn't appreciate, for him to reverse the demise to some extent. On the training pitch there was no love lost between player and manager, both of whom had vastly differing ideas when it came to how the game should be played. Never frightened of letting people know exactly what he thought of them, even at that age, it was a fractious relationship at the best of times. But Sexton knew that Chelsea were a weaker side without Alan.

'The Kings of the King's Road', as they were affectionately becoming known, needed to up their game because European football beckoned the following season in the form of the – now defunct – European Cup Winners' Cup. The Chelsea 'Kings' kicked off the 1970-71 campaign in impressive style, losing only three First Division games before New Year, and crowds at Stamford Bridge only dipped below 40,000 on four occasions.

Chelsea were big business and Huddy was the conductor of the orchestra. This was never better evidenced than in front of *The Big Match* cameras just three games into the season. Down by two goals away at West Ham, Alan ran the show and would provide two identical crosses for Osgood to head into the path of Keith Weller, both resulting in goals. On each of those occasions, Chelsea's number eight went hunting for the ball, probing at the Hammers' defence and drawing them out of position with effortless ease. Alan was playing beyond his years, putting in a hard shift for his team. His snake hips might well have been more at home in the nightclubs of Knightsbridge, but for the moment they were certainly a star turn for the west Londoners.

Not known for his own goal scoring prowess, when he did get on the score sheet, it was invariably always headline news. The opener against Ipswich on September 26, 1970 garnered as many column inches as his strikes against Coventry and Sheffield Wednesday from the previous season. Peter Houseman's trickery on the touchline had bought him a yard of space and as he moved in-field, he teed up Huddy who was advancing just outside the area. Allowing the ball to drift across his body, a venomous shot was unleashed goalwards.

With the keeper beaten, the ball sailed agonisingly wide, caressing the outside of the net and hitting the stanchion before bouncing back into play. Perhaps it was the reaction of the crowd in certain parts of the ground that convinced the referee otherwise, but TV cameras would later show – on the Saturday night highlights programme – that the ball had clearly gone past the post. Nonetheless, referee Roy Capey awarded the goal to chaotic scenes on the pitch and on the touchline.

The Ipswich manager, the late Bobby Robson, was livid and led extensive on-field protests to no avail. Chelsea would go on to win 2-1, thanks to Osgood's winner, while Capey's reward for his unfortunate gaffe would be a demotion to officiate in the Newcastle and District League, Division One, the following weekend.

"I knew It wasn't a goal and I just turned round to face up for the goal kick," Alan explained to *Chelsea FC* magazine in 2004. "Suddenly, though, the ref was pointing to the centre-spot. The Ipswich players went mad, they were furious. Dave Webb said to me, 'Tell them it didn't go in', and I replied 'Fuck off Webby, we're on £30 a point'. That was the difference between having a meal in my favourite restaurant – Alexandre, on the King's Road – or not. Anyway, I'd had a couple disallowed so I thought that I deserved a bit of luck."

Despite his fluctuating weight and fitness issues, Alan was still holding it together on the pitch, even if he wasn't doing so away from the club. The injury would give him constant grief but each and every week he would play through the pain barrier.

"I was drinking for all the wrong reasons by now, my head was totally gone. Whereas usually I'd go on a run every morning, I remember playing table tennis instead as I just couldn't run. Against all the odds though, I played really well – particularly in Europe – against some great teams with outstanding players. FC Brugge were brilliant and, in Robbie

Rensenbrink, had the best player in the tournament. He was a complete magician with wonderful skill, balance and the ability to ghost past people, George Best-like. And CSKA Sofia were unbeaten at home in Europe until we played them."

In an age where wall-to-wall TV coverage was non-existent, British clubs playing in Europe had to rely on the eyes and ears of their – often understaffed – scouting network. Playing European teams 'blind' wasn't uncommon, and however unprofessional that may seem now, it was more of a help than a hindrance to Chelsea.

"No team talks about the unknown – it helped us enormously. Not that some of the boys were bothered, because it wasn't until halfway through our European mission that they actually got serious about it all. Why? Because they were intent on scoring in Europe in an entirely different manner.

"Most of our players only enjoyed it because they were having very exciting relationships with air hostesses, which eventually led to three or four divorces. I always say that the boys involved saw getting through to the next round as the bonus – not for the money or the kudos of winning, but for the girls – and for once I wasn't interested. I had enough on my plate back home."

A busy March and April in the league saw Chelsea lose three games in the space of 10 fixtures, and that late drop-off in form no doubt contributed to an eventual sixth-placed finish. By no means a poor season, but not perhaps what Sexton was looking for. The campaign would, however, be salvaged by a win in the Cup Winners' Cup final against the mighty Real Madrid. In truth, for all of Chelsea's artistry and will to win, no one really expected them to triumph against Spain's finest in Greece. The Karaiskakis Stadium in Piraeus was full to bursting, with 45,000 crammed in to watch what turned out to be a tentative affair on the part of Sexton's side – which might've had something to do with the shenanigans from the previous day.

"I was with four of our best players, all drunk before the biggest game of our lives. Osgood was the main instigator, drinking in the Athens Hilton as if the world was coming to an end, and telling me as I left the bar: 'Go back to the room and sleep well and I'll have another drink and score tomorrow.' Can you believe it? He did just that! What incredible belief he had in his own ability."

Osgood's second-half strike just before the hour was cancelled out at the death by Ignacio Zoco, who'd come up from the back in a final desperate attempt to get something from the game. Referee Rudolf Scheurer blew the whistle shortly after, meaning the teams would have to do it all again just two days later, when most of the supporters of either side had already traveled home. Less than 20,000 were there to witness a tetchy but slightly better spectacle.

"They were better than us in that first match, with Pirri the master in midfield. In the replay however, Pirri – who was now Real's captain – played with his arm in a sling after breaking his collar bone in the first game, and Charlie Cooke and I ran the game. We won via a great John Dempsey volley and, of course, Osgood promised another goal and delivered."

As he collected his medal, ran a lap of honour with the cup and enjoyed the now customary celebrations with his teammates and the faithful Chelsea fans, little did Huddy know that this would be the pinnacle of his career as a 'King of the King's Road'.

3

Marriage and the 'Good Life' Don't Mix

"He was supposed to represent the club as captain but he was no good at that, bloody awful in fact."

You might have thought that after such a stunning victory, the players would be the toast of the west London club. After all, it trumped the FA Cup win from the season before, when Chelsea had reveled in the kudos that beating a hugely successful Leeds side brought them. Not on this occasion though.

"There was no 'thank you' from Sexton. Nothing at all," recalls Alan. "Although we had won the trophy I was unhappy, mainly because I felt that we were all unappreciated. I never once saw Dave Sexton put his arm round Osgood and say, 'Thanks Os, you were brilliant.' Had he done so, we might have gone on to bigger and better things, not just as a team but as a club. Even our unsung heroes John Dempsey and John Boyle were never, ever given the credit they deserved."

To outsiders looking in, Chelsea were the team that every opponent wanted to be, and to beat. Football was still an entertainment business and, week-in week-out, the likes of Hutchinson, Osgood, Hinton, McCreadie and Hudson would

MARRIAGE AND THE 'GOOD LIFE' DON'T MIX

turn on the style. Supporters were happy to part with their hard-earned cash, yet for all of the fantastic value that the Blues were providing, and not just for their own fans but to football connoisseurs generally, something still wasn't right behind the scenes. Dave Sexton's autocratic style had put him at odds with just about everyone, including Huddy.

"All of these British-born talented young men making history, but earning peanuts and getting absolutely no credit whatsoever from the manager, will forever be unacceptable. I have vivid memories of our wonderful team spirit and togetherness – something that Sexton never understood – which came from our ability to not only work hard but play hard too. We were unbelievable on and off the field – and proud of it."

The summer break couldn't come soon enough, but the hangover from it continued throughout pre-season and into the first few games of the 1971-72 campaign. Winless in their first four and having conceded 10 goals, the pressure was on Sexton who, unsurprisingly, diverted the blame. The drinking culture inside the club was now common knowledge outside the Bridge, and it was much easier for the manager to pin his own failings on the playing staff. But, like poking a dog with a stick until it eventually retaliates, he'd fail to understand the significance of his words and actions. The tide had turned against him, and even Sexton's most trusted lieutenants were getting to the point where they'd had enough.

"Ron Harris was stripped of the captaincy for urinating in the bath after training. Sexton had then got in and washed his hair without knowing what 'Chopper' had done, until someone informed him about the extra 'bubble bath' the captain had added. The players felt Sexton got what he deserved and, for the first time, I think he understood the depth of feeling that was building up against him."

The team would go on to lose just three more games until the turn of the year, but that was in spite of Sexton rather than because of him. A 21-0 aggregate win against Luxembourg part-timers Jeunesse Hautcharage in the first round of their defence of their European title – including the club's record victory of 13-0 – formed part of this run, but there were no real celebrations amongst the team.

"I felt so very sorry for those players because they were bank managers, builders and milkmen, yet tried their hearts out. At the Bridge their captain ran on to the famous greyhound track to get the ball and take a throw-in. I stood there wondering if I was watching a Marx Brothers movie, not knowing whether to laugh or cry. Why? He only had one arm! I mean, they were about 16 goals behind and here was their main player with one arm, showing fantastic courage by chasing a lost cause. They were wonderful people."

Work continued to be a chore and a drain for the players, with the local hostelries more of an attraction than having to accede to Sexton's requests. As if to emphasise the point of a manager completely out of touch with his players, assistant Ron Suart was bizarrely asked by Sexton to gather all of the team together in the boardroom – to choose a new captain.

"We were about to travel for an away match and as we walked in, Ron handed us a piece of paper and a pencil and we had to write a name on it and fold it up. On the bus going to Euston station we all laughed about it and asked each other who they'd voted for. I was the only one who said myself, and I meant it. By then in my third season, I thought that I was the right man for the job: I got on with the older players, had their respect and was completely honest. I think Dave Sexton, had he chosen me, wouldn't have found a better player because I loved responsibility. Ron Harris was the wrong choice for a number of reasons, but especially for his behaviour when we

MARRIAGE AND THE 'GOOD LIFE' DON'T MIX

were on tour. He was supposed to represent the club as captain but he was no good at that, bloody awful in fact. Whereas I could mix with anyone."

Things came to a head during the journey home from Åtvidaberg on October 20, the second round, first leg of Chelsea's European Cup Winners' Cup defence, after drawing 0-0.

"The wheels were falling off and there were regular fallings-out between Sexton and Osgood. They had very heated words on the aeroplane, ending with the manager saying, 'I'll see you behind the North Stand when we get back.' The long awaited 'big fight' was on. We got to the Bridge and I talked Os into going into the Imperial Arms, Matthew Harding's pub in years to come. We had a few drinks as he calmed down, but he still really wanted the bout to go ahead. Can you imagine if it had actually happened?! The front pages would have been incredible, especially in the days of the legendary Frazier and Ali battles.

"Dave's father, Archie Sexton, was a famous boxer and Dave was a handful too, although a very nice man when he wanted to be. I often wondered who might have won, because Os loved a tear-up and the gaffer was a very fit man for his age – but I'm pleased to say that I had a big part in stopping it."

Huddy was always a lover not a fighter and his intervention on that day placated the centre-forward, but it was never going to be a long-term solution because Osgood thought of himself as both. At the Bridge two weeks later, the Blues would say goodbye to their European adventure, going out on the away goal rule after drawing 1-1. It was, by a distance, one of the biggest upsets in European football history at the time.

"We had to get our act together in the second leg and we absolutely battered the Swedes. I scored a wonderful 25-yard volley and then stood behind John Hollins as he smashed a penalty wide, which would have made it 2-0: game over. Somehow we conceded a late equaliser and were knocked out on the new away goals system. I was devastated and it led to things within the club falling apart.

"One of the biggest problems was that Sexton had his favourites, and I always thought that he should've given others more responsibility for taking penalties. Had Osgood, Cooke or I taken the penalty we would've gone through, but Sexton simply loved Hollins and it turned out to be costly. Every time I see John Hollins, even today, I can't get the vision of him putting the ball on that spot out of my head. There was no thought process or calmness in his play and he seemed to rush everything, which became a feature of his coaching and management style in later years."

The newspapers speculated for days afterwards as to the cause of such a seismic defeat, but none were close to solving the mystery of why the Kings of Europe were dispatched by unknown Swedish minnows. As if to defy their manager further, some of the players would make a point of being seen in all of the right places socially, with all of the right people. Michael Caine, John Alderton, Sean Connery, Raquel Welch, Denis Waterman, Richard O'Sullivan and Rodney Bewes were among the film and TV stars that Hudson, Osgood and the like were rubbing shoulders with on a weekly basis on the King's Road.

"I remember, around the same time, Sexton putting a notice on the dressing room board: 'Any player seen drinking in the East Stand will be fined and reprimanded'. To us, it was like something out of Colditz, but remember that Dave was a teetotal church-goer."

Had Alan been on top of his game at this point there's a slim chance that his manager might've turned a blind eye, but he was nowhere close to being the player he could be as that

MARRIAGE AND THE 'GOOD LIFE' DON'T MIX

season drew to a close. Speaking to Clive Batty for *Chelsea FC* magazine in 2010, Huddy was philosophical.

"My form dipped badly and I fell out with the managers of both Chelsea and England. The ankle was still playing up, and I was picked for an England under-23 summer tour to Europe, but I didn't go. I had other valid reasons for not touring because of the problems I was having at the club, and with my wife who was having our first child. We'd also just moved into a new house and I don't think I'd have done myself justice had I played. I spoke to Ramsey on the phone about my decision but he wasn't having any of it and told me that I'd have to accept the consequences. I ended up with a ban from international football which pretty much wrecked my England career. Looking back, I think the ban was very harsh and a slapped wrist would've been enough."

As was to be expected, one of the darlings of the football press quickly became news for all of the wrong reasons, and the associated meltdown was entirely predictable. A drink was never far away and it became a mistress for Alan. A drink, a glass or two to loosen him up and make him feel loved and wanted. He knew all of the pubs, clubs and restaurants in and around the King's Road like the back of his hand and if he didn't find solace in the bottom of a glass, it would be via the latest fashions from boutiques like Cecil Gee, Just Men and I Was Lord Kitchener's Thing. Huddy was christened the 'George Best of the South,' because of his long hair, love of clothes, women and night life. It was a reasonable comparison even if Manchester United's 'El Beatle' was in a class all of his own, on and off the pitch, but it was very alluring to Huddy who was five years Best's junior.

"We regularly played Manchester United at Old Trafford on a Wednesday night and then head for Slack Alice where George was always at the bar. He and I hit it off from day one.

HUDDY

Our team was a great bunch of socialisers – once we did the business on the field – and by the early 1970s George wanted to play for us and be a part of that scene. The players wanted him too but, of course, Sexton had other ideas."

Not even exploring the possibility of bringing Best down south was another nail in the coffin for Sexton's relationship with his players and it's a wonder that the Blues were still a semblance of a team by this point. A seventh place finish left them ahead of United on goal difference and 10 points behind eventual champions Derby County. Both Chelsea and United were much better on paper than their results had shown but, in the case of the Londoners, the decline was almost terminal, a League Cup final appearance notwithstanding. A sense that Sexton had lost the dressing room long before it absolutely became public knowledge was palpable, due in no small part to the nocturnal activities of the majority of his squad. To the players, it was a rebellion solely of Sexton's own doing.

"The restaurant, Alexandre, was pretty much the Chelsea FC restaurant, and run by some great queens from Malta who I got to know through my brother cleaning their windows. Camilla was a wonderful, wonderful man who I was very close to, as were my mum and dad. They knew nothing about football until John took me there and then I brought our 'Rat Pack' into their lives. Within a few weeks, I remember them travelling to Burnley for an FA Cup replay to watch us. They loved David Webb and screamed 'Butch' whenever he walked in. There was also all the flirting from the gay waiters, it was hilarious.

"Upstairs was the Markham Arms, another drinking den that I introduced the boys to. It was where we would go on a Saturday night after travelling back from away matches before finishing off in the Cromwellian Club. The 'Crom' had another gay character – 'Harry Heart' – who was the life and soul of the club, and if you asked him to have a drink he'd say, 'I'll

MARRIAGE AND THE 'GOOD LIFE' DON'T MIX

have a Camp Heart' and pour a Campari into a huge glass behind the counter. He would sip it as he looked seductively at his prey. I loved Heart dearly, a very funny man who really loved us going there. He embraced us more than Sexton.

"At Chelsea we hardly ever had team meetings, which was odd in itself, but I remember one night after returning to London from an away match we got to the Markham, which was really hotting up with the local talent, but all we did for an hour was have a meeting about what was going wrong. Osgood held court and told us how he loved the success, adulation and living up to expectation but also how much he cared for me and the rest of our inner circle. We were a very loveable bunch, something Sexton never ever understood.

"Tommy Baldwin and Charlie Cooke would drink elsewhere on the King's Road with Oliver Reed, Peter O'Toole and Richard Harris. It was one big ball of fun in the late '60s and early '70s with mods and rockers, Hari Krishna and 'flower power' hippies. We just had to be a part of that, whether Sexton liked it or not. Freddie Mercury often frequented The Coleherne, a gay pub, but that place wasn't for us – there were no women in there. The King's Road was one of the reasons why George Best wanted to play for us and although he finally moved there some years later, my greatest regret was him not signing for us and making up a forward line of Best, Hudson, Osgood, Hutchinson and Cooke – simply scintillating!"

Away from the good life on the pitch and the high life off it, long-suffering wife Maureen did her best to keep things ticking over. Like Sexton's, her's was also a losing battle.

"I never ever recovered from my injury and was at war with management over it because I was looking for treatment outside of the club; something I paid for myself which cost me a quarter of my £75-a-week wages. I fell out with Chelsea because I was seeking help and because our physios and medical staff in the treatment room just didn't understand my condition. I'd spend many hours in my bathroom using the hot and cold water treatment which, although it helped me in later life, tormented me at the time and led me to more drinking and more womanising. This was worsened by the feeling that I wasn't getting any sympathy or understanding at home.

It was probably not the type of marriage Maureen O'Doherty had envisaged when she tied the knot on July 17th, 1971. Huddy was besotted from the moment he laid eyes on her, in the Chelsea Bird's Nest, now The Ivy. Her beauty was stunning, but he never thought she'd fall for him. That she did rang alarm bells for some, but Alan fell in love immediately. Always a sucker for a pretty girl, Maureen was just about the prettiest he'd ever seen. From day one, however, she was never liked by any of his family and that was what ultimately drove a stake through the relationship he had with his mum and dad. Things turned very spiteful, very quickly, and their ire was likely to do with a rather novel career choice that Maureen had in mind for herself.

She wanted to be a Bunny Girl, and came straight out with it not long after they began courting. Bub was none too enamoured with Maureen's ambition and her presence at the prefab often turned it into a warzone. As savvy as they come, Bub had worked out the bigger picture long before Alan realised Maureen's infatuation with him was more about the *cachet* it brought her, and less about the love she had for her man. A leg up in certain social circles would make her dreams easier to achieve but that's not a situation Bill and Bub would allow. They believed Maureen adored their boy's money and lifestyle but wasn't in love with him. Bub was convinced that she could sense it in the way Maureen looked at Alan and in her demeanour towards him, and Bub believed Maureen knew that she knew this. A family rift was inevitable. For a man who thrived on the love and support of his nearest and dearest, this was an unexpected turn of events which would ensure his form for Chelsea continued to suffer.

"Not long after I met Maureen we all fell out because the family were very much against her, but their suspicions actually proved to be correct. At the time I thought 'just let me work it out,' and so I moved out and lived with my Uncle George the season after the FA Cup win. One night I saw Mum and Dad when I was with Maureen at Alexandre and I crossed the room to offer an olive branch. Bill met me halfway and he was really mad. 'If you love her then marry her,' was all he managed before storming off. I went back to our table and said, 'Maureen, we're getting married,' and that was it.

"It was horribly contrived and I only did it to please them. Otherwise, I would never have got married. That night, things happened so quickly. One minute we were sitting eating and drinking with Danny Gillen and ten minutes later, after Bill and Bub came in, we were getting married. Bloody ridiculous. You might say I had to sacrifice my freedom to have a relationship with Mum and Dad again."

On the face of it the family rift had healed, to the extent that everyone was back on speaking terms again. The plain truth of the matter was that an open wound still festered as far as Alan's parents were concerned. He was going to make the biggest mistake of his life, in their opinion, and there wasn't a single thing they could do about changing the mind of a headstrong man of 20, who knew his own mind and was free to do as he pleased. Not that Huddy identified with being free at that point in time. He felt he'd been coerced into something purely since it would get him welcomed back into the family unit with open arms. With enough on his plate elsewhere, and having had enough of the constant stress and animosity, it was a decision that needed to be made.

HUDDY

The wedding was less than two months after the Real Madrid victory, swiftly turning summer 1971 into the best of Alan's life. Or so he thought. Nothing would really prepare him for the discovery, not long into his marriage, that his parents had been right all along. Being a proud man, it was impossible for him to go back with his tail between his legs, he'd need to tough this one out. The bed was made and he'd have to lie in it.

"I was warned about her by others because she was never out with a girlfriend, always with a young man or two – almost as if she was looking for the right one – whereas I was only out to enjoy myself. In those days, although marriage was the 'in thing,' it was madness to throw away your youth: 'sow your seeds' and all that. If she hadn't wanted to be a Bunny Girl, I think we might never have got married. My parents would've been fine if she'd been a local girl from Chelsea but she came from Forest Hill and, to them, it just looked like she had arrived out of nowhere, looking for her golden goose. I didn't have any money, but I was becoming a big name by that time.

"She wasn't a naïve girl either, she'd dated several footballers before me, and at such an early age. I think she might've been the original WAG, a term which was unknown in those days. I'd heard it said that girls did target players, rock stars and film stars to secure their future happiness – or should I say for their money. Today, it's a fact. You've only got to look at tennis players, racing drivers and golfers – they all have beauties on their arm. I can't believe I was so stupid. Like George [Best] I made the mistake of getting married far too young, without really knowing the person, and for all the wrong reasons."

Huddy only ever wanted to do what came naturally to him and to make the most of the gift he had been born with, but it was becoming a blessing and a curse all rolled into one. Chelsea were now on the slide but were still attracting crowds of over 50,000. Every week Alan's name would be sung religiously

MARRIAGE AND THE 'GOOD LIFE' DON'T MIX

and, intoxicating though it was, it contrasted sharply with his home life.

Those peaks and troughs go some way to explaining why Alan preferred the company of teammates and hangers-on rather than the awkward and uncomfortable atmosphere at home that was alien to someone who had lived in the happiest of households as a young man. For a talented professional footballer who enjoyed the spontaneity of the high life with his teammates and the night life with a never ending supply of willing women, the reality of married life and the routine that accompanies it was not something that Alan was used to or enjoyed.

Despite being in its very early days, the writing was already on the wall for his marriage, as Alan soon sought an escape from home life by heading back to the lights of the West End and the company of the many young glamorous girls eager to be in his presence. He was also sure that Maureen knew what he was up to and accepted it, as long as he came home after his boozy and amorous nights on the town. There appeared, to Alan, to be an 'understanding' between them.

Popular with the other players' wives and girlfriends, to whom she was just another dutiful home-maker, Alan saw an all altogether different Maureen. Behind the 'Bunny Girl in-training' façade, he quickly came to see her as a calculating and 'street-wise' manipulator who knew that by falling pregnant she'd secure her grip on him.

"In the early days, Maureen met some famous people through me and was having a better life than if she'd married an ordinary 'Don the Decorator' in Forest Hill. She was smarter than anyone gave her credit for and, in the end, got exactly what she wanted."

Life in general quickly became a constant battle for Alan, which drove him to further excesses. His mood swings were such that even the 'Hello Darling, I'm home' as he came through the door would strike fear into Maureen. What mood would he be in? Had he been drinking? How long would he be home for? Most of the time, she knew the answer and most of the time she wished she didn't. Theirs had quickly become a marriage in name only: a mere piece of paper.

Drinking ever more heavily by now, Huddy was unable to put in a decent shift on the pitch, and his fall from grace was noticeable. Maureen hadn't signed up for that either. Having a husband who was barely around was one thing, babysitting a drunk was another. Not that Alan really cared too much at this point. Falling pregnant was a lifesaver for her but the pregnancy wasn't without the usual complications. Whilst Alan has never regretted Allen's birth, and that of Anthony later – and loves both his sons as any father would love his children – during her pregnancy his regular hangovers and mood swings meant he was unable and probably unwilling to support Maureen through her pain and discomfort which made the tension in the house even more unbearable.

Allen's birth in 1972 – at the Queen Beatrice Hospital, Earl's Court – was an event deemed newsworthy enough to feature in all of the papers. It would only heap more pressure on a man who was really struggling mentally and emotionally. In truth, at just 21 years of age, the birth of his first-born had probably come too early for Huddy. How on earth was he going to cope with the pressures of being a parent on top of everything else? If things were bad at home already, and remember that this was barely a year into his marriage, then they were about to take a turn for the worse.

But Chelsea were now foremost in Alan's mind. How was he going to make them great again? Home life had changed for the worse, there was simply no getting away from that, and trying to convince everyone otherwise was becoming futile.

MARRIAGE AND THE 'GOOD LIFE' DON'T MIX

Even Dave Sexton had begun to start asking more awkward questions, and no amount of flannel was going to gloss over the truth.

The drinking was never really going to be tolerated, but it's possible that Sexton might've turned a blind eye if everything had been working well on the pitch. Problems outside work were starting to be brought to work and that was unacceptable to Sexton, a manager who was already looking at ways to stifle Alan's extra-curricular activity. This was the final straw.

An exasperated Sexton gave Alan a final warning and it initially appeared to do the trick. Despite being some way off of his best, Alan could still influence the game and he and his colleagues were at least grinding out the results. By mid-December, Chelsea had only lost five league games and were looking a decent bet to enjoy some success during that 1972-73 season – against all odds, it must be said.

However, from December 12th to January 12th, Chelsea wouldn't win again, a full calendar month before a victory arrived. Worse was to come as the Blues would only get four more victories before the final few weeks of the season. A great run all the way to the semi-finals of the League Cup lightened the gloom that was enveloping the club at the time, but a two-legged defeat by Norwich put paid to any optimism. For a team that had been deified not long beforehand, this was embarrassing.

Chelsea FC magazine in 2004 notes Alan's words on why exactly Chelsea were spiralling downwards, seemingly at a rate of knots. "Eddie McCreadie was past his best, his eyes were going and that affected him a lot. I think we'd seen the best of David Webb as well, although he went on to do well at QPR. George Best definitely wanted to come to us at that time so if an Abramovich had been around then, we would definitely have got him, even if we'd had to smash the transfer record."

Reference to Best is folly really, because there's no doubt whatsoever that Sexton would've vetoed any such move. At least the Irishman would eventually don a Chelsea shirt – albeit for Peter Osgood's testimonial – almost two years after Alan and Os had left the club!

Another reason why Huddy wasn't enjoying his football was because, after signing Steve Kember, Sexton insisted on playing his midfield maestro out on the right – a position that he disliked – in order to accommodate Kember. The February 2001 issue of *Chelsea FC* magazine is a good reference for Alan's feelings.

"I needed to be where the ball was. I didn't mind going out there now and again, but I didn't like being stuck out there and only getting the ball when other people felt like giving it to me. I had to go looking for it and that would annoy Sexton. When I played in the middle, I was always in the thick of it. Moving me out wide was like asking a marathon runner to be a sprinter. I wasn't being selfish or anything like that and I thought I was helping the team. He was effectively expecting me to play as a wing-back – to track back and pick up a full-back, and then get forward to join in the play. It just wasn't me and that was one of the things that led to me leaving. I was brought up and educated to play as an inside-forward by my father, who told Sexton at the very beginning, 'Don't try to tell him how to play, he already knows.' From then on, things became much more personal than professional with the manager."

The point of no return really came at the beginning of the 1973-74 campaign when another summer's worth of drinking and womanising had quite obviously taken its toll, even more than the previous summer's shenanigans had. Alan was sluggish in pre-season again, but this time he didn't appear overly bothered about getting back into shape. Although he may not have realised the extent of it at the time, Alan was

MARRIAGE AND THE 'GOOD LIFE' DON'T MIX

now clearly suffering from depression, which was seeing him sink to lower depths and by now he'd lost the appetite for the game he loved. Not only that, he couldn't be bothered with the responsibility of being a parent nor a loyal husband. Drink continued to be his best friend: the difference this time was that recovering from a good session on the sauce wasn't really on his agenda.

He was still only 22 years of age and hadn't come anywhere close to reaching his peak as a player, but neither had he fully matured as a man. Too much, too soon, is a far too simplistic way of accurately describing the descent into what was by now a serious mental illness. Alan was a sick man but to admit it wasn't really the done thing in those days, and he may have suspected that he'd get little sympathy from his manager. Sexton was too busy trying to keep Chelsea afloat, and failing. Only three wins in the first 13 games of the season didn't bode well.

How could a team boasting some of the greatest talents in the First Division – Charlie Cooke, Tommy Baldwin, Peter Osgood and Alan Hudson – be underperforming so badly? The pundits in the media were also now pondering why Sexton's team, awash with such quality, were imploding. Sexton refused to discuss the matter, preferring instead to let rip at his players behind closed doors. These dressing room show-downs became increasingly prevalent and by Christmas 1973, mutiny was in the air. Sexton had, without any doubt whatsoever, 'lost the dressing room'. His tactical changes and coaching influence weren't reflected by positive performances on the pitch, and his brusque manner off it was now falling on deaf ears.

Four losses in December prompted the manager into some surprising changes, which saw Huddy dropped for the trip to Sheffield United on New Years Day 1974. Osgood joined him, as did Baldwin and goalkeeper Peter Bonetti. The papers loved it, and prior to the game were unanimous in their view that Sexton had essentially cut his own throat. As it was, Chelsea played as well as they had all season – which in truth wasn't that well at all – and came away with a vital 2-1 victory. Sexton thought he had now got it right, but was this a one-off or would a Chelsea team without Osgood and Hudson be better than one with them?

Alan couldn't have cared less by this point. He'd had a Christmas to forget and within a fortnight he was gone, with Stoke City signing him for a then-record fee of £240,000. January 1974 would therefore prove to be a watershed moment in both Alan's career and Chelsea's immediate prospects.

"Sexton was livid during training the week before I left because, after being dropped from the team to go to Sheffield, Os and I chose to train with Dario Gradi who ran the reserve team. It was about 10.25am when Sexton sent a message over for me and Os to get back to the first-team, but then met us halfway where nobody could hear the conversation. 'You're on your way out of this club,' he told Os. Standing ten yards away, the manager also confronted me – and he didn't hold back – 'As for you, I've been trying to get rid of you for ages, but now you're going with him.' When he'd finished, Os and I showered and went to Alexandre in total shock. I was not too bothered because I was totally bewildered by both my football and my marriage, and nothing was going to plan. Os was completely shattered though, he was 'The King of Stamford Bridge'."

Although Alan had wanted out, there was no doubt now that the club needed him and Osgood gone. "Personally, I blamed the board," Alan would tell *Chelsea FC* magazine some time later. "The directors near enough demanded Sexton sell Os and myself and I can understand their reasoning: 'We'll get rid of Hudson because young Ray Wilkins can play like him, and as for Osgood, who needs a troublemaker?' It suited me,

MARRIAGE AND THE 'GOOD LIFE' DON'T MIX

to be honest, though, I was done with the club and still am bitter at the way they treated me."

Although there's also likely to be some truth in the assertion that both players were sold by Sexton to help pay for the new East Stand, their relationship with the manager had been at breaking point for months. Someone had to go and it clearly wasn't going to be Sexton. That he used the ground expansion as a plausible excuse for their removal worked well within certain circles, even if the truth was widely known by the media, 'off the record'.

Osgood would leave two months after Huddy, but not to Stoke as had been expected. Southampton ended up being the grateful recipients of his services and, shorn of two of their best players, Chelsea finished the campaign teetering on the precipice and just one point above relegation in 17th position. They had won only four more games after New Year's Day and failed to score in four of their last five matches. They were lucky, Sexton not so. A few matches into the following season he would be sacked.

By contrast, Alan became reinvigorated by the words and deeds of a special man. A man who would become the one person, apart from his father, who would shape his personal and professional existence like never before. The difference in Tony Waddington's personality to Sexton's was incredibly marked – like two different sides of the same managerial coin. If Chelsea were on the way down, Alan Hudson was clawing his way back out of the abyss – and about to produce the best football of his career.

4

Mr Waddington

"I crossed the road and entered this dark, bleak park looking for someone I'd never met and as I walked past a phone box, the red door opened and out stepped Waddington."

Alan's media-driven persona – one he believes was created by Fleet Street – no doubt authored his next playing destination. As someone who was, by common decree, one of the best players in the country at the time, why weren't the likes of Derby or Leeds coming in for him?

It could only be for one reason, that Alan was trouble and damaged goods. He certainly couldn't be trusted to deliver a consistently high level of performance at that point in time, because he wasn't really in any fit state – physically or mentally – to do the business. Yes, he was outspoken and wasn't the type of personality or player that wanted to be moulded into something or someone else, but he was still a fine footballer. Even a long way from his best, he was still better than most of his teammates or opponents.

The loss of the more fashionable clubs was, as it turned out, very definitely Stoke City's gain. It's true that the Potters wouldn't necessarily have been Alan's first choice, but they

MR WADDINGTON

were prepared to break the British transfer record to land him, with the result that Alan felt something he hadn't experienced for years, either in his home or working environment. Being wanted again was a wonderful feeling.

In Tony Waddington, he had met a kindred spirit and someone who 'got' Alan from the first moment. A manager who was well known for making the seemingly impossible, possible.

Anthony Waddington was born in Openshaw, Manchester on November 9, 1924. A stocky youngster, he quickly derived most enjoyment from having a football at his feet, something that, not unlike a certain Mr Hudson, would lead to hours of endless fun with friends in the back streets of the city. Cobbled alleyways between the gardens of row upon row of red-brick houses became pitches. It was Wembley for Tony and his friends one day, Old Trafford the next. They didn't have a care in the world, all that mattered was there were enough young boys to get a game started.

Such enthusiasm for football never wavered, continuing throughout his childhood and early teens. He was never City, mind, always United, and so it was a very easy decision for him and his parents to make when scouts from the Red Devils came calling. It wouldn't be until 1941, as a 17-year-old, that he would lace up sporadically as an amateur for the youth team during the Second World War, whilst serving as a telegraphist on board HMS Hound, a minesweeper which took part in the D-Day landings.

A serious knee injury during his Navy days appeared to have put paid to any dreams Waddington had of making it to the top, but he confounded the experts with an iron will and determination – much like his record signing would do 20-plus years later. At the end of the war, Crewe Alexandra were prepared to take a chance and their faith was handsomely repaid. As a wing-half, Tony would amass over 200 appearances across seven seasons, scoring eight goals, before leaving to join Stoke, the team where he would eventually build his legend.

Once playing was no longer an option – his knee far too battered to allow him a career at any level – but known within football circles as a fearsome competitor on the pitch, there was interest in whether his knowledge and application of the game could translate into a youth coaching role at the Potters, something he would undertake in 1952, aged just 28.

Any initial fears were soon put to bed, for it was quite obvious that Tony had an aptitude for the other side of the game. Not afraid to take risks with his team selection or in allowing his youngsters to fully express themselves, Stoke quickly gained a reputation at youth level as being a team to watch, something that would later become a feature of his senior squads. A plethora of hard men were the minders in the team, but there would always be room for a luxury player or two who wouldn't necessarily track back and help the team out, but could turn the game on its head in the blink of an eye. Some games were lost as a result of this insistence on mixing flair with grit but that was a price he was prepared to pay. That wouldn't go down well with the hierarchy at the Victoria Ground, but Waddington was only interested in getting his staff to play a certain way. His way. Over the course of the next few years, his teams won many plaudits and there weren't any raised eyebrows when he was named assistant manager of the first team in 1957.

A little too keen to impress upon manager Frank Taylor on which players he should be looking at from the lower reaches of the club, he often wasn't the most popular choice with Taylor himself or in the dressing room. Yet he always received a healthy dose of respect from the players when out on the

MR WADDINGTON

training pitch and, very importantly, from the supporters who'd followed his progress from the youth set-up. Supporters who were starting to turn on Taylor.

The team spent another season – 1957-58 – in the old Second Division, and it looked to be going well as the Potters maintained their position in the top two from the beginning of the campaign until Christmas. However, a shocking second half saw them finish a lowly 11th, 15 points behind eventual champions West Ham United. No signings that summer wasn't the most popular of moves either, but it was entirely necessary as the costly redevelopment of the Victoria Ground took priority.

The 1958-59 campaign began with a 6-1 opening day humbling at Fulham and despite losing two out of the next four, Taylor managed to rally the troops. Stoke would then go on a nine-match unbeaten run which lifted the team to third in the division, but any designs on continued success were again swiftly removed as they lost four of the next five. Six unbeaten would briefly lift the spirits once more, but the remainder of the season was disjointed and largely forgettable. Given the lack of investment in playing staff, it wasn't really a surprise that another campaign had fizzled out, and a fifth-placed finish was certainly not what Taylor, Waddington, the board or the Victoria Ground faithful wanted.

Four victories in the opening five matches of the 1959-60 season was nothing more than a false dawn because Stoke's final season in the 1950s was an absolute shocker. Crowds were well down and the football fare being served up wasn't the best. Although Taylor became ill towards the end of the season, thus making any decision to remove him a little more difficult, the board had already made up their minds. The team lost 10 straight games between March and April sending them plummeting down the table, and new chairman Albert

Henshall was left with little choice. The manager couldn't continue, no matter the extenuating circumstances.

Taylor would later tell the media that he couldn't understand why, after eight years service and always giving his best, he was being shown the door. It was an odd statement to make and probably turned any supporters he had left at that point against him. Before the official announcement came that Waddington would step into his former mentor's shoes, many in the locale had already predicted it. However, it might never have happened. Years later, Waddington was interviewed by the *Stoke Sentinel*.

"I assumed I never needed to apply for the post when it became vacant long-term. Just a short time before the meeting, Mr Henshall took me across the ground and said that unless I applied quickly there was no way that the board could consider me under their articles of association. I felt it wasn't necessary, but I quickly penned an application and I was appointed manager shortly afterwards. My wage was £13 per week and £2 of that was a win bonus. Stoke offered me £11 and for that amount they had their pound of flesh out of me."

A lesser man would've turned them down, but he loved the club and was looking to its future. Perhaps if the Potters had been on a more stable financial footing, a more acceptable level of remuneration would've been forthcoming but, as it was, Waddington had a simple decision, to take it or leave it. He was only too aware that times were difficult and there was no room for negotiation.

"There was a huge stove in the centre of the dressing room and coke [coking coal] was constantly shoveled on, resulting in fumes all over the place. The stove supplied the hot water for the communal bath and sometimes the water wasn't changed for a week – you can imagine the colour of it some days."

Money was so scarce that there was a fear that creditors were closing in and if things didn't change quickly, then bankruptcy was a very real possibility. Waddington needed to pull the proverbial rabbit from the hat on the pitch if Stoke City were going to have any hope of surviving. Although unpopular initially, 'Waddington's Wall' as it became known much later, was an overly defensive tactic that managed to keep a very poor Stoke side, who lacked confidence and coherence, in the Second Division by just three points. In the summer, the manager would make a move which divided the town's opinion of him, but re-signing the great Stanley Matthews for a £3,500 outlay seemed a risk worth taking, even if he was 46 by now and had left the club some 14 years earlier.

Waddington was 10 years Matthews' junior, so there was instant pressure. How well would this manager cope with integrating and getting the best out of the biggest name in English football? The paying public were intrigued and instantly the tills were ringing. When 15,000 extra fans came through the turnstiles for Matthews' first game back, against Huddersfield, Henshall and his colleagues on the board were unanimous in their opinion that they needed to trust their manager and let him get on with it.

Although the Potters had yet to gain promotion back to the top flight, Waddington had changed the mood. Players were happy in their work and supporters were buoyant, believing that under this manager the club could go places. Convinced in his own abilities and those of his squad, and with man management skills that were second to none, Tony Waddington had just about everyone eating out of the palm of his hand.

He had that special gift of making people feel good about themselves and if there was a way in which he could flip a negative on its head, for the sole purpose of getting a player to give another 10 percent, then he'd find it. Genius may be pushing it a little too far at this stage, but he was certainly a man manager *par excellence*. Henshall was happy enough to accede to almost every demand that Waddington made, knowing that by so doing, he could only enhance the manager's dream of taking the club back to where they belonged. A dressing room upgrade was only the beginning.

The latter half of the 1961-62 season saw him pull off another transfer coup. Manchester United's Dennis Viollet was, at 28 years of age, still regarded as being in his prime. 179 goals in 293 games spoke volumes and his character was in keeping with that which Waddington liked to have about the dressing room. Matt Busby would take some persuading but an eventual £25,000 move to Stoke was a masterstroke. Promotion would again prove beyond them, but the manager was only just getting into his stride.

Skillfully working within a tight budget and with a superb blend of youth and experience in the side, 1962-63 – Stoke's centenary year – would become memorable for all of the right reasons. Not that anyone had an inkling of what was to come after the first half-dozen matches. No wins in six, not scoring in three and only managing a single goal in two more: for the investment that the directors were making it was only right that Waddington justified a return, and Henshall was beginning to ask questions for the first time since appointing him. Thankfully, he was a manager who wasn't prone to panicking, and continued to work in the same way as always, knowing that, eventually, things had to turn. They did of course. And how?!

On September 12, 1962, only 11,596 fans bothered to turn up for the visit of Charlton Athletic. It was well below the attendance from their three previous home matches of the season but by the end of the game, those that had stayed away were the ones kicking themselves. The south Londoners were taken apart with Viollet the destroyer-in-chief. The striker

MR WADDINGTON

had plundered four of Stoke's six in a sensational attacking performance, albeit Charlton's three in response had given Waddington a defensive headache, the second time in four games that the Potters had conceded so many.

The second coming of the Waddington Wall was an obvious tactic and though it didn't please some, it had the desired effect. It would be almost Christmas before they'd let in so many again, coincidentally their first defeat after an epic 18-match unbeaten run which had seen them climb up the Second Division table, and stay there. The crowds were flooding back too, 20,000 or more guaranteed for each home game. Stoke were surfing the crest of a wave now and even that 1-3 defeat by Leeds on December 15 was brushed off as a 'blip'. A 2-1 victory away at Rotherham on Boxing Day only served to highlight that the Leeds performance was indeed a one-off, but no one was prepared for what happened next.

It would be March before Stoke could play again after the harshest winter in over 200 years totally disrupted the football calendar – and Waddington was livid. His team were 'in the zone' so to speak and Mother Nature had intervened in his master plan at the worst possible moment. There was nothing he or anyone else could do of course. League games were on the back burner, whilst the FA Cup had never seen anything like it.

David Miller of *The Guardian* wrote, 'When Middlesbrough beat Blackburn 3-1 in a replay at Ayresome Park on 11 March, this brought to an end the most chaotic third round in the then 91-year history of the FA Cup. The round had begun on 5 January and lasted 66 days through frost, snow, ice, power cuts, thaw, rain and mud. The third round was spread over 22 different playing days and there were 261 postponements. Sixteen of the 32 ties were called off 10 or more times.

'Topping the list was Birmingham v Bury, which stretched

through 14 postponements plus one abandonment and a replay, while Lincoln v Coventry was postponed 15 times. The record was set in Scotland, where the Stranraer v Airdrie cup tie was postponed 33 times, while in Yorkshire, Barnsley played only two matches between 22 December and 12 March. It was Britain's coldest winter since 1740 and also caused mass postponements in both rugby codes and the loss of 61 days of National Hunt racing.

'The FA Cup third round of 1963 gave birth to the Pools Panel which, on four successive Saturdays under different chairmen – Lord Brabazon, Sir Alan Herbert, Group Captain Douglas Bader, and Sir Gerald Nabarro (the Tory MP) – gave results for the postponed games, of which there were more than 30 on 26 January.'

Fortunately, during this time Stoke players were able to keep their fitness up by training indoors. It wasn't ideal but it gave Waddington what he needed when normal service resumed. Jackie Mudie's hat-trick against Walsall on March 2 was a perfect way to restart the campaign even if overconfidence from both manager and players would prove their downfall a week later. Carrow Road witnessed Norwich's best 90 minutes of the season as they tore into their opponents from the first whistle. Waddington's Wall was blown to smithereens as the Canaries romped to a 6-0 victory.

The match also saw Jimmy McIlroy's debut for Stoke, having just completed a cut-price, and controversial, £25,000 move from Burnley. Bob Lord, the Clarets' Chairman and a man renowned for being a larger-than-life character, had sold the player to Henshall without telling either the player or Waddington. It was a move that worked, but the uproar it caused in the national press was almost certainly the main reason why nearly 26,000 supporters turned up at the game. That, and the chance to see a 48-year-old Stanley Matthews still doing his thing. Unfortunately, Matthews was well below par on the day and it was, by a distance, Norwich's best result of the campaign.

The shock of such a reverse allowed Waddington to use it as a motivational tool, and a 10 game unbeaten run was the result. Stoke had conceded only three times until the last game of that run, against Huddersfield, where they'd let in as many as they had during the previous nine games. A late-season wobble saw them lose three out of the next four, but with only a win needed from their final two games to secure top-flight status, Stoke took 12,000 supporters to Bury on May 14. Spurred on by what was almost half of that matchday crowd, Stoke could taste glory. However, the win would ultimately elude them on the day, a crushing 2-1 defeat bringing them back down to earth.

This is where Tony Waddington came into his own. On the coach back to Stoke, there was no talk about the loss. None whatsoever. Only how, in four short days, his players would fulfil their destiny against Luton Town, who were mathematically relegated. How fitting it would be that Stanley Matthews would score the second and deciding goal – his only goal that season – in a 2-0 victory to send the club back into the big time after a decade away. 'Waddington's Wonders' were headline news, the board's faith finally justified.

Peter Dobing was brought in over that summer for a record transfer fee – later usurped by Alan's move from Chelsea – and John Ritchie would also sign from Kettering Town. In keeping with a long-held practice of working within his means, Waddington wouldn't go overboard and throw money around unnecessarily. An astute business, as well as footballing brain marked him out as special and although strengthening the side was required, he wouldn't do so at the expense of upsetting the financial equilibrium at the club.

HUDDY

Two wins from two at the beginning of 1963-64 season had the Potters' faithful dreaming of reaching greater heights but it was another 11 games before Stoke would taste victory again, a winless run that included seven losses and three draws. The last of those draws, a six-goal epic at Stamford Bridge on October 5, 1963, was watched by 29,204 spectators, one of whom was Huddy.

"I recall being there at the Bridge and Tony was standing by the tunnel just below me, the Chelsea fans abusing him because of his tactics. I remember looking down from the old East Stand and watching the look on his face as Stoke snatched a valuable point. Something stood out about his manner. An unshakeable belief in his players and the style he was cultivating at the club. It was clear that the abuse – and it was shocking let me tell you – didn't bother him, and I liked that. I might have only been 12 years old at the time, but I was streetwise enough to understand football culture and the vile nature of the language I was listening to. That Waddington wasn't rising to it at all stuck with me. When it happened to me later in my career, I was already ahead of the game and *au fait* with how to brush off such abuse. Tony had been an inspiration in that respect.

"There were only a few minutes to go at Chelsea and he was desperate to hang onto a draw, which Stoke got. Waddington's Wall had done the trick yet again, only this time he was building a new team with old heads like Maurice Setters at the back, players who would kick their own granny if necessary. A tough bunch of battlers sprinkled with one or two great footballing minds. I also remember Eddie McCreadie getting booed during the match by his own supporters for kicking Stanley Matthews, but Chelsea's manager Tommy Docherty had congratulated Eddie because his job was to kick whoever wore that number 7 shirt no matter how old they were – and Matthews was just three months shy of his 49th birthday!

MR WADDINGTON

"I brought you down here to kick wingers and if you don't get out there and do your job you'll be going back to East Stirling," was the essence of Docherty's tirade. For all of 'The Doc's' histrionics, it was actually Tony's demeanour that really stood out for me. He looked every inch the very serious football man. When I first met him years later at the Russell Hotel in London, I remembered that October day."

Not too long after the Chelsea game, just before New Year in fact, Matthews would succumb to a serious injury which meant he would miss the rest of the season. Waddington would have to get used to life without a player who, despite his advancing years, could still be the team's talisman. Stan would spend the 1964-65 season in the reserves, playing just one first-team game – his last ever – against Fulham on February 6, 1965. That it came five days after his 50th birthday was of little consequence to the man himself, but the significance remains to this day. The evergreen Ryan Giggs would last until his 40th year, Gary Speed retired at 41 whilst Billy Bonds was still playing for West Ham at 42. They're probably the only modern day examples of players that will come anywhere close to the 'wizard of the dribble' in terms of top-flight longevity.

Matthews' absence from the team continued to be felt, with Stoke losing five straight games at the back end of 1964, and then two more from the next four matches. Waddington's pragmatism and *nous* would again see to it that Stoke could overcome even the most adverse situation and only three more defeats before the end of the season saw the Potters earn a respectable, if not overly impressive, 17th place finish: 10 points clear of relegation, but only 12 behind 5th place in the division.

"Stan was the only player I have ever heard of that changed his boots at half time," recalls Alan. "He thought that every ounce counted. Every piece of dirt collected in a first half was left in the dressing room. He was that concerned by carrying extra weight that by taking a heavier pair of boots off, he would gain the extra inch needed to get past his full-back. I only ever had one pair of boots and coped just fine. It made me think, and I must be honest here, that Matthews was a total lunatic. I mean, a piece of mud giving him an advantage: come on!"

In that season's League Cup, Stoke were inspired, and their participation in the 1964 final against Leicester City was a reward for the hard work of everyone at the club. From the tea lady to the boardroom, everyone was pitching in. The two-legged affair – on April 15 and 22 – sandwiched the destruction of Manchester United at the Victoria Ground. The Red Devils were put to the sword by three goals to one, in front of 45,697 fans, the largest attendance of the campaign and over double that of the first leg of the League Cup final.

Keith Bebbington's follow-up, from Bill Asprey's rasping 30-yarder that was too hot for Leicester's Gordon Banks to hold, looked like it had given the Potters a decisive lead to take to Filbert Street. Then Waddington made a rare mistake. Clearly on top in the game and with over 20,000 fans roaring them on, the manager instructed his players to go for another against the tiring Leicester players. The Foxes managed to soak up immense home pressure and, as has been seen so many times on a football pitch, they hit Stoke with a sucker punch and grabbed an undeserved equaliser through Dave Gibson.

The way in which Stoke dismantled United however, left those in attendance purring and in no doubt whatsoever that they would bring home the trophy. It was a feeling that was shared by the team and their manager too. The dream turned into a nightmare before the second leg could even take place, after regular keeper Lawrie Leslie was ruled out with injury. Calvin Palmer being stretchered off during the game did nothing to aid Stoke's cause and despite a valiant effort from

MR WADDINGTON

first until last, Leicester would triumph 3-2 (4-3 on aggregate). It would bring the club back down to earth with a shattering thud but, as had been seen so many times before, Waddington didn't give in to the negativity. Even his famous 'Wall' was, for him, a means to a positive end rather than what might be termed 'anti-football'. Defence was and still is just as much a part of football as attack, and Waddington had to ensure his team played to its strengths.

For such an unfashionable side, Stoke had the knack of regularly playing above themselves and that was down to the way in which Waddington fused the talents of his side together. Walking the walk as well as talking the talk was a speciality and it's easy to understand why such a mind-set, allied to his managerial talents, were manna from heaven for his players. Think of the hold that Sir Alex Ferguson had over his Manchester United charges and we're definitely approaching the same territory. Without the incessant pressure that would often accompany some of the bigger teams in the top flight, Waddington was largely able to go about his business untroubled. Local media were firm but always fair with him, whilst fans were intelligent enough to understand and realise that their mid-table berth was probably going to be as good as it got. The tills were still ringing so Henshall and the board remained content enough.

Some mediocre years followed, but things kept ticking along. Stoke were never fantastic during the mid-to-late 1960s but neither were they rubbish. An average team playing average football but as long as they could keep themselves afloat financially and in the top flight, that was good enough. Waddington was continuing to develop players as best he could, and it would eventually pay handsome dividends.

Gordon Banks, one of the heroes of England's 1966 World Cup win and a thorn in Waddington's side during that 1964

League Cup final loss against Leicester, was bizarrely dropped in the aftermath of England's finest hour. Never one to stand on sentiment, Waddington pulled off another transfer coup to match that of Matthews' return years earlier. Just nine months after lifting the Jules Rimet trophy at Wembley, Banks would leave the Foxes in April 1967 and sign on the dotted line for Stoke at a cost of £50,000. Huddy clearly remembers that it was an extraordinary coup for Waddington.

"Gordon and I spoke years later and he told me that Tony had gone to Filbert Street to sign him and had met with him just as he was going into the manager's office to get his loyalty payment. Banksy came out sullen and told Waddington that 'You've had a wasted journey. They won't pay me.' As I would later come to understand, there was never any panic in Tony's demeanour, and he said, 'Gordon, slow down and wait here, I'll talk to him.' Ten minutes later he was back out with the contract which Gordon subsequently signed. Tony advised Gordon that he'd got Leicester to pay up and it was only years later that a Mr Crow, one of the Stoke directors, had let the cat out of the bag that it was actually Waddington himself who had paid it to ensure that the deal went through. That was the measure of the man, and he would do exactly the same thing for me later on."

The *Stoke Sentinel* takes up the story: 'With very little money available to spend, Waddington drew on the pool of talent that the city was generating. Several local-born players were also brought in, among them defenders Eric Skeels, Denis Smith and Alan Bloor, who went on to amass a combined total of nearly 1,600 appearances for the club. The team was improving every season and reached their peak at the turn of the decade. They made it to the 1971 FA Cup semi-final only to lose to Arsenal, Waddington going on to cement his position as Stoke City's greatest manager in 1972.

MR WADDINGTON

'An 11-game cup run (this included four games with West Ham United in the semi-final; the two-legged match was replayed twice) culminated in a trip to Wembley for the League Cup final against Chelsea. Waddington fielded an ambitious 4-1-5 attacking formation and was duly rewarded after a scrambled Terry Conroy header beat Chelsea keeper Peter Bonetti for the opener. Despite a sterling performance from Gordon Banks, Chelsea equalised through Peter Osgood. As the second half progressed, Bonetti failed to hold on to a driven Jimmy Greenhoff shot, allowing George Eastham to slot home the winner.'

Huddy would be on the losing Chelsea side at Wembley of course and would see at first hand the virtue of utilising your back line in such a way as to stifle the life out of the opposition. Whilst it might have been anathema to his own style, he would later come to appreciate Waddington's methodology.

"The 1972 final was something a little different. The loss to Stoke never affected me anywhere near like missing the Cup Final versus Leeds United.

"In a way it was the greatest result of my life because had Stoke not won, Waddington wouldn't have had enough money to buy me, and that move changed my life.

"That was the day, I think, that Waddington realised I was the perfect man to replace George Eastham, and although I was not at my best, he could see that I could control the match like he wanted.

"He was a master tactician, who knew players inside out and he also knew Jimmy Greenhoff and I would complement each other perfectly. He was right."

Continuing their good form, Stoke were on the verge of an unprecedented cup double, only to be undone, for the second successive season, by Arsenal in the FA Cup semi-finals. The Division One title was Stoke's next target as far as

Waddington was concerned but in order to set about achieving that ambition, he would need to spend, and spend big. By January 1974 both Stoke City and Alan Hudson had reached a watershed and it was a bittersweet day when Huddy got wind of the Potters' interest.

"I was sitting in Alexandre with Osgood a day or two after being told that we were no longer wanted at the Bridge and I remember us laughing, thinking that there would be a host of clubs coming in to sign us. We told Christine Matthews, the Chelsea secretary at the time, where we were, and if any clubs were interested to call the restaurant. We joked about going to Liverpool with Shankly, Manchester United with Bestie and Busby and even Spurs or Arsenal, but the phone on the wall didn't ring.

"Just after we'd finished our meal and the place was ready to close and set up for the evening, the phone finally rang. It was Christine and she asked Camilla if she could talk to me. I laughed at Osgood saying, 'Unlucky mate, no-one wants you,' and grabbed the phone in anticipation. 'Alan, are you okay?' Christine asked. I was fine after a few glasses of red and a beautiful steak pizziola. 'Lovely Chris, what's up?' I said. 'Tony Waddington wants you to be at the Russell Hotel at seven.' Immediately my mind turned back to that day 11 years previously. Watching him revel in the negative draw-at-all-costs tactics and the terrible and constant expressions of hate and anger he received from the stands as a result.

"Anyhow, I said to Christine, 'That's Stoke City isn't it? No one from Liverpool, Manchester United, Arsenal or Spurs?' I was a little taken aback, I have to be honest. The Saturday prior I had been to QPR thinking that their chairman Jim Gregory wanted to sign me but nothing came of it. I spoke to Terry Venables afterwards but it was clear that a move was a non-runner which was a shame as it would have suited me down

MR WADDINGTON

to the ground and would've stopped the subsequent upheaval of moving in with Geoff Hurst – a man who would later refuse to sign me when manager of Chelsea after I returned from Seattle.

"I didn't even know where the Russell Hotel was at the time although I would come to understand later that it was Waddington's London HQ. I got there and walked up towards the front door. About three steps from the top the doorman said, 'The man you're looking for is over there, in the park.' I crossed the road and entered this dark, bleak park looking for someone I'd never met and as I walked past a phone box the red door opened and out stepped Waddington. He was hiding from the press and anybody else that might have cottoned on about his interest. 'Alan, come and sit down over here,' he said walking towards the park bench. It was like a Hitchcock thriller! I liked him immediately, he was a gentleman and now I saw what I'd seen at the Bridge. A man of morals, who did things his way. I couldn't fail to be impressed, especially after putting up with someone like Sexton for all those years. Tony's style was immediately engaging, warm and sincere and our deal was all done and dusted within minutes.

"I hadn't been used to that sincerity at Chelsea and I was in a total daze as I made my way back to my parents' prefab. Although by now I was living in Southfields, near Wimbledon, I had to discuss the move with my dad. I recall Bill standing next to the fridge in their tiny kitchen and after listening to me explain the situation – and being fully aware of all the speculation in the papers – he was, as always, straight to the point. 'Sign for this man, he knows a footballer when he sees one plus it will get you out of this place. The bright lights of London will be the death of you.'

"He was absolutely spot on with his advice but what he didn't know, and neither did I at that time, was that Waddington was a genius in an old fashioned suit from the Potteries. I mean a real genius, one who seemed to know everything.

"Tony's last words to me had been, 'I'll see at you at the Bridge in the morning at ten.' I went home and told my local publican, Tommy Hunter, 'Not under any circumstances must you sell me a drink after the last bell.' Tommy threw me out at 11.30pm and I went home thinking that I would impress my new manager. I was there at ten, he wasn't, and I thought the deal had fallen through. All of a sudden at 11am, in walks Tony with his tie halfway round his neck and looking like he had just drunk London dry. I found out later, by a good source, that he had been in an all-night club until 6am. It was then that he told me, after I signed the contract, that he was going to sign Osgood. I can't even remember us talking about money. All he said was 'Don't worry Alan, I'll look after you, you just concentrate on playing for Stoke City.' I've always thought that he bought me because we were so alike, both on and off the pitch. He was also an inside forward, he loved 'proper' players and loved everything I did. A true perfectionist in football and in life."

If Alan had any doubts whatsoever as to just how badly his new manager wanted him, he'd find out in the *London Evening Standard* later that day. A fee of £240,000 had been agreed with Chelsea and he would be Stoke's record signing. For a player with as big an ego as Alan possessed at that time, being 'cock of the walk' suited him perfectly. Knowing that one of his best pals was also on his way to Stoke gave him a sense of well-being he hadn't experienced for some time. Waddington had, almost in the blink of an eye and without knowing, boosted Alan's confidence and he would celebrate in the only way he knew how – with a night on the town. As it turned out, Osgood's move to the Victoria Ground never materialised. There was no doubt that Stoke wanted him and had conducted initial negotiations with the player, but it would be to no avail.

The *Stoke Sentinel* noted that: 'Peter Osgood seemed certain to be on his way to join his old Chelsea pal Alan Hudson at the Victoria Ground. He was an interested spectator as Stoke played Liverpool, and then had a night out at famous nightspot, The Place. We don't know what happened in Bryan Street that night, but instead of signing for Stoke, Osgood announced he was going to quit football after Chelsea refused to sell him. Then, just as suddenly, he signed for Southampton. 'I had great hopes of Osgood lining up alongside Hudson,' said Waddington, 'but from what he told me he joined Southampton because he would not have to leave his home in Epsom'.'

Chelsea's reluctance to sanction that particular deal would hammer another nail into the coffin of the relationship that Huddy had with the club. The club that had given him his big break, and that had nurtured his talents from his youth, was dead to him now. He was going to make it his business to show the Blues what a horrendous mistake they'd made by selling him and as Chelsea continued sliding down the table, Stoke City and Alan Hudson started to flourish.

5

Stoke

"I know what I was. But I always produced the goods. People forget that."

"This is Alan Hudson."

Four words that Tony Waddington uttered to signal the arrival of his new signing to the Stoke first-team squad. As if Huddy needed an introduction. They all knew *who* he was, but they also thought they knew *what* he was: a diamond of a player on the field, a disaster off it. Did they really want someone of that ilk alongside their tight-knit group? As was his way, Alan bowled in like he owned the place. Not quite Lord of the Manor, but not far off it. Geoff Hurst, for one, wasn't impressed. New signings needed to be looked after and welcomed but Hurst, a World Cup winner, wasn't going to kowtow to this West London upstart.

In he came with a swagger, surveying the scene and eyeballing each and every one of his new teammates. All expensive aftershave and Saville Row threads, he stood there in the middle of the horseshoe that the squad had made looking like a peacock fanning its tail feathers. It really wasn't the way that the 22-year-old should've announced himself, and within

STOKE

the space of 30 seconds, he'd already made enemies. The lack of warmth that greeted such arrogance and pomposity wasn't quite hostile, but there was certainly an atmosphere. Huddy was still revered, despite his loss of form and off-field activities, but an element of jealously was bound to rear its head once the club had decided to break the British transfer record for him. It goes with the territory. Alan didn't give two hoots of course. They were only work colleagues after all, and they'd soon understand his value to the side. Quicker than perhaps even they realised.

No one could get near him in his first training session. None of the anger at his arrival was meted out, because Alan was simply too good. Denis Smith, who'd already been at the club for six years and would go on to make over 400 appearances for Stoke, remembers the day clearly. "My first impression of Alan was that he could play, after he left me on my backside in that very first training session. Not many players ever did that to me and I didn't like it at all." It might also go some way to explaining why the pair never really saw eye to eye throughout Alan's time in the Potteries.

"We would *always* have different opinions because we were both such strong characters. We didn't have a personal relationship because of that, and Alan and I certainly had a few disagreements – he was very sure of himself and had a big personality. Not my cup of tea. As a player he was very good but in my opinion he should've been better – his lifestyle stopped him from being a great player. I mean, I liked a drink but I was never in his league. The real shame is that when he wasn't too drunk he was an intelligent bloke. I was fortunate enough to play with a few good players, and Alan was up there with the very best, but I learned from him that you can have God-given talent and waste it. He should've played more than 100 times for England."

HUDDY

It didn't help Alan's introduction to life at Stoke City that Waddington had singled him out again before the training match which would conclude that first session. It was another reason for his new colleagues to dislike him, their minds already made up about him before he'd even showered and changed.

"We had a practice match, like teams did back then. Once the first team was announced, they would play against the second XI. They were matches I hated playing in because players who were left out might take it too seriously and I might end up getting injured. Anyhow, on this occasion – my first day – as we were standing in a circle, I was handed a different coloured 'bib' from the others. I was the only player with this certain colour on.

"The idea [from Waddington] was that when a first team player got the ball he *must* give it to me. Well, as you can imagine, that went down like a lead balloon and Mickey Pejic in particular, hated the idea. Every time he got the ball he'd run it down the left side ignoring me, and a few of the others followed suit. Although this was embarrassing for me and made us enemies in our dressing room from the off, at least I knew on the Saturday against Liverpool who was going to pass to me and who wasn't, which was a massive help! I wasn't a mug and I knew from day one that my team mates weren't happy with my signing, but that helped me because I was fighting for not only my career but my life at that time – and so a few more enemies did not bother me."

However, Alan did absolutely need to be settled off the pitch and to have some stability that would ensure as little stress as possible. Hurst had been approached to be some sort of minder to Alan and, in his autobiography *1966 and All That*, he recalls: 'Tony Waddington asked Judith and me if we would help Alan settle in his new environment. What this meant was simply this – could he live with us? Please! It was a slightly unusual request but Judith said that she didn't mind having a lodger in the house, so we agreed."

It was an odd relationship on the face of it, and in actuality. A player who had been there, done it and was still one of the most celebrated English footballers thanks to his World Cup final treble, babysitting a strapping young buck who thought he deserved to be in such esteemed company but yet had never come close to hitting those highest of heights on the pitch. Regardless, the arrangement appeared to work – thanks to Judith. "I wasn't happy about it at all to be honest, but Judith made me feel very welcome," Huddy recalls. "It was a relief because at the time I thought that Geoff was only doing it for the money. It had been patently obvious from the beginning that I wasn't really his type of bloke, but he got paid by Stoke for having me there. I also heard a rumour – although I don't know if it was true – that the club paid to have his house redecorated instead of paying the cost of putting me up in a hotel."

Before Alan would have a chance to showcase his talent in his much anticipated debut, Hurst would at least do his bit for morale and, probably against his better judgment, take his new lodger out with the team.

"That first night I was completely exhausted after the weekend partying in London to celebrate my move, by having another party round my house in Sispara Gardens and then travelling up north by train. I thought, 'If I have a nice early night I could get four good days training in.' Just as we finished dinner in the bungalow, Geoff dropped it on me that 'We're going out to meet the boys at The Place.' I knew The Place nightclub through playing in Chelsea's midweek matches up at Stoke and I recall one night in particular, which was a League Cup match on Wednesday night.

"There was a bust-up between Osgood and Sexton at half time, which led to Os not coming out for the second half – a serious mistake as we lost 1-0. After the match Os disappeared immediately, so once I'd changed at the hotel, I jumped in a mini-cab and asked if anyone had heard about his whereabouts? The minicab driver said, 'Yeah, it's the talk of the taxi rank, a cab took him to Hanley, to The Place.' I walked in and there was Os standing at the bar with my friend Johnny Fennell, drinking champagne and orange out of a washed-out bucket. Typical Os!

"In any event, Monday night was apparently when most of the Stoke players went out, The Place was where they would always end up and it was where I was off to with Geoff Hurst to chat bollocks with people who clearly didn't have time for me and who, bar one or two, had made no effort at even small talk during training. At that point I couldn't have cared less. Put it this way, I wasn't one for making friends for the sake of team harmony. I got chatting to a blonde soon after walking in there and, scanning the room, I could see that as far as women were concerned, I wouldn't be missing London too much. It also meant I didn't need to socialise with players who, with just a few exceptions, hadn't bothered to say a word to me in training that morning. To give you an idea as to the 'welcome' I received from some of them, one player came over and said, 'It's quite fitting we should meet in a night club after what we know about you.' What he knew about me! The cheeky so-and-so knew nothing about me. That kind of summed it up.

"On the Thursday, Geoff and I went out with Osgood which meant that I'd been out 'on the town' until the early hours on two of the four nights during my first week, before making my Stoke debut. So much for staying with Geoff and Judith to help me get plenty of rest after training!"

By the time Liverpool arrived at the Victoria Ground that

STOKE

Saturday, however, Alan was ready. He had played against them only three weeks previously for Chelsea, and had had a stinker. It was January 19, 1974 and 32,789 fans, including all of Alan's family, crammed in to see what all the fuss was about.

"I was very nervous as I'd only had one real, what I'd call 'proper', training session, on the Friday in the gymnasium with sweat bags and everything on. I was so bad for Chelsea when we'd played Liverpool, it was like I was in a coma – I was shocking. So I thought, 'Take it easy, play a few short passes and don't give the ball away,' because if I did, the crowd would've got on my back immediately. And of course, Tony would've got abuse for spending on all that money on a womanising, playboy boozer.

"After I got through the first 20 minutes though, I began to open up the play, not misplacing a single pass. I ran the match after that and got rave reviews in what turned out to be the most important match of my life. I would've been called the 'record transfer flop' but instead I won the fans – and even some teammates – over from that game forward. I think even the London press came up to report on 'the biggest gamble of all time' because nobody was interested in signing me apart from Waddington. It was immediately obvious to me that he knew how to handle me, and what buttons to press to get the very best out of me. I remember seeing all of my family afterwards and being totally relieved. I'd not played that well for so long and here I was, back to my best, after just five days under Waddington's management. In the dressing room, post-match, he just looked at me and nodded as if to say 'You're worth every penny'."

It's not through rose-tinted glasses that Alan recalls that day either. His debut was so good that it's still fondly remembered by those who were privileged enough to witness it. Stories can be embellished over time but this was one performance that needed nothing extra added for effect. Huddy was unplayable. "On the field, his impact was immediate," said Hurst. Wolves manager Stan Cullis, who'd been in the crowd, said later the same evening on BBC radio that, "It was the best performance, as a debut, I have ever seen." A conductor supreme who ran his opponents ragged for 90 minutes. The 22-year-old with the world very much at his feet.

Things would get better and better on the pitch, but were still far from satisfactory off it.

Maureen hadn't made the move from London, and it would eventually cause problems all round. She didn't like the idea of Stoke. It certainly wasn't the glitz and glamour she'd been used to and perhaps it was a little 'down market' for her liking. "What we originally thought might be weeks turned into months," Hurst recalled, and the strain of trying to keep tabs on Alan meant more stress than was necessary for England's hat-trick hero and his wife.

"Alan had a rebellious streak. He wasn't a bad lad, but he was too easily led astray. A bit cocky, but vulnerable. There was a bit of the George Best about him. You couldn't meet a nicer guy than George, but he had a self-destruct button. There was nothing malicious about Alan either, but he invariably seemed to make the wrong decisions. My task, as a senior professional, was to keep him on the straight and narrow."

It got to the point where Waddington himself had to visit London to persuade Maureen to bring herself and son Allen up to the Potteries. That Huddy hadn't suffered in a professional sense was missing the point. He needed to be with his family. Ironically, by the time she had acceded to Tony's request, Alan had already got himself acquainted with regular female company from The Place and could've done without the inconvenience of having a wife in tow.

STOKE

On the pitch he became a real darling of the terraces, fully deserving of all of the plaudits that were coming his way. It's not a disservice to any one of his colleagues to suggest that his arrival at the club, and his subsequent level of performance were the main reason behind why Stoke finished the campaign so successfully. "It was quite something, as if I'd been reborn at 22, whereas Matthews was turning 49 when Waddington bought him. The two of us are still compared in Stoke as to who was the best signing but Tony always said that I was!"

Even Hurst admitted as much in his book. "It was a remarkable revival and [Alan's signing] proved to be the defining moment of the season for us. With him prompting from midfield, we climbed steadily upwards. We beat Leicester, Tottenham, Chelsea – Alan scoring the only goal at Stamford Bridge – and finally Manchester United in the last game of the season."

Indeed, when Huddy had joined, Stoke were languishing fourth from bottom yet, by the end of the season, they'd lost just twice more and ended up qualifying for Europe. One of the best games during this period was against Leeds United on February 23, 1974. The visitors to the Victoria Ground were on a mammoth 29-match unbeaten run that had begun on the opening day of the season – August 25, 1973 – against Everton.

The Toffees had been blown away 3-1 at Elland Road in a sparkling display and when Arsenal had been defeated at Highbury two days later, followed by their north London neighbours Tottenham being swept aside 3-0 before the week was out, there was a sense of bewilderment at the standards of Don Revie's team so early in the campaign.

His pre-season boast of suggesting the ambition for his side was to go unbeaten throughout the season was dismissed at the time as being fanciful, disrespectful and incredibly naïve, but by the end of September, having won eight of nine games – drawing the other – the chattering classes amongst the football fraternity were full of it. Talk began to turn to who was actually good enough to beat them rather than the notion of an unbeaten campaign being completely dismissed. For a modern day comparison, think of Leicester's rise to the 2015-16 Premier League title and the 'will they, won't they' discussion that was a common theme throughout.

Leeds were playing far and away the best football and even though some games were close in results terms, Revie's side always seemed to have things under control. Incredibly they were still unbeaten at Christmas and closing in on the top-flight record – at that point – of 30 matches without losing. There was a sense of it very definitely being achievable, more so when, in the space of seven days in February, Leeds would draw with Chelsea and beat Arsenal at Elland Road whilst taking the points at Old Trafford with a 2-0 win over Manchester United. Then came their trip to Stoke.

Lifetime supporter Fred Ball, recounted his memory to the *Stoke Sentinel*;

"Leeds were unbeaten in 29 league games and hoping to equal the record, so there was a considerable build-up of interest before the game. The bookies gave odds of 9-2 on a Stoke win and hundreds of supporters, including myself, had a bet. We felt if anyone could beat Leeds it was Stoke. They could always turn it on against good teams. Incidentally, Stoke had an interesting 4-2-4 attacking formation, with John Ritchie wearing the No 11 shirt, and they were confident, having been undefeated in nine games themselves. That ebbed away in the first 20 minutes though when Leeds were two goals up.

"After 15 minutes Bremner scored a cheeky goal at the Boothen End from a quickly-taken free kick as [Stoke goalkeeper] John Farmer stood by his right-hand post organising Stoke's

STOKE

wall. He put the ball down just outside the penalty area and immediately stroked it along the ground into the left-hand corner. To the astonishment of the Stoke players the referee signaled a goal and waved away all protests. With Stoke still in a state of shock, Alan 'Sniffer' Clarke scored a second for Leeds with a typical effort, whipping the ball past Farmer after dashing clear of Stoke defenders. At this stage Leeds looked arrogant, but the game changed completely when Alan Hudson got into it and started to play.

"Hudson played a little one-two with Greenhoff before pushing the ball through a gap for Mike Pejic, who beat Harvey with a terrific left-footer into the top corner. Then, just before half-time, it was 2-2 when Hudson scored his first goal for Stoke. Ritchie headed the ball down and Hudson shook off a man before coolly slotting it home. As Stoke went in at half-time, you'd have thought from the roars of the crowd that Stoke were already winning. In the second half it really was a battle of the titans – blood and thunder stuff like a cup tie – with the ball going from end to end, and some crunching tackles. Stoke had the fire power up front in Hurst and Ritchie, yet ironically it was the marauding Denis Smith who got the winner in the 73rd minute.

"He put a diving bullet header past Harvey after Ritchie had headed the ball back across goal to the far post. I thought Ritchie had a fine game. He was always a threat. Towards the end Leeds were agitated and after Bremner chopped a Stoke player down there was a *melee* involving a dozen players. That night the game was on *Match of the Day*, so we could relive the thrills."

Huddy was in his element. Just six weeks or so after his transfer, here he was, running the show against the best team in the country. Prompting, probing, little 'give and goes'. If the footballing public hadn't already, they sat up and took notice of Alan Hudson again – and of Stoke City. "Regarding that goal of Bremner's, he put it into the net as a joke. Even he couldn't believe it when the referee gave a goal and neither could we. But once we had pulled a goal back, I knew we were going to win. I'd forgotten that my goal in that game was my first for Stoke and in the second half, there was only going to be one result. For the rest of the season we felt we could beat anybody. They were happy days."

Although disappointed, Leeds still only lost three more games in the space of a March fortnight and won the league at a canter.

Although untouchable in a footballing sense, Alan was a divisive and prickly character in the dressing room when he wanted to be and Denis Smith was still none too impressed. Perhaps Waddington turning a blind eye to Alan's extra-curricular activities wound Smith and the other players up. It was an open secret in the dressing room that Alan would often be out boozing heavily the night before a game, something that bothered everyone else more than the manager or Huddy himself.

"Tony Waddington knew alright, but always gave me the look as if to say, 'You can do it, but if you dare let me down.' To me, that is the sign of a top-class manager. We're all human beings and each one of us is different. To be a manager – not just in football circles – you need to have the *nous* to know your staff. How they work, what they do outside of their working hours, what makes them tick, how do you get the best out of them. I know what I was. But I *always* produced the goods. People forget that."

The self-destruct button that Hurst referred to was never more evident than during the summer of 1974. Alan was back down in London for a period and was swiftly reacquainting himself with his old watering holes, even taking Hurst himself to one or two during a pre-arranged meet. By the end of the night, it was probably nearer to five or six different pubs, and it gave a real insight into the life Alan had been leading whilst at Chelsea. Hurst left his colleague to it, a full day and night's drinking wasn't for him.

As that summer came to a close and with Alan by now back in Stoke, he asked Hurst if he could borrow Judith's car and of course the striker thought nothing of it. "We had given him permission to borrow it, expecting to get it back in once piece," Hurst wrote. "He wrote it off in a country lane." It wouldn't be the only car crash he would have that year either, and the second had much more far-reaching consequences.

Eleven days before Dutch masters Ajax were due at the Victoria Ground in the first leg of Stoke's maiden UEFA Cup match, and after a comfortable 2-0 victory over Carlisle, a game in which Alan had scored, Waddington invited him and Hurst for a drink at his local in Crewe. At closing time, Alan foolishly decided to drive back and took Hurst home, before setting off to Barlaston where he now lived.

Not too long afterward, in Newcastle-under-Lyme, Alan slammed his car straight into a bush. Cut and bruised, he called Maureen from the nearest local pay phone. "You fucking idiot," she yelled. "Why do you keep doing this to yourself? To us." If it was sympathy he wanted, he wasn't getting any, but he did need someone to get him the hell away from the scene of the accident before the police turned up. Maureen still hadn't moved from London at this point in time so she had little choice, and when Geoff Hurst's phone rang in the early hours, he instinctively knew something was wrong.

"Maureen explained where Alan was," Hurst recalls in *1966 and All That*, "and I dressed quickly, climbed in my car and set off to find him. The car was buried in a thicket. When I found him, he was shaken and bleeding but not enough for a hospital visit, I took him home where we cleaned him up, bandaged his wounds and put him to bed. It was nearly 4 a.m. before Judith and I finally went to bed. The police knew Alan had been in an accident because they found the car ... but they were very understanding."

Alan was ineffective in the following week's win over Coventry City as was to be expected, his head and hand injuries received in the accident severely hampering his effectiveness in what was a disjointed individual performance. And it was no better four days later.

"I was in the best form of my life and my confidence was sky-high but, to be honest, that crash left me in a bit of a mess. I had to play against Ajax but that was a poor decision on my part, it was like they were playing against 10 men. I wasn't at it, and I knew I'd let myself down, my teammates down, and most importantly Tony."

The Potters held Ajax to a 1-1 draw in that first leg on September 18, a remarkable score line in a match where Piet Keizer was majestic for the visitors. Although Johan Cruyff had left for Barcelona by this point, Hans Kraay's team still boasted talent throughout the side, including Johnny Rep and Ruud Krol amongst others. It was Krol, the captain, whose bullet saw the Dutch side take the lead but Waddington's half-time team talk did the trick. Denis Smith's equaliser, and the way in which the team had played in the second period, had given them genuine hope that an upset might be on the cards in the replay a fortnight later.

Alan would be back to his mercurial best in that game, but Stoke just couldn't score. They held the Dutch masters 0-0 but went out on away goals and although he'd partly redeemed himself with a performance of genuine quality, some of Alan's teammates would never forgive him.

Despite the initial fall-out over the repercussions of the crash,

STOKE

Huddy wouldn't learn his lesson and crashed another car into a new roundabout. Alan slammed his car so hard into it, that it embedded itself in the centre. Even now it's known locally as the 'Alan Hudson' roundabout! That he walked away with barely a scratch is remarkable, but he even had the brass neck to write and complain to the council that it should have been better lit, conveniently bypassing the fact that the skinfull he'd consumed was ultimately the cause.

Initial opinions about Alan had changed, certainly in a football sense, over the course of the first few months after he had joined Stoke. How could they not after the way in which he had reinvigorated the team. Yet a niggling and understandable annoyance at the way he treated his body never really went away. Alan's father had seen the move as the right one because it would keep his son away from the bright lights of London and the temptation of the wrong type of company – more so because he would be 'looked after' by Hurst. The reality of the move was that if there was somewhere that served alcohol, with pretty ladies in abundance, Alan would find it as easily as he would a 50-yard pass to Jimmy Greenhoff.

Teammate Terry Conroy liked an occasional drink too but Huddy was a law unto himself. "He was very consistent in his habits and never came back on the same day he went out," Conroy remembers fondly. "Huddy had stamina in abundance. After an evening out with him you suffered for a week, but his own powers of recovery were remarkable. He would roll up for training on a Tuesday morning, never late, cover his body in black bin bags and sweat all the fluids from his previous night's exertions. The great thing about Alan was he was always at the front, leading the way. Some of the other lads had gone to bed early, but suffered when the session got tough. Not Alan. Bloody incredible!"

Huddy continued to wow the crowds, his colleagues and

fellow professionals as the 1974-75 season got underway. The understanding that he built with Greenhoff in particular was an art form, poetic and majestic. The brushstrokes with which he caressed the ball and threaded eye-of-the-needle passes with alarming regularity were a total joy. Always with a steely edge, mind. For all of his evident quality, he could, and would, still mix it with anyone who wanted to stand toe-to-toe.

There was still just one small, nagging issue. Alan's chronic ankle trouble, which had been playing up for some considerable time, was beginning to get much worse. Puffy and sore after matches on pitches that hardened as winter set in, it was so bad by Easter weekend that Alan seriously considered resting himself for fear of further damage to his ankle and his career. Two gruelling draws in London: 2-2 at Upton Park on Good Friday and 1-1 at Highbury the following day, weren't the best preparation for Stoke's next game.

"On the Easter Monday we were due to play Liverpool after those two matches in London so on the train home I told Waddington that I couldn't play a third game in four days on those hard pitches, my ankle just wouldn't take it. He just said for me to report for the game as usual, and the pitch would be fine as he'd heard that rain was forecast. It didn't rain at all, of course. I knew Tony was a genius, but a rain maker?!

"He'd persuaded the Stoke-on-Trent fire brigade to turn up early on Easter Monday and give the pitch a 'good watering'. The best part was that I arrived at the Victoria Ground for the game – having skipped my Sunday lunchtime drink, as he'd suggested – with no intention of playing, even after going through my normal pre-match routine. As always, I'd pulled into the car park at 1.45pm and, before going into Tony's office, I thought I'd pop my head into the dressing room where I saw my boots on my bench next to my number 10 shirt.

"The crafty old sod – I knew he'd do something like that

because he told me how he used to do much the same with Sir Stan. So, off I went to his office but something stopped me. As I passed the tunnel I looked at the state of the pitch, and to my absolute amazement the entire pitch was drenched. My heart starting pumping like never before and when I walked straight into his office his face was a picture, as if nothing had happened. 'How many tickets do you need Alan?' was all that he said. I took my 16 tickets for my family and friends, who had all travelled up from London, and thought that one great deed deserved another. The old maestro had done it again. What a master of man-management he was.

"Before the game, Kevin Keegan came up to me and said 'Huddy, this pitch is amazing, we're only 45 minutes from here and the sun's been shining for weeks on Merseyside!' 'Stoke has its own climate, it's always raining here.' I cheekily replied. I repaid Tony with one of the finest footballing performances of my life, which had the Boothen End singing, 'Alan Hudson walks on water'. On that particular day it could not have been any truer. The rain-soaked pitch was perfect for me and we outplayed Liverpool, who had by now taken over Leeds' mantle as the team to beat.

"As we were taking in the magnitude of the win and the manner of it, there was a knock on the dressing room door. Bill Shankly, who'd recently retired as Liverpool manager had popped his head in and said, 'Can I come in Tony?' to which Waddington replied 'Our dressing room is your dressing room Bill.' I was still taking my boots off and out of the corner of my eye saw Shanks heading towards me. I looked up and he offered his hand. 'Son, I thought I'd seen the greatest ever performance by Peter Doherty but you were bloody fantastic, well played.'

"As I looked around Tony simply gave me that knowing look, whilst those teammates who despised me were gutted, and I revelled in their discomfort too. I couldn't wait to shower and tell my father and Uncle George – who were waiting in the North Staffs Hotel – what Shankly had just said."

Although he wouldn't show it at the time, the emotion of that particular moment – the great Shankly placing him above a player who was one of the first to ever be inducted into the Football Hall of Fame and who had once been described as "*the genius among geniuses*" by England striker Len Shackleton – moved Huddy to tears. It was an acknowledgment from one of the very best in the game, and that meant everything.

Alan would've jumped at the chance to play for Shanks, but hardly anyone else. Many has been the time since the end of his playing days that Alan has been vocal in asserting that Bill, Bub, Waddington, Uncle George, and friends Leslie May, Tony Davis and Bobby Eyre were the only people who he wanted to play for. People who truly meant something to him. Not those Stoke City colleagues who would only pass the time of day with him if they absolutely had to.

"On match days I'd get as many as 16 tickets for those coming up from London. They all joined the Stoke City Supporters Club, and never missed a match home or away. Bub would even get all her shopping done in and around Stoke Market before kick-off, leave it in the Conservative Club and have it carried onto the 8pm train to Euston. She, Bill and the rest loved every minute of my journey with Stoke."

A journey which, with three games left of the 1974-75 season to play, still saw Stoke in with a chance of winning the title. They had followed up the Liverpool victory with a 3-0 home win against Chelsea and, if they could finish the season by defeating Sheffield United, Newcastle and Burnley, there'd be nothing anyone else could do – little old Stoke City would be lifting their maiden top-flight championship. Perhaps the pressure became too much because not only would they fail

STOKE

to win any of those games, they failed to score as well. It was quite an anti-climax and a big disappointment to the players and their faithful fans.

Stoke never really got going after an average start to the next campaign. The hurricane that battered the area in January 1976 had an enormous impact on the club, and not just structurally or financially. The roof of the Butler Street stand was blown off, and the cost of the repair work would eventually see to it that Messrs. Greenhoff, Pejic and Hudson were sold in order to satisfy the banks. What started out as the greatest adventure of Alan's footballing career ended in utter sadness. Waddington didn't want him to leave, he didn't want to go, and he was still only 25 years of age. In football parlance, Alan hadn't yet 'reached his peak'.

Like it or not, Huddy had to accept that the money he would make for the club – £200,000 as it turned out – would help them enormously. With a heavy heart he would bid his mentor, manager and friend, Tony Waddington, a long goodbye. It was horrible but necessary, and teams that previously wouldn't take a chance on him were now queuing up to sign him. The bright lights of his home town beckoned once again, and Arsenal would be the next recipients of his services.

6

England

"I was now the England captain, be it only at under-23 level, but I loved it because now I could do a little bit of what you might call revenge work. Making up for lost time."

Like much of Huddy's mesmeric footballing career, there were as many downs as ups as far as England were concerned. From being a 19-year-old about whom Sir Alf Ramsey had declared, "There's no limit to what this young player can achieve," to Tony Waddington's famous, "Alan Hudson will play for the World XI before he does for England" quote, there always had to be a story. He couldn't just be allowed to get on with showing his country what a mercurial talent he was and, given half a chance, take them back to the heights of 1966. Two caps is all that Huddy had to show for his dalliance with the national side.

It has to be one of Alan's biggest regrets that he didn't shine on the world's biggest stage, because that's absolutely where he belonged. Hypothetical now of course, but reflecting on just how far England might have gone with Huddy in the side is a worthwhile endeavour. A few years of experience on the international scene might also have seen his club form pick up because, frankly, it dipped again once he'd left Waddington and Stoke behind. Nick Hancock of *They Think It's All Over* fame agreed years later with friend and club director Keith Humphreys that "We were in danger of becoming a one-man team," as they both recalled the Potters' golden era.

There aren't too many footballers throughout the generations that evoke such beautiful memories, but Huddy was definitely one of the chosen few. Even Michael Parkinson acknowledged that "Anyone who saw Alan Hudson play when he was young and intact will remember a talent to amaze, and will feel sad it was so wilfully squandered. In the final analysis, the greatest calamity to befall him is the one suffered only by those greatly gifted people who take their talent for granted. He will never know just how good he could have been." Never a truer word spoken, but Parky but wasn't the only one to see such virtues.

It's easy to understand why but incredibly disappointing that the 'great and the good' at the FA couldn't see past Alan's obvious shortcomings off the pitch. His international troubles began whilst he was still at Chelsea and Sir Alf Ramsey was still at the helm of the senior national side.

The serious injury that put paid to his hopes of making the 1970 World Cup squad made Alan extremely conscious of the levels at which he could perform, and he wasn't one for pulling out of games with minor concerns either. If he genuinely couldn't play, then there had to be a very serious issue to stop him from setting foot on the pitch, as when Alan played 89 consecutive matches for Stoke with a chronically bad ankle before having his leg broken by Bruce Rioch at Derby County. Rioch would join Huddy at Seattle Sounders three years later, where he was heard boasting to the younger players that he'd done it on purpose.

Alan was intelligent enough to manage his ailments and

listen to his body, but neither his club nor international managers realised it.

"It all began in 1969 when I was called up by Alf Ramsey to play for the England under-23 team, not too long after I didn't get a look in at the England Youth team trials. My first under-23 match against Scotland on March 4, 1970, at Roker Park, Sunderland – where I received my one and only sending-off in one of my final games for Stoke – was abandoned because of snow. We were leading 3-1 and with 28 minutes still left to play, there's no telling how big the score would've been by the end. They'd only scored through Colin Todd's own goal!! Osgood had a pair and Brian Kidd was on target too as I recall.

"I especially enjoyed the match against Wales on a very heavy pitch at The Racecourse Ground, Wrexham on December 2, 1970, [an entertaining 0-0 draw in front of 16,367 fans]. It was used as a great comeback vehicle by me as I was going through a bad spell with Chelsea with a shin-splint injury but I put in a brilliant performance. The *London Evening Standard* raved about it the following day, telling Dave Sexton via a veiled headline that 'Hudson proves he's ready to return'."

Not that the stubborn Chelsea manager ever felt the need to take advice from anyone. The sideshow at home at the time – Bill and Bub not getting on with Maureen – also provided Sexton with more than enough ammunition to throw in Alan's direction to suggest he just wasn't 'at it': that his mind was elsewhere. Whether Alan agreed with that assessment was beside the point but a grim existence at home certainly hindered rather than helped his general mental well-being.

At the end of the Wales game, Ramsey handed Huddy some very unusual advice. Even now Alan struggles to find the logic in the sentence that was uttered as soon as he walked back into the dressing room. "There I was, buzzing, chest out and knowing that we'd just produced a terrific ninety minutes, and then I hear, 'Alan, you covered every blade of grass, but preserve your energy.' I found that more than a little strange because us 'flair' players were always considered a luxury. The reason I ran for miles was because it was the first time I had played on a heavy pitch for a long time, and I wanted to test my fitness in order to win my place back at Chelsea.

"Three months later – on February 24, 1971 – I remember playing at Hampden Park along with Ian Hutchinson, my Chelsea team-mate. Scotland were 2-0 up at half-time, but we dug in and Larry Lloyd then Tony Currie silenced the Jocks to grab us a draw."

After missing out on the next two under-23 squads – against Switzerland on November 24, 1971 and against Wales on January 5, 1972 – Huddy was recalled for a titanic tussle against Scotland at the Baseball Ground, Derby, on February 16, 1972, in front of an impressive 18,028 fans. It was almost a year after his last appearance, but he showed no signs of rustiness. A Kenny Dalglish double cancelled out Mick Channon's brace, but the standard on show gave hope to everyone that this 'new generation' would be something very special indeed. And Huddy was on top of the pile that Wednesday afternoon, in a class all of his own.

"Tony Currie and I tortured Scotland, with Steve Perryman playing as a third midfielder. He enjoyed watching the pair of us as much as the crowd did, saying, 'It was a pleasure to sit back and enjoy seeing you and TC crucify that lot.' Brian Clough was in the stands that night and he can't have failed to have been impressed – I actually played well against his teams on a regular basis – I was unplayable."

When all seemed to be going so well, Huddy would be hit by the cruelest of blows. Not wanting to inflame his injuries any more than was necessary, he thought it the mature thing to do to turn down an invitation to an under-23 summer tour, in order to rest properly and give him a fighting chance of pulling the strings properly at the beginning of the following campaign.

"I remember Christine Matthews, our Chelsea secretary, calling me and telling me that Alf would be phoning the Bridge on one particular afternoon to speak to me about my pulling out of that tour. Christine took the call then transferred it to me in an office down the corridor. After hearing what he had to say, I remember walking back to the main office as if it were Death Row. I was totally shocked, although I didn't realise just what effect it would have on my international future. What's more, he didn't even have the balls to deal with me face to face. 'If you're not at Heathrow tomorrow, you'll take the consequences,' he said. I didn't turn up, of course, and along with Colin Todd who'd also pulled out, we were banished into the international wilderness for years. Can you imagine any other nation treating their promising young players in that way? No, neither can I."

The 'Boys of '66' were, by now, getting on and English football needed an injection of young, hungry, talented players to push the national side forward for a tilt at the 1974 World Cup. Ramsey's somewhat overzealous punishment was nonsense and the only purpose it served was to see the England manager – who not long beforehand had lauded Huddy, don't forget – in the 21-year-old's bad books.

"1966 was not the best thing that happened to Ramsey because it affected his ego. I had just won the FA Cup and European Cup Winners' Cup with Chelsea in my first two seasons, was instrumental in both of those triumphs and also runner-up to Billy Bremner for the Football Writers' Footballer of the Year in my first season, and yet here I was in the international wilderness. Ridiculous!"

Alan never did understand the scale of the punishment, and

still doesn't, because there was no one prouder to play for their country than this working class London lad. As it turned out, and just as he had expected, the lack of international action across that summer helped him at club level, certainly as far as the initial recovery of his injury was concerned. The completely irrational international ban however also contributed to the mental anguish that he began to suffer on a regular basis. England's most natural talent was not playing for his country at *any* level and that was bound to hurt.

The under-23 side only won four of the next 14 games over the two-year period that Hudson wasn't selected, clearly a ship without a captain. His comeback was something to behold, and if ever there was a player sending a message to those that needed it – flashing it in front of them in 10-foot high neon letters – this was it. Huddy was back. Alan played so well that, even now, it might be considered one of the better under-23 performances in an England shirt. The embarrassment that it caused Ramsey may have been overplayed at the time by the media, but no one can say that their treatment of him wasn't partly deserved. If anything, it showed the footballing world that Ramsey, like Sexton, didn't know how to deal with this new breed of player. A player of the future who England purposefully overlooked for two years, denying the obvious talent that could have lifted the national team out of its doldrums.

"I saved my best performance for my comeback from the international wilderness. March 13, 1974 at St. James' Park, Newcastle, when the Auld Enemy were again our opponents. And what do you know, I put them to the sword once more ... no one could get near me."

The failure of the senior side to qualify for the World Cup, and a staunch refusal to revitalise a tired squad, saw Ramsey dismissed on April 19, 1974, just over a month after Hudson's mesmeric 90 minutes. However, the actual announcement was delayed until May 1. With Ramsey out of the way, the FA were prepared to let bygones were bygones – not that Huddy ever had anything to apologise for – and a summer tour of France, Yugoslavia and Turkey beckoned. A certain player would definitely be going this time.

"We were at the airport and interim manager Ken Furphy, who was touting for the main job full-time, called the players in and we sat round on suitcases and anything else we could find as he said, 'Look, I'm only here to take you for this trip and don't know who to make captain, so I need your input.' It was like Suart at Chelsea all over again. At that time there was a big lad who played centre-half at Middlesbrough and he said, 'I don't think there is any doubt that it should be him,' pointing at me, adding 'Huddy's the best player here by a mile so he should be captain.' His name was Willie Maddren and I liked him and his attitude. I was now the England captain, be it only at under-23 level, but I loved it because now I could do a little bit of what you might call revenge work. Making up for lost time.

"Willie later announced that had he played for a more glamorous club he would've made it to the full England side, which I can both echo and relate to as I played with several lads at Stoke who were far better than those from Manchester United, Leeds United and Liverpool who played for the national team. Sadly, when Willie died in 2000, Hugh McIlvaney commented that, 'Willie Maddren was the best player never to play for England,' which was a fair shout but he forgot about Jimmy Greenhoff!"

The three-game tour turned into a bit of a disaster and, frankly, an utter waste of time. The first game was against Turkey on May 11, at the 19 Mayıs Stadyumu, in Ankara. England's trip, to a country not known for rain, coincided with a deluge that was biblical in scale, leading to the game being abandoned at half-time with the score at 0-0 and left the players with nothing more to do than look forward to their game against Yugoslavia four days later at Stadion Karadordev Park, Zrenjanin. A 1-0 loss certainly wasn't on the cards, but it was revealed afterwards that the Yugoslavs had played a large number of overage players. The final match in France at the Stade Georges Pompidou, Valence, couldn't come soon enough for Huddy.

"I was given the Everton centre-forward Bob Latchford as a room mate in France and, on arriving in Paris, his luggage had not arrived with us. So, my first job was to go and see the England secretary for some money to buy him some clothes. I offered him mine to wear but Bob would not fit into my clobber as he was a big and beefy striker. I soon found myself, the man who'd been banned for two years, knocking on the doors of the other players, asking for cash to help my roommate buy some new clothes. It was hilarious. After collecting as much as I could, I gave the cash to Bob which is when the funniest thing happened.

"I said to him, 'Look Bob, we'll go shopping for some gear for you and then go for a couple of beers,' and off we went. As we got to the main shops he stopped at this ladies boutique and began looking in the window, which had me thinking he was a cross dresser: 'Bloody Hell!' I thought. 'Hey Bob! What are you doing mate?' I said. 'Just looking for something for my wife. I always take her something back from trips,' which had me thinking 'there you are with nothing to wear and you're buying your missus a dress'- nutter! I pulled his leg about it for five days. Bob was a big, lovely lad, who had that wonderful season at Everton after signing for lots of money from Birmingham City."

It would be a proverbial game of two halves against the

French, goalless at the break followed by a stunning 45 minutes from both sides which saw the game end 2-2: Gillard and Fletcher for the visitors, Rampillion and a Larque penalty for the hosts. The 5,000 fans in attendance were entertained, especially in the closing stages. John McDowell was injured but the French bizarrely protested when West Ham team-mate Tommy Taylor was due to be substituted in his place. After considerable confusion and to enable the game to continue, Mervyn Day was brought on in place of Alan Stevenson in goal, and Stevenson then replaced McDowell as an outfield player. A comical way to end the tour.

Alan, naturally, was in the highest of spirits. Despite the trio of matches not quite turning out as he'd expected, being handed the captaincy was an honour that he cherished. All he needed to hear upon his return was that Furphy had been handed the senior job full-time because it would then be nigh-on impossible for him to be left out at the top level. However, events wouldn't pan out as he hoped.

"So, after my record breaking deal to Stoke City, I found the best club form of my life, Ramsey had been given the bullet and I thought that it was a foregone conclusion that a full international return was imminent. I was the best inside-forward in the country at the time, everyone knew it, George Best included. 'You're still the best player in the country, keep shoving it down their throats,' he wrote to me. A rare and lovely gesture from someone I loved both as a player and a man. I truly appreciated the sentiment because I can promise you that George didn't sit around writing letters to any Tom, Dick and Harry.

"After such a wonderful time, upon our return the news came that Don Revie had been given the job and not Furphy. It was like replacing Christopher Lee with Vincent Price, only this was no 'thriller'. Don and I had history through my taunting of Billy Bremner and Johnny Giles from whenever Chelsea or Stoke played against Revie's Leeds side. He'd made it quite clear that he didn't like me, but Waddington banged my drum loud enough to get everyone's attention – including Revie's – and I was back in England contention. I could see Revie had no intention of selecting the likes of me, Frank Worthington and Stan Bowles though. I've lost count of the number of squads I was in without getting a look in on the pitch."

Indeed, almost a year had passed before the stubborn ex-Leeds manager would play Alan, with no adequate explanation given as to why that was the case. When Revie eventually did get around to selecting him, there was more than a whiff of something underhand from the England manager. Picking a player for his first senior game against the reigning world champions? That was bound to show him up as not good enough wasn't it? Revie would then have some justification to never have to pick Huddy again. But his masterplan didn't quite work out in the way it had been intended.

England's 2-0 friendly victory over the seemingly invincible Germans, at Wembley on March 12, 1975, was as comprehensive as you're ever likely to see and even included the Kaiser himself, Franz Beckenbauer, being put on his backside by Huddy. Cheers greeted his every touch and *Oles* rang out as Alan taught his contemporaries a footballing lesson, and then some. England's nemesis in the 1970s, the fearsome Gunther Netzer, was famously quoted after the game as asking "Where have you been hiding this player? He is world class!" His manager Helmut Schön was in full agreement, telling reporters that "at last England have found a replacement for Bobby Charlton."

Huddy had destroyed the opposition, and it was evident that such an incredible display, after being snubbed for a year, would embarrass his manager. So it proved, because in the papers the following day none held back, even those who were essentially Revie sympathisers. But rather than bestow upon him the praise that his performance deserved, his manager didn't even offer Alan a single word of congratulation. Not one. Not that it would've come as any surprise whatsoever to the entire group of England players, most of whom took an instant dislike to Revie and his methods. Even Alan Ball, a player revered by his peers and loved by his managers, couldn't get on with 'The Don', which gives some perspective to just how wrong the FA had got this particular appointment.

A 5-0 victory over Cyprus in the European Championship on April 16, 1975, would be the last time Huddy pulled on a shirt for the senior national team. Although he again played superbly alongside Ball, it was Malcolm McDonald who would grab all of the headlines with a five-goal haul. Yet McDonald was also none too happy with Revie and, writing in *The Guardian* some years later, stated: 'A month and four days before the Cyprus game we played West Germany, the world champions, in a friendly at Wembley. It was the first time Don Revie had called me up and when I arrived at the team hotel, the first thing he said was I was only there because the press were demanding it. He said if I didn't score he would never pick me again. It was a really outrageous thing to do but I kept it to myself. At least I didn't have to worry about whether I was playing – he'd basically told me I would be starting. I got prepared as best I could and, as it happens, I got our second goal in a 2-0 win. I'd done what was asked of me. Next was the Cyprus game.

'So, when we got back to the team hotel, I let Don know I hadn't picked up any kind of injury and, without saying hello or anything like that, he said: "If you don't score this time, I'll never pick you again." It was a repeat of what he'd said before. I thought: "How dare you, you bastard." I told Alan Ball, and he said: "You just leave it with me." On the day of the game we had a team meeting and at the end, as everybody was leaving, Alan got hold of Mick Channon, Alan Hudson and myself. He quickly related the tale to the other two. He said he had a plan. "Do you know what England's goalscoring record is?" he asked. We all shook our heads. He said: "Willie Hall scored five against Northern Ireland in 1938. Tonight, this man's going to score six." Pointing to himself and the other two, he added "we are going to make it happen. Now, are you up for it?" We all nodded.

'In the third minute, Hudson floated a free-kick in, I got on the end of it and I was on my way. When I got my third just after half-time he said: "That's your first hat-trick, now get the second." I scored five, had one disallowed for offside and hit the post before the final whistle. At the old Wembley there was an electronic scoreboard above the tunnel. At the end of the game it went blank, and then it flashed up: 'Congratulations – Supermac 5 Cyprus 0.' Wow! My eyes then focussed on Revie. There he was in his trenchcoat, head hunched down, hands in his pockets, heading back to the tunnel. I knew he couldn't hear me, but I pointed at the scoreboard and shouted at him: "Read that and weep, you bastard. Read that and weep".'

Those sentiments will have been echoed by Huddy. Revie was one of the most outspoken football people of the era, and so he was never going to see eye-to-eye with a player who shared many of the same traits he did, but to pick fights with the likes of Alan Ball because he wouldn't join in Revie's carpet bowling sessions in London – it was extraordinary! A short while after the Cyprus game, Jimmy Greenhoff was picked alongside Huddy – as an overage player – for an under-23 trip to Hungary but, once again, something was amiss.

"It was in Hungary that Revie played his ace card by trying to humiliate Jimmy and me because we failed to make a lunch appointment with the team. We were rooming together and chose to skip lunch because we both were a little weight conscious. Even in training, Jimmy and I would wear sweat bags in the gymnasium, but Revie would hear none of it. Our phone rang and Les Cocker, the biggest grass since Shaw Taylor, was on the other end telling us Don was furious. When we got to the ground floor, they were both standing there. 'Who the fucking hell do you two think you are?' Revie bellowed. I wasn't having that but as I said something back to him, he shot me down again. I felt sorry for Greenhoff whom Revie had sold whilst at Leeds, but that was it, we were finished as far as England went. A heated argument over a pitiful lunch and that was our international careers over – thanks to the co-star of *The Damned United*!"

Alan remains adamant that every conversation he had with Revie was not only completely negative but always felt like a set-up. Let's be honest, why would you go and play bingo or carpet bowls when you could hang out with Frank Worthington at Bernie Winters' house?! Revie knew he was placing unreasonable demands upon certain players in his squad because when they failed to meet his expectations – as they almost always did – he could offload them, no questions asked.

Of course, there were the occasions like Huddy's debut and McDonald's five-goal blast that put a spoke in the works, but Revie was a law unto himself. If the FA did know about his unusual motivational methods, then they kept their distance and allowed him to manage as he saw fit. As with Ramsey, there was still very much an air of the autocrat about Revie, a manager who never gave a moment's thought to understanding precisely what it was that did actually motivate this new breed of professional footballer.

The youngsters weren't being rebellious for the sake of

it. They were grown young men who expected to be treated as such. Arguably the best players of their generation, they just wanted to go out and express themselves in the way that they knew how, and not to be told "If you don't score, you're out" or inciting resentment because, if you didn't accede to his every whim, you could kiss goodbye to your England cap. When you're that out of touch with your dressing room – at any level – it's only going to end one way and, frankly, it's a miracle that Revie survived in the post until 1977.

Charlie George was another flair player of the time who deserved to be wearing the 'three lions' but, like Hudson, there appeared to be a mistrust of such talent. Evidently unwilling to accommodate these mavericks, the easy option was to not pick them at all, but dropping Ball and Emlyn Hughes – both former captains – from his European Championship squad of 1976, sounded the death knell for Revie's managerial aspirations and it was all downhill from there. Colin Todd was one of many to speak out and suggest that, despite what one or two in the top echelons of the FA thought, Revie was never right for the England job and was more suited to club management where, it's fair to say, he excelled. When Revie was eventually suspended by the FA for 10 years for bringing the game into disrepute, the egg on the faces of those in power was a delight to Hudson, Todd and their contemporaries.

"There is no other nation that would've banned Colin Todd and myself – two of their brightest youngsters since the Munich air crash – for something so trivial as not playing a summer tournament because of injury concerns. It was a whitewash on the FA's part but they'll never learn. They'd rather pick players that do and say the right things over those that could win them tournaments. Trevor Cherry in the 1986 World Cup best sums up our international scene. A safe bet. In a nutshell that is England past, present and future.

HUDDY

"Revie was an arsehole, full stop. Someone should've realised he wasn't right for the job as soon as he changed the kit suppliers to Admiral, who had been supplying Leeds before Revie took over the national team. Everyone, and I mean everyone, knew that Don had got something out of that particular deal. He earned from every person or company he could and it was sheer good fortune for all of us when greed got the better of him and he was booted out – exposed for what he really was.

"You have to remember that this was a man who kept wads of notes in his desk at Elland Road and if the groundsman or other staff needed 'helping out,' they'd go and see Revie. It's why you'll never hear a bad word said against him in those parts, and why Cloughie never really stood a chance there. He even had local cabbies in his pocket, paid handsomely in return for being appraised of when his players were out until the early hours. Who knows how much he was giving to all and sundry with the sole purpose of keeping control? Those of us that wouldn't play his game were kept at arm's length. No, he was never the fit and proper person to lead his country and I had to chuckle when it all came crashing down. He who laughs last, eh Don?!"

Although two pitiful caps is an absolute disgrace for a player who was in his prime, there's no possible way of knowing that Huddy would've gone on to become what everyone knew he was capable of. His good friend, and someone who he had the utmost respect for, Bobby Moore, probably summed it up best when he said, "Alan Hudson could've conquered the world ... but there was no guarantee he was going to conquer his temperament." It's a comment that would no doubt resonate with many of his contemporaries, supporters and pundits.

To this day, Huddy regrets not retiring from international football straight after that Germany match, knowing that

ENGLAND

Revie would somehow find a way to drop him. "I should have made my statement to the London press, a statement which would have staggered Fleet Street, but more importantly it would have opened a can of worms. I truly missed the boat, knowing that my international future was in jeopardy and anything I did would not be good enough for Revie. I could have walked away with my international head held high after beating Franz Beckenbauer and his friends at Wembley, leaving the press to digest why I had knocked it on the head after just one, magnificent, game."

Given how fragile his temperament was, being cast aside as a nobody by Revie was always going to play on Huddy's mind. The 'what ifs' whirred round and round his head for month after month as each squad was announced and his name would be absent. Not that he expected any different of course, but it was the polar opposite to the love he felt at the time from Stoke fans, which was probably the single most important factor in keeping him on an even keel at that time.

It's often forgotten how young Alan still was when his international dream became a nightmare – just 24-years-old. Even when Revie was ousted and Ron Greenwood came in, Huddy was still only 26, although clearly far from the player of a few years previously, but the blow of non-selection undoubtedly played a part in the mental anguish he was suffering from during that period.

Wayne Rooney's international career hit the heights that Alan's never did, but towards the end of it – against Malta at Wembley – the England captain was booed by his own fans. He at least had the excuse of age for a dip in form but 31 isn't old yet at the elite level, unless you've something extra special about you, it's obvious that you are going to be limited in your output compared to when you were in your mid-20s. Huddy never had that luxury, because by the time he'd reached his peak, his star was already on the wane. For a man who made it his business to train hard, to work hard, and yes to play hard, he didn't deserve some of the treatment that was meted out by Revie in particular.

It wasn't uncommon for Huddy to complete 2,000 sit-ups a day in his prime, with some bike work thrown in if he fancied it. This was on top of any training that Stoke would have in place for him. He was a person who, in the main, took great care of his body long before anyone had even heard of the term 'sports science'. If he wasn't match fit, fine, but everyone knew that the one thing he prided himself on was his dedication and professionalism to the cause. Off the field was a different matter entirely, but how many times have we heard from England managers – from the television age onwards – that England players 'are picked on merit?'

It's an indisputable fact that there was no one more meritorious and more deserving of an extended run in the national side from 1975 onwards than Alan Hudson. That was doubly confirmed by the way in which he marked his debut. You'd expect someone who was about to step out for their country for the first time to be a little nervous, but that was not even a question that needed asking in the post-match interview.

It's worth pondering on just what England lost out on when they binned Huddy. Some 15 years later, another mercurial player who had the football world eating out of the palm of his hand, would explode onto the international scene. There are too many similarities to list here but Paul Gascoigne was a breath of fresh air during the 1990 World Cup, and beyond. Although his manager, Bobby Robson, was also a bit 'old school' and expected certain standards from his staff, he was also astute enough to understand that with someone like 'Gazza' you took the full package: warts and all. You'd be hard

ENGLAND

pressed to find someone who could speak ill of Gascoigne the player, an exceptional midfield genius cut from the same cloth as Huddy, as Billy Hudson – Alan's nephew, who played in the Spurs youth team when Gascoigne was playing for the senior team – recalls.

"I was signed by Terry Venables and played with Paul Gascoigne and Teddy Sheringham, but once he was sacked I lost my focus. Before joining the club, however, I went to White Hart Lane on work experience from my school. All my mates went off to be chippies, sparks, plumbers ... and I went to Tottenham. All I was excited about was meeting Gazza, but it was just after he'd done his knee in the 1991 Cup Final. I told all my mates, 'I'm gonna meet Gazza' and they just fell about.

"I turned up on the first day wearing Al's football school top – at that time he ran a clinic with Don Shanks up in Stoke – and I walked into the treatment room. Gazza's sitting there with Gary Lineker and Gary Mabbutt and shouted, 'Where'd you get that shirt from?' so I told him that Al was my uncle. With that, Gazza's literally jumped off the treatment table, dived at my feet and started bowing. 'His uncle's the Guv'nor', he kept saying over and over!! I was just a 16-year-old kid and when my school friends asked me if I'd met Gazza, I said 'Met him? He was bowing at my feet!' It was incredible but it showed the esteem that Al was held in."

Greatness always recognises greatness of course, so it's not a surprise that the most naturally gifted footballer of his generation would say to someone that he and Alan shared many similarities both on and off the pitch. Before Venables took over the England job and 'Gazzamania' took off again in 1996, if Gascoigne played well, it defined how well the England side of the Bobby Robson era played. Everyone knows he was *that* influential. And that's the real issue here. Qualifying for the 1976 European Championships and the 1978 World Cup may have come a little bit easier for England had they taken advantage of what they had at their disposal – but decided to overlook – thus allowing personal battles to shape the make-up of the England set-up rather than seeing the much bigger picture.

That Alan's silky skills and tactical genius were only rewarded with two caps is scandalous.

7

Arsenal

"Huddy played in millimetres when others played in inches. He didn't play football, he danced it."
Malcolm McDonald

"In terms of technical ability, the man was brilliant. Alongside the likes of Brady, Bergkamp and so on, he was one of the most skilful players I've ever seen in the shirt. He was so talented that I almost feel cheated that he played fewer than 50 games for Arsenal. If I had to sum up Alan Hudson's ability in one word, that word would be 'genius'."

Bernard Dowling from Hertfordshire, an avid and lifelong 'Gooner,' certainly wasn't alone in his assessment of Huddy's fleeting contribution to the north Londoners. He was 25 by the time he'd left his life in the Potteries to come back down south. Not that he ever wanted to go, nor did Tony Waddington want him to leave, but having him stay was never an option once the Victoria Ground stadium improvements needed paying for. Almost a year after the roof had blown off, many had expected that the club were over the worst of it financially but the stark truth was that Stoke's directors had wanted to keep things from Waddington for as long as possible because of the impact. Everyone knew that their best-ever team would have to be broken apart for the club to survive.

When the day came that Alan was sold, he was so choked up by the magnitude of the situation that he didn't even say goodbye to his mentor, Waddington. How could he? He was already in bits at the thought of having to leave what for him had become a utopian footballing existence. Now it would be back to the same old haunts from yesteryear, the same faces, the same troubles. There was no 'off switch', and the bright lights of London were only ever going to mean one thing – party time. Wine, women and song, Alan's favourite pastimes other than the beautiful game.

December 13, 1976 was the day that Huddy finally arrived at Highbury, although he would not make his debut for another three weeks. His £200,000 fee went some way to helping Stoke out off of the pitch, but on it they would eventually fall away and be relegated – just as the directors had feared they would. Alan was the glue that held everything together, and the effect of him moving on was like a deck of stacked cards falling in on themselves.

"Waddington told the directors that, 'if you sell your best players, Hudson and Greenhoff, you'll go down,' and he was spot on. They didn't have a clue, all they were interested in was the money and looking after their cronies in the directors' suite with a gin and tonic. They were the morons who ran football clubs back then, with no idea about the game, and no feelings for those that were making them money on a Saturday afternoon. Fans flocked to see the 'Hudson & Greenhoff' show on match days, but it went over the heads of those dumb directors.

"My move happened so quickly. It was early one Saturday night and I received a call from Jimmy Robertson, who knew Terry Neill from his Arsenal days. I'd missed that day's Stoke

ARSENAL

match through an abdomen injury so was resting at home, and when Jimmy called to tell me that Terry would be contacting me about joining Arsenal. I was completely dumbfounded because I didn't know that I was available – but neither did Waddington. My best guess is that Neill must have spoken to a director at the game, and before I knew it, Terry and Ken Friar were at my door. By the following evening I was an Arsenal player.

"I recall Ken speaking to Tony on the phone from my Barlaston home, and Tony refusing to come and sign the papers so they had to get Stoke's secretary Bill Williams to do it. I didn't have time to think about anything other than 'How can they sell me after all that I've done for them? They were fourth from bottom when I arrived and I helped them into Europe and almost won the championship. What's going on?' Then I thought 'be positive' because Arsenal are a great club and they had Alan Ball and 'Chippy' Brady – two wonderful players – and I'd enjoyed playing with Bally for England so very much.

"Just like with Chelsea, it was 'now you see me, now you don't' and all because of money again. At Chelsea they couldn't afford to pay for that East Stand, and now Stoke couldn't afford to pay for the Butler Street Stand. Arsenal, like Spurs, were my two favourite clubs outside of my Chelsea 1970s team but my family were all devastated about the move, as was Waddington. When Maureen and I went to the ground the following morning to collect my boots, Maureen told me she bumped into Tony and he pleaded with her to talk me out of it, but it was already done. She said he cried outside the ground. He knew that Stoke City were finished, although I don't think that he or I thought that Jimmy Greenhoff was next – getting the same treatment to Manchester United."

Regardless of whether the deal had been concluded in a

slightly underhand manner, Huddy was now an Arsenal player and needed to focus on that above everything else. Stoke, and Waddington, were already in the past – as hard as that was to accept – and the Gunners and Terry Neill were the immediate future. Such is the business of football. As a player, you're a pawn in the bigger picture and there's absolutely no point in pretending otherwise. *Every* player is for sale if the price is right. It was the case back in the mid-1970s and it remains the case today. The big difference now is that top level players can walk away from the game and never have to worry about money again. On the back of the huge transfer fees many young footballers become millionaires overnight.

If Neill thought he could just step into Waddington's shoes, he was sorely mistaken. The Stoke maestro was a second father to Huddy and the effect of being taken so swiftly from that environment was going to have consequences. To what extent would only become clear in the coming months. In the meantime, Alan just wanted to get his head down and concentrate on giving his best for his new club. At least he was now at one of the big teams he'd wanted to come in for him before Stoke changed his life.

He was still a great player, and the news that he'd signed for Arsenal was greeted with part disbelief and part utter joy from the locals. For Alan, it was a chance to put himself back in the international shop window as well. Although Revie was still at the helm, it wouldn't be that long before he was relieved of his duties.

With a spring in his step and in a positive frame of mind, Huddy believed that this was a new beginning and another chance to fulfil the promise he'd shown throughout his career. What he didn't bargain on was falling out with Terry Neill quite so soon after he'd put pen to paper. The Irishman was incredibly quick to judge and, within a couple of weeks, Alan

Top left: Holding the cup with his Park Walk school teammates after their successful 1960-61 season.

Top right: Alan at 10 months, already looking for a bottle - of milk!

Middle right: A happy Huddy as a 10-year-old boy.

Bottom right: As a 15-year-old in 1966, Alan's first year as an apprentice at Chelsea.

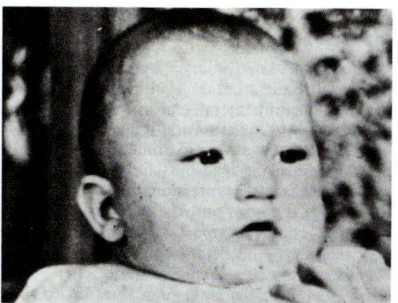

Left: Chelsea Boys Club won the National Association of Boys' Clubs trophy at Craven Cottage in 1965. Alan, with his brother John, cousin Anthony at very bottom, and the great Johnny Haynes who presented the trophy.

Proud brothers, John and Alan, with their baby sister Julie.

Alan and John outside their parent's prefab in 1970.

CHELSEA FOOTBALL COMBINATION TEAM 1966-67

Standing (left to right): **Dick Spence (Trainer), Allan Young, Brian Brown, Pat Purcell, Tommy Hughes, Jim Thomson, John Hudson, Alan Nelmes, Frank Blunstone (Coach).**
Seated: **Joe Fascione, Tommy Harmer, Warren Tennant, Barry Lloyd, Tommy Robson.**

John was signed by Chelsea before Alan, but his path to a career as a professional footballer didn't go to plan.

Alan's sister Julie treating the injured ankle that kept him out of the FA Cup final, and World Cup, in 1970.

When it came to fashion, Alan was the George Best of London ... or was Best the Alan Hudson of Manchester?

The 18-year-old Alan was quite fashion conscious about his hair as well.

Flying from Heathrow as a young kid with his new Chelsea teammates

Alan and his mum in 1970. The photo was taken for an American magazine, so Bub insisted that he cover up the word F**k.

Parading the FA Cup at Stamford Bridge with David Webb.

In Athens, straight after the Cup Winners' Cup final replay win in 1971, with Ron Harris and Keith Weller, celebrating Chelsea's historic victory over the mighty Real Madrid.

Top Left: With 'marvellous' Marvin Hinton and Stewart Houston in Athens. "I wasn't letting go of that trophy."

Top right & Middle: Memorable scenes in SW6 as players and fans celebrated the European Cup Winners' Cup victory.

Bottom: Recording *Blue is the Colour* before the 1972 League Cup final against Stoke City, with Peter Houseman, Ossie and Eddie McCreadie.

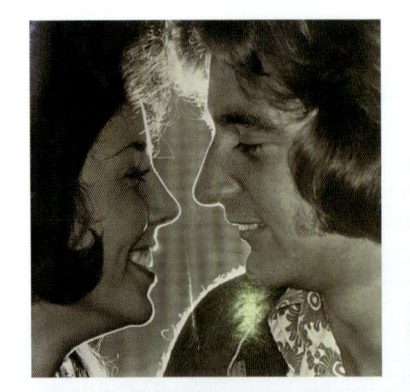

Alan and Maureen embarking on married life. They both loved their sons but their affection for each another didn't last.

A 'King of the King's Road' with his Prince: Alan and Allen

The beginning of the end. The Chelsea team photo at the start of 1973-74 season.

Top left: Alan, with Tony Waddington, signing for Stoke City in the Stamford Bridge car park: "The man who'd change my life forever."

Top right: Leaving the Bridge with his boots after signing for a record fee of £240,000 – "I was in a daze!"

Middle: "One of my greatest ever performances." Turning it on in front of the Boothen End on his debut for Stoke. Liverpool were European champions and Stoke 4th from bottom.

Bottom: "I only captained Stoke a handful of times; all victories against Chelsea. I remember saying here to Johnny Hollins that I was going to 'run you ragged', which I did."

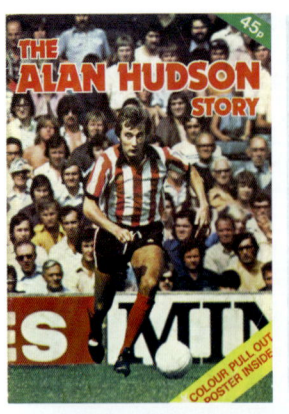

ALAN HUDSON PERSONAL FILE

FULL NAME:	Alan Anthony Hudson
BIRTHPLACE:	Chelsea, London
BIRTH DATE:	June 21st 1951
HEIGHT:	5' 11"
WEIGHT:	11st 10lb
EYES:	Blue
HAIR:	Brown
FAMILY:	Wife: Maureen / Son: Allen
HOME:	Barlaston, Stoke-on-Trent
CAR:	Audi
FAVOURITE FOOD:	Steak, Spaghetti Bolognese
FAVOURITE DRINK:	Milk

Top left & middle: In full flight in the red and white of Stoke, as seen on the front of The Alan Hudson Story magazine, which included Huddy's 'personal file'.

Top right: "My favourite Stoke City strip, the one we wore in Amsterdam when we lost to Ajax on away goals in 1975-76."

Left & bottom left: Bleary-eyed after late nights when Alan was drinking more than milk.

Bottom: Stoke City 4 Southampton 1 – "What a shame Osgood and I didn't reignite our double act in the Potteries. He'd have been a legend in Stoke."

Alan's debut for England under-23s at Roker Park against Scotland. The game was abandoned after 62 minutes due to the snow.

Alan won nine caps for England under-23s and was destined for a glittering international career, or so he thought.

"I trained as hard as anyone, but when I told Ramsey I needed a rest he banned me and I didn't play for the senior side until 1975!"

"With Alan Ball - my favourite midfield player - on my England debut. We went on to prove Revie wrong by beating the Germans."

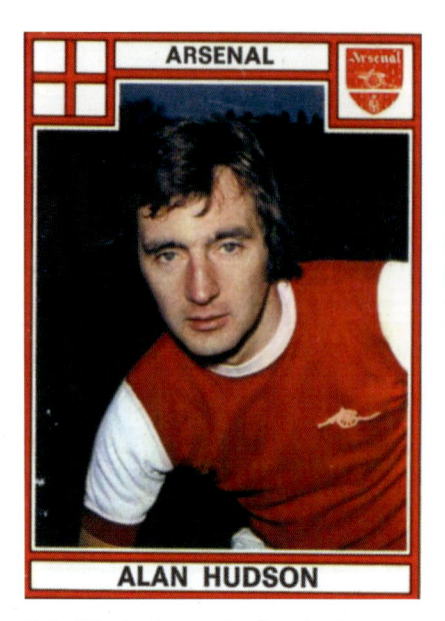

'A brilliant player who has had a stormy career' noted the Panini Football '78 sticker book after Huddy's move to Highbury in December 1976.

"George Armstrong and I grew beards, which was against the norm at Arsenal but we were only doing it to 'wind up' Terry Neil."

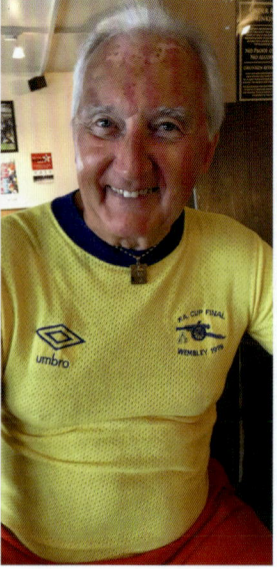

After missing out on the 1970 FA Cup final and losing to Stoke in the 1972 League Cup final, Alan was at Wembley again in 1978 with Arsenal.

"A truly dreadful experience. I wasn't very lucky in cup finals at Wembley."

The Gunners lost 1-0 to Ipswich but Alan still wears his shirt with pride.

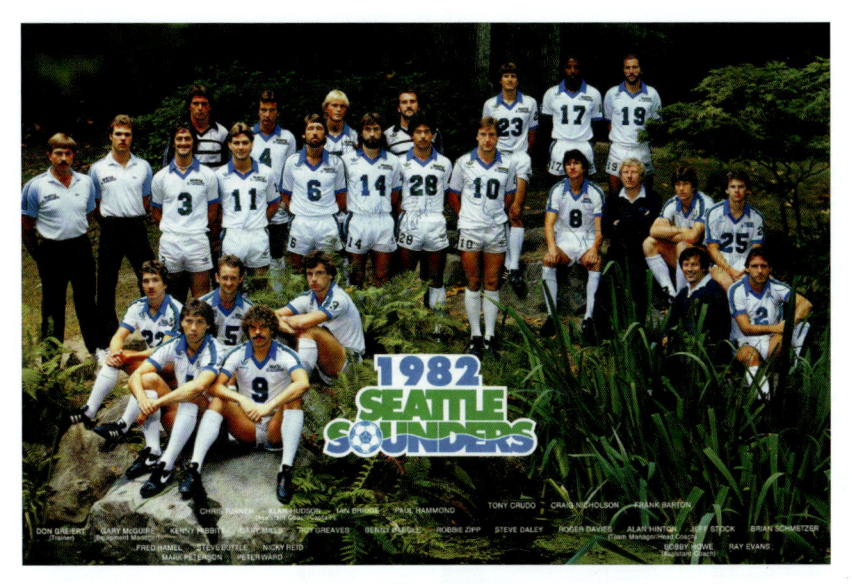

"I adored Seattle and the Sounders. I knew immediately, after my first evening overlooking that marvellous city from the restaurant in the Space Needle, that I was falling in love. We played to win, but we also played to entertain."

Taking on his old friend Frank Worthington, a star for the Tampa Bay Rowdies.

"Huddy 'didn't play football, he danced it," said Malcolm McDonald.

Top left: Celebrating another goal with his Seattle Sounders teammates John Impey and Frank Barton.

Top right: Visiting Tony Waddington and watching a Crewe match with Maureen and Allen after a flight from Seattle.

Left: One of the many boozy days in Seattle with friends Tony Davis and Ray Evans, the former Spurs, Fulham and Millwall defender.

"Back at Chelsea in 1983 - an absolute disaster ... but an incredible return to Stoke who were 14 points adrift when I arrived in January 1984 but, from then until the end of the season, we picked-up more points than eventual champions Liverpool. I'm pointing to the nearest pub to celebrate staying up!"

Despite all the ups and downs in his private life, Alan is very proud of both his sons and what they've achieved. Top left: enjoying a cool drink while on holiday with Allen. Top right: Anthony has forged a career in football and has enjoyed success as manager of the New Zealand national team, the All Whites.

The Hudson brothers John and Alan.

Happier times at Stamford Bridge with his father Bill, and cousin Jimmy Damons.

"His recovery thus far has been nothing short of spectacular"
Mr David Goodier (MBBS FRCS Orth.)

SKULL: Depressed frontal skull fracture!

BRAIN: Major problem! The blood clot and head injuries could have caused permanent brain damage

NECK: This procedure was normally performed via the groin but as there was so much local swelling and clotting in both legs Dr Otto Chan had to position the filter via a vein in his neck passing through his heart into the Inferior vena cava

HEART AND LUNGS: To prevent further blood clots a plastic filter was put into the Inferior vena cava to prevent blood going from his legs up into his heart and lungs!

LUNGS: There were severe complications due to blood clots from the legs travelling up into the lungs!

RIBS: Fractured sternum with multiple rib fractures on left bilateral haemoneumothoraces!

PELVIS: C-Clamp was removed and the internal fixation of the pelvis was performed! The most immediate problem was the bleeding from the pelvic injury!

ABDOMEN: Ruptured left kidney with massive retroperitoneal and pelvic haematoma!

KIDNEYS: On the 8/1/98 were put on dialysis, while the BLADDER had two catheters, one via the uretha, and one through the ABDOMEN wall!

RECTUM: Recurrent problems with widespread sepsis!

NERVES: On 22/01/98 Neurophysiologists diagnosed widespread damage to the lumbosacral plexus of nerves, and such was the severity of the damage to the lower half of his body, it was unlikely he would ever walk again!

LEGS: Needed relief in his legs, otherwise he may die if he gets sepsis!

Alan Hudson

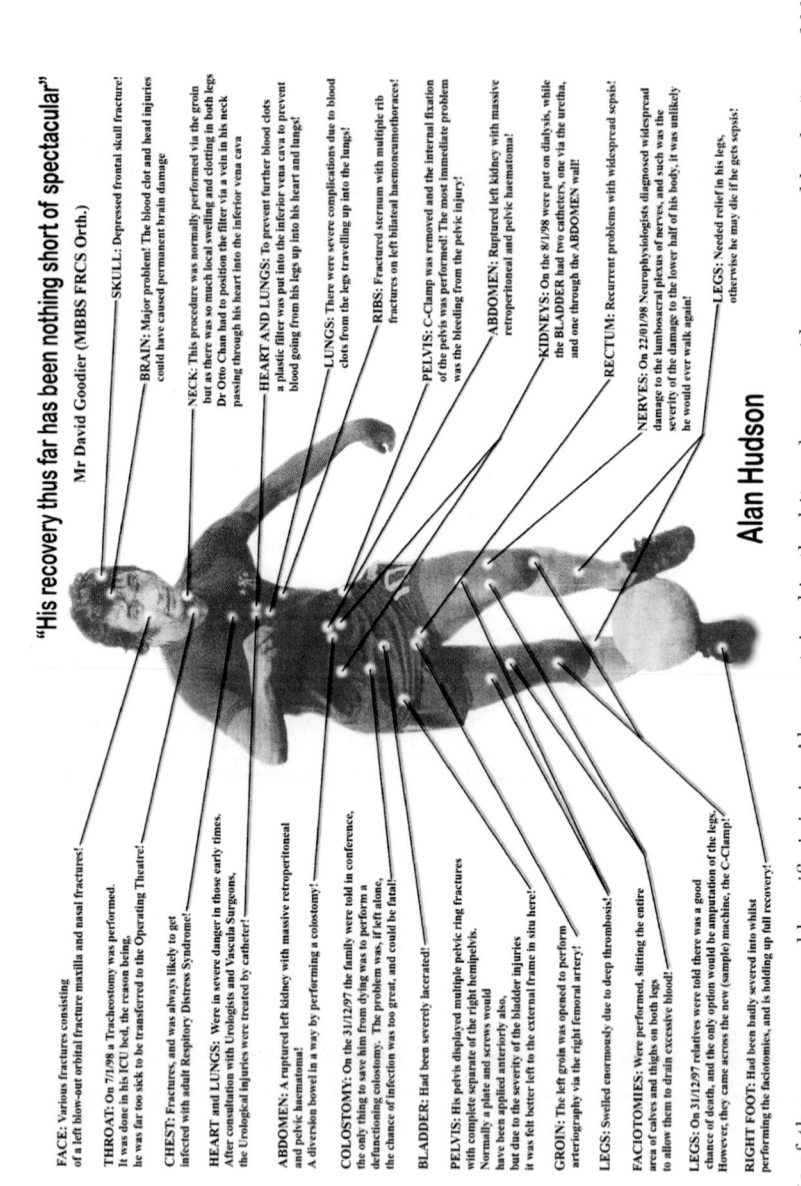

FACE: Various fractures consisting of a left blow-out orbital fracture maxilla and nasal fractures!

THROAT: On 7/1/98 a Tracheostomy was performed. It was done in his ICU bed, the reason being, he was far too sick to be transferred to the Operating Theatre!

CHEST: Fractures, and was always likely to get infected with adult Respitory Distress Syndrome!

HEART and LUNGS: Were in severe danger in those early times. After consultation with Urologists and Vascula Surgeons, the Urological injuries were treated by catheter!

ABDOMEN: A ruptured left kidney with massive retroperitoneal and pelvic haematoma!
A diversion bowel in a way by performing a colostomy!

COLOSTOMY: On the 31/12/97 the family were told in conference, the only thing to save him from dying was to perform a defunctioning colostomy. The problem was, if left alone, the chance of infection was too great, and could be fatal!

BLADDER: Had been severely lacerated!

PELVIS: His pelvis displayed multiple pelvic ring fractures with complete separate of the right hemipelvis.
Normally a plate and screws would have been applied anteriorly also, but due to the severity of the bladder injuries it was felt better left to the external frame in situ here!

GROIN: The left groin was opened to perform arteriography via the right femoral artery!

LEGS: Swelled enormously due to deep thrombosis!

FACIOTOMIES: Were performed, slitting the entire area of calves and thighs on both legs to allow them to drain excessive blood!

LEGS: On 31/12/97 relatives were told there was a good chance of death, and the only option would be amputation of the legs. However, they came across the new (sample) machine, the C-Clamp!

RIGHT FOOT: Had been badly severed into whilst performing the faciotomies, and is holding up full recovery!

A graphic of the numerous and horrific injuries Alan sustained in the hit-and-run accident, prepared by the "incredible Dr David Goodier, who saved my legs and my life."

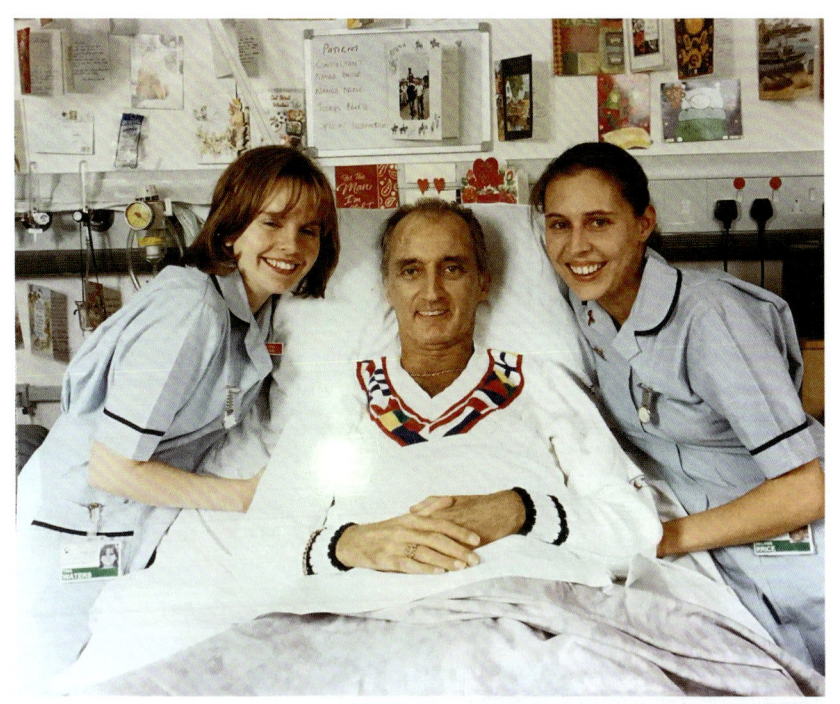

Huddy recovering in hospital in 1998, not long after coming out of his coma.

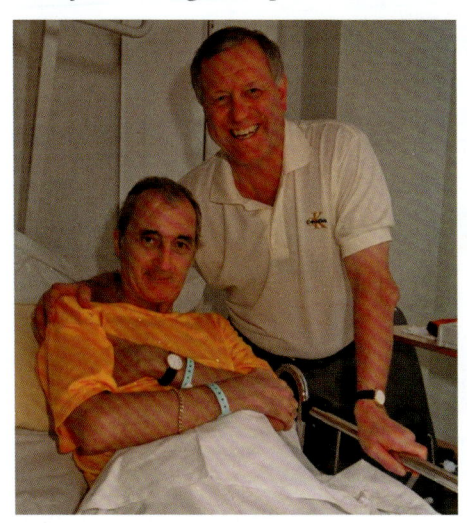

Inseparable friends. Peter Osgood visits Alan in hospital in 1998.

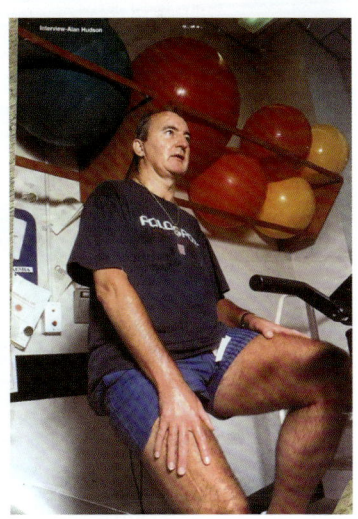

Back to the old routine. Alan in the gym after coming out of hospital.

At the Chelsea Arts Club with friends Ron Brunton and Tommy Wisbey, the Great Train Robber.

Catching up with Frank McLintock and friends.

Alan and author Jason Pettigrove in Riley's, celebrating the completion of *Huddy*.

Full circle. Alan adored living in Stoke and Seattle but loves being back home in Chelsea, where he grew up.

had already made up his mind about his new boss. He didn't like what he saw or heard. Not one bit. In a sign of what was to come, their problems began with an argument over housing.

"I refused to move to north London and returned to the Southfields area where I'd been living before going to Stoke. In fact, looking back, that move to Stoke has cost me a fortune as, unlike players today who can afford to simply buy a new house near the club where they've been transferred to and keep their existing one, back in those days we couldn't stretch to two mortgages so had to sell our homes when we were signed by a new club. I loved that house and it broke my heart to have to sell it. By now it's worth almost £3 million, which would have been my pension today.

"Terry and I started off on the wrong foot and although I really liked him initially, it very quickly turned into a farcical feud, was very facile and, to be perfectly honest, pathetic. I loved Arsenal and wanted to show those fans that I could play but, not long after I signed, there was more bad news: Alan Ball was leaving. I thought I'd been signed to play alongside him but it was soon made clear that Neill had bought me to replace him. How could I replace my favourite player? A midfield of Ball, Hudson and Brady: Wow! Can you imagine that?"

By the time of Alan's debut on January 3, 1977, against a Leeds side that included old England youth colleague Tony Currie, he was already at loggerheads with his manager. This may go some way to explaining why his first match was instantly forgettable – and certainly not what the paying public were expecting.

Gerald Sinstadt wrote in the following day's newspaper; 'Arsenal may have to wait a while before Hudson is ready to fulfil a similar role [to Currie's for Leeds] for them. The newcomer from Stoke introduced himself to his new supporters with a volley that cleared the bar by about eight feet. Later, he had a shot comfortably fielded by Harvey and another uncomfortably deflected by Jordan. Otherwise, Hudson contented himself with simple and safe passes. That he was able to run himself in gently reflects much credit on his colleagues.'

Alan would totally agree with such an assessment and he was angry that – when all eyes were on him, and only him that day – he fluffed his lines. Worse still, he was ordinary. If there was one thing that he despised, it was being thought of as ordinary on the football pitch. Like a '70s Cristiano Ronaldo, here was a player that could be utterly brilliant on his day and didn't mind telling everyone either – something which, as could be expected, clearly grated with many – he simply didn't perform on his debut for Arsenal. Not anywhere close. 'Simple and safe passes' indeed! Since when has such a description satisfied a player with a reputation for elegance and showmanship.

Just a handful of games into his Gunners career, Alan suffered an injury, and Terry Neill's lack of understanding as to how Alan dealt with injuries came to the fore. The Arsenal manager should have known, as was shown with Alan's decision to drop out of the England under-23 tour several years earlier, that only when he was really injured would he spend time on the treatment table. The rest of the time Huddy would grit his teeth and play through a niggle, but Neill displayed his 'know it all' attitude which destroyed their fledgling relationship.

"I was injured but Neill doubted me, so I lost any trust or faith in him immediately, and I should never have played for him whilst unfit. In the early days I even felt the lads thought that I was kidding because, not long after signing, I was regularly seeing the physios and medical staff. I was getting a little conscious of this myself and, if truth be told, rather embarrassed. The thing with Terry became more of a standing joke at Highbury: although I didn't find it funny as I wanted to regain my fitness. Terry and the club doctor even wanted me to see a 'shrink' about one injury they believed I'd invented. I was livid with him.

"Surprisingly, I was to become very close to two players who were nothing like me, Peter Simpson and George Armstrong. They were both introverts, whereas I was the opposite. I think it was through us playing in the reserves in a couple of away matches that brought us close but we also had another thing in common. None of us could stand Terry Neill, and so we all griped about him in our spare time. It was refreshing to realise that others shared your opinion. To make things worse, in a match where I felt my form retuning – just a little – I over reached for a dodgy pass at Villa Park and heard and felt my shin crack. It was not like a break, a simple snap like a twig sound, but I knew that once again Lady Luck was not on my side."

The speed of just how quickly this move would turn sour shocked even Alan. Towards the end of the season his relationship with Neill was at breaking point and as a result, general communication went through Don Howe, the assistant manager and one person who Alan always respected and had time for, right up until the day of his passing in December 2015.

Neill was angry. Raging in fact. Huddy's ongoing injury concerns clearly were not acceptable to him. Not that it could've been foreseen, but that was of no consequence to the manager who then made it his business to keep pressuring Alan, expecting him to crack and confess that the injuries were fabrications.

After the kind, charismatic Waddington, this managerial style didn't appeal to Huddy in any way, shape or form and it was no surprise when, he too, dug his heels in, ready for battle. For all intents and purposes, Alan considered Neill a bully and, if there was one thing that was guaranteed to get Huddy riled, it was someone with exactly that attitude. Having already taken on Sexton, Ramsey and Revie, Neill was going to be a pussycat in comparison – and Huddy would relish the chance to stand toe-to-toe with his manager.

"Once I got back playing in late February or early March, I was in and out of the side because my injury would start playing up after an hour. You know, like when you get a stitch, but this was unbearable, like a knife being stuck into my abdomen. The problem had come about after I'd overdone my sit-ups – whilst at Stoke – when I thought we had a free weekend but, after doing this extra training, I got a call to go and play in a testimonial at Stamford Bridge and after an hour it was like I had been stabbed." Being stabbed in the front was a new experience for Alan given that most of the time he'd felt the knife in his back!

Arsenal's loyal supporters demanded more, and they deserved it too. Be in no doubt that Huddy wanted to perform for them but an instantly forgettable first half of the season in the famous red and white could only get better; couldn't it? There was something about summer tours that Alan couldn't abide, and the official Arsenal website currently states that: 'Although his Highbury start was promising, Alan never quite delivered in the red-and-white. He was dogged by disciplinary problems throughout his career and they surfaced during the summer tour of 1977 when he was sent home by manager Terry Neill.'

Huddy had known for some time what a mistake he had made in signing for Arsenal, but he still consistently did his very best to remain professional at all times. It was widely known he was a big drinker and it was precisely that which gave Neill the perfect excuse to rid himself of his 'trouble' whilst on that tour of Australia. However, as teammate Malcolm McDonald recalled, Neill just ended up making himself look a fool over the whole situation.

ARSENAL

"I asked for Arsenal to let me go to Australia at the beginning of that summer, because I'd already got myself organised and I needed to stay in shape. I explained to Terry Neill that I had to keep ticking over, to keep playing and training because long lay offs were no good to me. Neill agreed, so I played for a side in Melbourne run by the Greek community. As we were approaching the end of the summer break I was contacted by Arsenal, who said we were going on a pre-season trip to Singapore and Australia. As I was already at the latter, I said, 'Look, I've got to come through Singapore on my way back [to England], can I not just fly from Australia to Singapore and meet you all there?'

"At first they said yes, then for some bizarre reason Terry Neill changed his mind. So I had to fly all the way back to England from Australia and a couple of days later report for training. I worked hard on the training pitch for two or three days, jet-lagged up to the eyeballs, then flew back out to Singapore. The night before our last game there – we were due to play against the Singapore national XI – we had Singapore TV on. They were showing a music programme, a pre-record of a group singing. There were three backing singers, all lasses, and the cameras panned in for close ups of the three. Two were black and the other was white. I couldn't believe it and turned to Huddy. 'Good heavens above. I know her,' I said pointing to the white girl, 'I used to sit next to her at primary school! It's Nita Selby.' Huddy turned around and said, 'Bloody hell! I used to go out with her'.

"We played against Singapore, kicking off at 9pm. The timing was daft considering we were expected to be playing at our physical peak. After the match, we went back to the hotel, had showers and went downstairs to have some food. A few of us decided to quickly nip out for a few beers. We had played in 100 degree heat and 98 percent humidity and I'd lost 12 and a half pounds in that game alone. We drank but couldn't go to the toilet because our bodies were absorbing all the liquid we'd just lost. This wasn't a session as such, we'd remembered clearly being told by the club doctors that when in Singapore we were not to drink Coke, or the local water, and not to drink too much bottled water. 'The best thing to drink is beer' they said. I know it seems hard to believe these days but that is what we were told. It could be due to the water having been boiled during the brewing process, I'm not sure.

"We got back to the hotel late and, because we were flying at 5am the next morning, we all missed out on a good night's sleep. However, once we had arrived in Australia and the usual formalities had been completed it was early evening by the time we arrived in the hotel restaurant, without even having had breakfast. As Huddy went in to eat, the chairman, Denis Hill-Wood, a lovely, lovely man said, 'Come on boys, wonderful game last night. Come and have a drink.' We explained that we needed to eat, but he insisted we had a drink in the bar first. So we spent a short while with the chairman, making small talk, and he bought three beers handing one to me and one to Huddy. After a few minutes of chit-chat, we politely made our excuses and went to the restaurant. As we approached our table, Terry Neill came over and picked up mine and Huddy's drink, smelt them and said, 'I thought so, you're both going home'.

"We were both stunned and said, 'What are you talking about?' but it was obvious he wanted to pick a fight. Then, out of anger, just like that, he made all of the rest of the squad go out and do a night-time training session. It was utterly daft. I never really got to the bottom of it but the episode really upset Huddy's equilibrium. I couldn't see the sense of it but I could let it ride. Not Huddy though. Oh no, no, no!

"When we arrived in the Middle East on the way back, there

was a whole host of journalists waiting for our plane. We decided to keep our counsel until we got back to London, where Huddy had arranged a car to collect us. We went straight to his local pub and had a bit of a battle plan as to what to do and how to go about it. With the press having been told, we thought we've got to have a right of reply. He did a deal with one paper, I did a deal with another and we told our story, our side of things."

Huddy remembers that chain of events only too well. So scarred was he by them that it's as if he were recounting something that had happened only yesterday.

"That Australian experience was too ridiculous for words. Terry flipped after our long overnight flight and Mal and I laughed our heads off before going back to our room, because we really didn't believe he was serious, Geordie Armstrong came in fuming saying, 'I've just been in to see him and told him "If they're going home I'm going too, because everything they've done, so have I," but he wouldn't have it.' That was Geordie to a tee, as honest as the day is long. Terry knew that had he sent Geordie packing as well, the directors might suspect that it was him who was in the wrong, because Geordie was the model professional and an Arsenal legend. The directors most certainly would have smelt a rat.

"Ken Friar, Arsenal's managing director and secretary, came to the rescue by bringing a little sanity to it all. He met us in the bar that night for a drink and to sort out the formalities of our trip home. The directors who we'd had a drink with earlier were in the bar too. I know that they thought that I was trouble but doubted that Malcolm was, so we had a drink and a laugh with them, mocking the manager saying things like 'He's bringing the club down' and 'What the hell is he doing?' Malcolm and I then caught the plane home. Remember he'd already flown back from Australia to England not long before and now, here he was, doing the same trip again just a few days later: he was livid. Before we knew it the Fleet Street gang were on the case. Brian Madley of the *Sunday People* contacted me and I arranged for Ken Montgomery of the *Mirror* to get in touch with Malcom at the Park Tavern in Southfields.

"We flew three eight-hour legs home, even holding a press conference after the first in somewhere like Beirut. It was hilarious but we kept our cards close to our chest. Malcolm and I had everyone in stitches having drank all through the flight. We slept through the next eight hours, and planned a party on the last leg with champagne bottles all over the place. I recall three elderly ladies getting drunk with us and standing up in the aisle saying, 'Cheers lads, the best flight we've ever been on. Who says that you're trouble?' We got back to Heathrow where I was picked up – literally – and carried over a barrier and into the waiting car. Malcolm and I were in my local, The Park Tavern in Merton Road, Southfields, at about 8.30 am. Brian Madley met me and we sat there all morning telling this incredible, but ridiculous story. Terry then banned and fined us when the team arrived back. It was an unbelievably bizarre episode.

"Terry Neill did us a right favour really because he stopped my wages, which for two weeks was £600. The following day I was in Fleet Street meeting the editor of The *Sunday People*, the great Neville Holden, who agreed on £5,000 for my story. That paid for my family holiday to Marbella. Before the weekend the stories were due to go to print, Terry got to hear about both our stories and in his wisdom, went to see Neville. In typical Neill fashion, he stormed into his Holden's office ranting and raving. As cool as you like Holden, I'm reliably informed, retorted, 'Get out of my office. When you can run your own business come back and see me, in the meantime don't waste my time,' and he sent Neill away with his tail between his legs."

ARSENAL

As rifts go, this was a monumentally huge mistake by Neill because if he wanted to take Huddy on, he was always going to lose. The underlying issue, of course, was that Alan didn't think Neill had a clue how to run a football club. That notion was confirmed when the manager hired Wilf Dixon as his first-team coach. Dixon had worked at Everton and, by all accounts, was decent in his role, but Huddy never gave him a chance, due in no small part to the advice of Alan Ball, who was the King at Goodison Park when Dixon was there.

"Bally warned me about him. His favourite story was that Wilf believed he'd invented five-a-sides, something he told a young player once during training!"

McDonald also vividly remembers the way in which Huddy used to shut Dixon down as soon as the latter would try to instigate a training drill or some such. "Alan was a straight talker alright. When you're in a football dressing room or out on the training pitch, there's that moment you need to be silent and listen to what someone has got to say. Huddy wouldn't always respect that, particularly if he thought they were talking nonsense. He would just jump down their throats and say, 'You don't know what you're talking about'.

"One of those on the receiving end was the first coach that Terry Neill brought in, Wilf Dixon. Literally every time Wilf opened his mouth, Huddy would sound off. He had no respect for the fella whatsoever and thought he talked utter nonsense. At least at the beginning of the 1977-78 season, Neill made one of his greatest decisions by getting Don Howe in as coach, with Dixon taking a back seat. Huddy and Don really hit it off, they were two great minds of the game. The problem was that too much water had gone under the bridge with everyone else at the club and it was all getting a bit too messy. If Don had been there at the beginning, I think Alan would've had a long, long career and seen his days out at Arsenal."

HUDDY

After the debacle of that summer tour, Huddy rarely spoke to Neill, preferring for messages to be passed back and forth through Howe. He could barely look his manager in the face, let alone talk to him for any length of time. The wider problem was that the wheel had turned full circle again, and Alan was at breaking point mentally. Not even a year had passed since the transfer but he was back to square one. Unhappy, constantly boozing and not really paying enough attention to the job in hand at home or at work.

"He fell out with Terry Neill, he fell out with the club, he fell out with just about everyone and he was dreadfully upset by it," McDonald said of his colleague's change in personality by autumn 1977. "Me, I wasn't happy with certain aspects of the club, but I withdrew and looked at it from afar to see what the best thing was for me to do. Whereas Huddy was a bit hot-headed and he wanted to start a world war with Arsenal Football Club – all over a drink that was bought for us by the Arsenal chairman in the summer – that was the bizarre thing about it. He just wouldn't let the matter rest.

"It seriously affected him mentally and when Huddy wasn't right, you weren't going to get the energy from him or the great performances that he was absolutely capable of producing. He had to be happy and comfortable in his mind, and he wasn't because things had really upset him. The reality was that the relationship became a war between him and Terry Neill and no one at the club was going to be able to pacify him in any way. When Neill made some strange team selections, Huddy criticised them because he had an amazing footballing brain. His vision of how to play the game was as good as anyone's and he was articulate enough to verbalise his thoughts, even if it went over the heads of many of the players.

"Terry couldn't live with him and started to get short, snappy and sharp as a result. Alan just wanted to put his thoughts across, and you could see it getting more and more fraught in the dressing room. It was such a shame because I could stand at the bar or sit on a coach, sit on a plane or in a hotel room, and I could listen to Huddy all day long. Not just a wonderful knowledge, but a wonderful way of expressing it with words. He had this love of the game, of what he might be able to do that was completely new. New tactics, new shape ... he was forever experimenting."

It was clear to everyone inside the club that Huddy's time there would come to an end sooner rather than later. From a personal standpoint, it was probably for the good of all concerned because, as anyone who goes to work knows, trying to get through the day when there's an antagonistic atmosphere amongst colleagues isn't the most comfortable environment to be in. Alan had made it his business to ensure that there was tension, so there had to come a point when things had run their course. From a professional perspective, him leaving was going to be a disaster for everyone. Players enjoyed playing with him because he was a delightful exponent of the art. McDonald was a goal scorer supreme, but was entirely self-deprecating when noting that it was players like Huddy and Bally that did the donkey work – all Supermac had to do was stick it in the onion bag. The loss to their midfield was going to have a real impact on how Arsenal played football. Not only that, but it was going to sound the death knell on a relationship between McDonald and Huddy that had blossomed right at the beginning of their respective careers.

"The first time that I was ever aware of Alan was when he signed for Chelsea as a teenager. He and I were pretty much the same age and we were kids in Fulham – he was at one end of town and I was at the other. I had been watched by Chelsea, at round about the time Alan signed, and I was looking for the same. Unfortunately, they sent me a letter saying that with regret they couldn't continue with me because they'd decided I was too small. Strangely enough, that was exactly the same reason why Alan was rejected by Fulham, where I ended up. So, he got his break, was there at Chelsea and had a brilliant time going through all of the age levels. I was left scratching my head trying to find a different route into the game which, as it turned out, was in the Southern League with Luton. Alan had made it whilst I was left playing catch-up and not knowing whether I'd ever get an opportunity in the Football League itself.

"The irony is that after two years at Luton, having scored a lot of goals and having beefed up a bit, I was told by Alex Stock – Luton manager – that there were three clubs interested in me: Manchester United, Newcastle and Chelsea! Newcastle had won the Fairs Cup a year or so previously but a lot of southerners were still unsure about heading to the north east, something I well understood, but it felt right and didn't worry me. So at this point, there had already been a rivalry between us without Alan and me ever having actually played against each other.

"What I did know was that he was a total one-off footballer. There's never been anyone quite like him in his ability, and what he was able to do with a football. He was way ahead of his time – as any great player is. He had that incredible skill of just being able to take all the pace off the ball with the slightest, deftest of touches. The ball would come at him in every way, and he would just kill it stone dead. Every time. And don't forget the pitches were crap then, but it never affected him. The pitches nowadays are better on the last day of the season than they were on the first day in my era.

"Our first opportunity to play together was for England in that game v Germany – Huddy's debut. A few weeks later we entertained Cyprus under the twin towers and he was

ARSENAL

absolutely supreme on the ball, setting up my first goal with a wonderfully flighted free-kick. I finished up getting five goals of course. I did score another but someone else was offside. Revie never picked me again to play at Wembley and that curtailed my national team relationship with Huddy, Bally and Mick Channon. Over 18 months later, when Newcastle – following a change in manager – were looking to move me on, I signed for Arsenal and joined up with Bally again. Soon afterwards they signed Huddy. What a midfield we had: Ball, Huddy, Geordie Armstrong and a lad called Trevor Ross who later went to Everton. It was a wealth of talent and I remember thinking wow, how lucky will I be playing up front with this lot feeding me, even though Bally soon went.

"During games, Huddy would cover the pitch across the 90 minutes many, many times over – but you never saw him running. I know that might sound daft, but he was always fairly still when receiving the ball. He made his space and would always receive the ball with just one touch and with his head up, looking. He didn't have to take any more than one touch, whereas others would take two or three. His head was up and he was looking around ... I look at the sorry state of recent England squads with Wayne Rooney withdrawing to the middle of the pitch to do two roles. It was exhausting and too much for even him to handle but Huddy could go in there, marshal it, general it. He'd get from where he was to where he needed to be in good time so he was nicely relaxed when he received the ball. He frightened really good players with that air of complete control and his footballing skills were made for Arsenal – he was a dream to play with.

"Arsenal's pitch at Highbury was that couple of yards narrower than all other pitches, and therefore your skills had to be absolutely top notch. That's why Huddy was made for it, because the games were always tight. There was no space.

HUDDY

Manchester City's Maine Road was probably one of the widest, and so your game could change if you were afforded space. At Arsenal it was tight so it pushed opponents nearer to you. It was a must to have a decent touch, and Huddy's was the most perfect I've ever seen.

"Bally once made a point to me. He said, in a stage whisper so everyone could hear, but doing it for the youngsters within earshot: 'Mal, listen to me carefully, when the ball is coming to me make your first run. If it doesn't come with my first touch, alter your angle, it will come with my second touch – because I've never had a third touch in my life.' Huddy's was instant, one-touch perfection. I never saw him miscontrol a ball, never saw a ball run away from him. He'd stand over a ball and you'd see defenders fall all over the place, because they'd go with his body movements and he'd just unbalance them. His second touch would just be a little pass into the runner.

"Arsenal played a very specific 4-4-2 and it was rigid. And that absolutely suited Huddy because a tackle would come flying in but he just knew everyone's position, would give a little flick with the outside of his foot and a big clumsy opponent would go flying between ball and Huddy. The ball was on its way to his teammate and he was out of harm's way with the defender looking a fool – perfect timing.

"Dear me, the number of times I winced, thinking he was going to get caught, but he always got the pass off first and then evaded the tackle by a fraction. Huddy played in millimetres when others played in inches. He didn't play football, he danced it. It's the best way I can describe him."

By the time of the 1978 FA Cup Final, Huddy was desperately looking for a way out, and had hardly spoken to Neill since their bust-up at the beginning of the season. On the Thursday before the final, he'd also fall out, briefly, with Howe.

"We were training at Wembley and as I was walking down

the tunnel after the session Don pulled me aside and said, 'Are you all right, Al? You seem a little concerned. If you're worried about whether or not you're playing Saturday, you are.' I thanked him and thought no more of it. That evening I received a call from Bob Driscoll of *The Sun*, who I used to drink with. He asked me about the match and did I think I'd be playing, which, like a fool and not thinking, I told him that Don had said I was. The following morning it was all over the back pages, and when I got to Highbury the first person I bumped into was an irate Terry Neill who let me know he was far from happy with me divulging team selection to the media. 'I ain't bothered about you,' I told him, 'I'm only bothered about Don'. 'He's waiting for you in his room, and he's raging mad,' Neill replied. He wasn't lying either, Don was like a man possessed, tearing into me like I'd never seen. 'You've let me down. I trusted you. Fuck off, out of my sight.' He was incredibly upset and I knew I'd made a big mistake. I tried to explain that Bob was an old friend and it'd slipped out, but the damage was done and Don wasn't interested."

Alan's favours for old friends extended to the Cup Final itself as when the Arsenal coach made its way into the back of the Wembley tunnel, Huddy's lifelong friend, Tony Davis, was there. The players made their way off of the coach, and Tony managed to divert attention and squeeze in with them past security. Once in the team's inner sanctum Tony managed to grab a seat on the team bench behind Neill, and watched the game from there. The Arsenal subs thought this was hilarious: "How did you manage that," one asked. Watch the final again and take a good look at the bench. There's Tony, having the time of his life in amongst the Arsenal squad. All players try and get match tickets for their mates but a prime seat, on the team bench? Huddy had excelled himself this time.

The loss to Ipswich wasn't expected and there was an

almost funereal atmosphere in the dressing room directly after the game. Once the dust had settled, and reality was swiftly washing over this illustrious group of players, Neill was looking for a scapegoat. Somewhere to shift the blame. After almost everyone else had chimed in with their two-penn'orth, it was the perfect opportunity for Huddy to let rip.

"After the FA Cup final, when in a team meeting run by Don Howe, I blamed Terry for his team selection in front of a full dressing room. It brought the house down. I told him bluntly that, 'You should've picked Graham Rix instead of Alan Sunderland.' I apologised to Alan when saying it but continued, 'You only left him out because he was the youngest. He played brilliantly in the semi-final and you leave him out? That cost us the match.' It was a little over the top but Neill had it coming to him anyway. It worked too. Don looked me straight in the eye as I pointed at Terry and gave me a look of approval – at least I think that's what it was. That was exactly why Don called the meeting. He wanted someone to stand up and show a little fight and passion. Something was missing on the pitch earlier in the day. I felt I needed to let Terry have it with both barrels and by heck, he got it.

"I was also annoyed by the sheer brass neck of the guy. Before the final, we'd had a meeting in the Players Bar about tickets. Malcolm was the man who dealt with this side of things – being close to the tout Stan Flashman – and he took all of the players' tickets to Stan. All but mine because I dealt with David Brown who I knew from Battersea. When I spoke to Malcolm about it, he told me that there had been a mix-up and it looked as if Stan also now had some of the directors' tickets. After some frantic calls and conversations between Stan and Ken Friar and a period of confusion when Ken was trying to get hold of Terry to see what had happened, it appears that the Arsenal chairman had to make Stan an offer to get them back otherwise the directors wouldn't have had seats for the Cup Final.

"Stan was a staunch Arsenal fan but can you imagine if he hadn't called Ken and he'd sold the tickets on to buyers? I can see it now, on the day of the final, the television cameras zooming in and seeing complete strangers, sitting proudly yet confused, in the Royal Box. Ken Friar got someone out of trouble that day and the directors finally got their tickets, completely oblivious to the chaotic scenes and panic after the 'mistake' came to light. If only they knew the real truth..."

After that post-Cup Final outburst, Huddy knew there was no going back. The white line had been crossed and this balletic, majestic footballer was destined for pastures new. He'd upset too many people for too long and despite the skill that he possessed, so eloquently described by Malcolm McDonald, Huddy's off-the-field behaviour meant that clubs were not exactly rushing to sign him. He was, once again, his own worst enemy. Potentially having to face up to being on English football's scrapheap at only 26, a chink of light emerged as *La Liga* club Hercules got in touch. They were willing to sign Huddy, and let him relaunch his career. It was the lifeline he was looking for. He'd take the whole family to sunny Spain. It was perfect for Alan, but Neill intervened yet again as McDonald recalls.

"Hercules of Alicante wanted to sign Huddy. They were prepared to pay decent money for him and he was given permission to talk with them. I waited outside Highbury but when Huddy came out he was beside himself with rage. I've never seen a man more angry. He explained that he'd discussed the deal with Hercules and they'd agreed to pay him a big whack up front – a signing fee of about £100,000. Not surprisingly, Huddy was up for that but he made the mistake of telling Terry Neill what the Spanish club had offered him, and apparently the manager wanted a 'cut'. 'I'm not giving that bastard any of my money, why should I?' Huddy said to me, visibly livid and frustrated. That really was the final straw for him at Arsenal.

"The one thing I always respected Huddy for was that he was always fair. First one at the bar, never lingering at the back, and he had a big circle of friends because he was just so warm, honest and sincere. You could trust him with your bank account, your chequebook, your daughter. He would look after everything perfectly for you but he could not abide people not being equally straight and fair with him. What he gave, he wanted back in return. When he met someone who wasn't to his liking – and he had to do business with them – it sent him up the wall. And I watched him go up that wall – it wasn't pretty.

"From that point [of the failed deal], Huddy had no interest in anything to do with Arsenal. No interest in training, in playing, no interest in putting an Arsenal shirt on. In fact, no interest in anything at all ... it was such a shame."

Alan decided his purpose in life would now be far better served wallowing in any number of hostelries and establishments that served alcohol. There wasn't even a hint of remorse for his actions which took a few people by surprise – even those who were used to his outbursts. Taking the manager to task – on Cup Final day – that took some bottle. But then Alan was never shy in that regard was he? Hercules was his salvation, so why did it have to go so wrong again? At least he remains philosophical about the whole episode.

"That Hercules situation was the strangest yet funniest thing I have ever experienced. I had gone AWOL from Arsenal, and Terry kept calling and pleading with me to come back, supposedly because of pressure 'from upstairs' but I'd refused. He doubted my injury, which is something that still annoys me, because if there's one thing I don't do is cheat or make excuses. Anyhow, I received a phone call from Ken Friar, although I cannot really remember where I was at the time. Ken was a great man who kept the peace when Terry was causing trouble and he told me that Arsenal had received an offer for me from a Spanish team, which I assumed would be Real Madrid or Barcelona!

"I walked into Ken's office to a very warm welcome. He was all that was good about the club, and knew I was going through a bad time with both Maureen and Terry which led to me drinking more – if that were possible. He was also aware that I wanted to get fit and back playing, and that deep down, I loved the club. Even as a Chelsea boy, my dad had taken me many times to Highbury for Wednesday night games.

"After welcoming me, Ken said, 'We've had a good offer from Spain,' to which I replied 'Wonderful, I've always wanted to play there.' That was mainly to do with my love of Di Stefano and Puskas as a young kid, and then there was Suarez – a Number 10 who was a brilliant player, a true inside-forward, not seen today. What came out of Ken's mouth next hit me for six. 'Hercules.' I laughed with Ken, as if he was kidding me, but he said, 'They've made a firm offer.' As the news sunk in, I began to think that actually it couldn't be any worse than working for Terry. I was cock-a-hoop and sought out Neill to tell him the good news; rub it in a little bit. I wouldn't say it backfired, but in the course of our chat I got the impression that there was no way he was letting me leave unless I 'shared' some of the fee. From that day on I never heard another thing, which remained as baffling and mysterious for me as it must've been for Ken. There are still things in print that say I played for Hercules but that's incorrect.

"I walked out but knew I was still obliged to play in a testimonial at Spurs for John Pratt. I really would rather have not done so but I knew that I should play for John, that I wouldn't have to exert myself and it would give me a chance to say a few goodbyes. Unfortunately, on the way home from the game I got breathalysed. It was a joke because I got to White Hart Lane early and was the first car parked outside the glass doors. I drove because my mate Tony, of the FA Cup final wheeze, would usually finish work and come over by bus, so I could have a few drinks afterwards and he would drive me home in my car. On this particular evening however, he didn't turn up because of working late. Because I had to wait until the car park emptied, and as I'd soon be leaving Highbury, I decided to have a few drinks with my mates and break the news.

"Tony had never ever let me down, this was the only time. I had no idea where I was over in that part of London, so when I saw a bus with the sign 'West End' on the back, I followed it ... down a bus lane and I quickly heard the police sirens ringing in my ears. I lost my licence, and I was never seen again at Highbury. Even in the courtroom, Don Howe got up and spoke on my behalf, suggesting that my attitude had always been spot on. He added that despite my obvious disappointment when losing in the Cup Final, I'd still been the best player on the day. The judge mentioned this is his summing up when saying, 'If he has a good attitude and was the best player, he should have known better. Three years.'

"Through training on my own, I shook off my injury and as luck would have it, between a couple of sessions, I ran into Bobby Moore one day at the Bridge. He talked me into speaking with Jimmy Gabriel, the Seattle Sounders manager who was having lunch there. I liked what I heard very much but I had to convince Maureen which was easier said than done, let me tell you. Allen was still young and it would mean uprooting everyone again, less than two years after the last time. I needed the move more than anything, and eventually she came around to my way of thinking.

"Ken Friar offered to talk to the Sounders' general manager, Jack Daley, and discuss my new contract, and he ended up getting me a lot more money than I would have done. He was brilliant in his handling of the whole thing. I regard Ken as a very good friend and have seen him at a couple of matches over the past couple of years. He remains a gentleman. Ironically, Don Howe was the last person from Arsenal who I saw. It was at London Airport when I was flying to Seattle. 'Alan, you're foolish going over there. You've far too much to offer us,' were his final words.

"It helped cushion the blow and my last words to Don said it all about my short spell with the Gunners. 'I've had enough Don. If only you'd been here when I arrived, things would've been so different.'"

8

Seattle Sounders

"I was over my Arsenal injury and this was a new chapter, so I was very excited about the future."

The original North American Soccer League (NASL) could probably be considered as the fore-runner to what we now know as Major League Soccer (MLS). Indeed, some of the clubs that played in the competition – which ran from 1968 to 1983 – now field teams for the latter. The popularity of the two competitions is comparable, as is the type of player. Although many of the big football names of the 1970s – Pelé, Johan Cruyff, Franz Beckenbauer, Carlos Alberto, George Best and Giorgio Chinaglia – all played a significant part in the rise of the game in the United States, they did so towards the end of their careers. Beckenbauer was 32, Carlos Alberto 33, Pelé was 35, and Cruyff was 32. In a similar vein, Frank Lampard, Steven Gerrard, Andrea Pirlo, David Villa were all household names and still with 'something' to offer – just not at their peak.

This is what makes Huddy's transition to American soccer so interesting as, at just 27, he was theoretically at his peak as a football player. The drink and mental problems had taken their toll and he was probably some way off where he initially needed to be, in terms of fitness and well-being, but it's still surprising that a player of his calibre and quality would at that age consider the NASL.

After playing with the likes of Osgood, Greenhoff and Brady, the standard of teammates – and most opponents – would be nowhere near his skillset, almost like asking a Premier League player today – at their peak – to drop down into League One or Two. Yet, in many ways, being one of the bigger fish in this particular pond was going to be a saving grace and an experiment that could only ever be positive. Plus he'd get to be reunited with his old mate George Best, who was already in the US and, at that time, playing for the San Jose Earthquakes after periods at the Los Angeles Aztecs and the Fort Lauderdale Strikers. Best had walked out on Manchester United at the same age as Alan quit Arsenal. Kindred spirits both on and off the pitch.

Even so, Huddy had never even watched an NASL match, much less set eyes on Seattle, before going to play there. It was only that chance encounter and endorsement from Moore that led him to Jimmy Gabriel, the Sounders coach.

Risky though it first appeared, to Huddy it all made perfect sense. He had to get away from everything and from everyone, and to make a new life in a completely different part of the world where no one knew who he was. A place where he could walk down the street and not be recognised. Where he could go into a bar and enjoy a beer without worrying that the papers would be watching his every move, hoping for a scoop.

It didn't take this proud Londoner long to feel right at home with everything that Seattle had to offer, and we're not talking nightlife either. For a start, the people were astonishingly courteous as one might expect. After all, our American friends have always been able to teach their British counterparts a thing or two about customer service. The scenery was out of this world, and it's no exaggeration to say that it was love at first sight for Alan and also for Maureen. Particularly for Maureen as it turned out. After the hell that had been his Arsenal move, this was paradise most definitely found.

"On our first night in Seattle, Maureen and I were looked after by Jack Daley, the Sounders' general manager, who took us to the wonderful Space Needle, the revolving restaurant in the sky. Overlooking the most beautiful of cities, I already had a sense that I wanted this to be my last move professionally, and also for it to be 'my resting place'. Somewhere that was a home from home, even though I'd return to London every now and then. Seattle was a breath of fresh air and now I was with another great man in Jimmy Gabriel, who was a great player at Everton and with Scotland. A man who would've got more caps if he hadn't shared the same era as Jim Baxter, one of my idols. My career had been on a see-saw, from Waddington to Neill to Gabriel – from the highest point to the lowest and back again."

Huddy also recalled it being a swing in the right direction socially. His next door neighbours were the aptly named Barman family, something Alan discovered on his first day when seeing their mailbox at the end of the drive.

"I'll never forget that. Not long after we'd moved in there was a knock on the door, and upon opening it there stood a lady holding a cake. She was very attractive, about the same age as me, and she introduced herself as Jean Barman, the wife of Bob. 'Welcome to Seattle' she said and passed over this gift. What a difference from London, where in Southfields, our first wonderful family home close to the famous All England Tennis Club in Wimbledon, we were faced by quite the opposite. The Barmans became our close friends and were invited to every gathering I threw, something that was a part of the American way of life. We embraced it and not only had some wonderful experiences, but appreciated that we lived in a wonderful society and country. If my love affair with Seattle began in the Space Needle, my passion for the place deepened upon being greeted by such nice folk. I take offence when the English call our friends across the pond 'false' – and this was living proof of it."

Huddy felt as happy as he'd ever been, and that showed in how he applied himself to training and in his early matches. The move had awoken what had laid dormant inside him for months at Arsenal, just aching to get out. Here was a player that still 'had it' and just wanted the platform to prove himself again. To be able to dictate the style and pace of a game, and bring all of those around him as close to his level as it was possible to be. It wasn't easy, though, and his new supporters clearly didn't understand his role. He'd tried to explain on many occasions that it was the equivalent of an American football quarterback, but it still took the locals quite some time to understand precisely what he was trying to achieve.

"I was now going to be playing with teammates drawn from the lower leagues in England, but I was over my Arsenal injury and this was a new chapter, so I was very excited about the future. I had bought a beautiful home – my 'House on the Hill' – and was about to meet some great people in this amazing city. My aim was to get back to my best and the new life of flying to every match was right up my street. I loved travelling and once those doors on the aeroplane shut tight I was going to Heaven, or as close to it as possible. We had built a truly wonderful team spirit, and I loved my new teammates, Steve Buttle, Adrian Webster, Mike Ivano, the strange but lovely Micky Cave who later, tragically, committed suicide, Tommy Jenkins of Southampton, who'd played with Jimmy Gabriel, and Dave Gillett, who'd been at Port Vale. They'd had careers like mine at Arsenal – mostly on the treatment table. I knew how they felt. When you're injured you can be ignored and feel completely out of it.

"Playing for Gabriel was easy because we had the same football brain. Jimmy was a real student of the game but he was tolerant too, because he knew us boys loved a good time. Actually no, they were great times, unforgettable in fact, but we trained hard and I was as fit as ever before.

Jimmy Gabriel was a hero with the Sounders, joining them as a player in 1974 – whilst Huddy was still at Stoke. He would go down in history for scoring their first-ever goal at the newly-opened Kingdome when Seattle moved there in 1976. Against their fierce rivals, the New York Cosmos, it's a goal that's still talked about to this day – a fabulous header from a Tommy Jenkins cross. On that day, April 9, a record crowd of 58,128 packed into the stadium – as much to check out their team's new home as to see how their heroes fared against the likes of Pelé and his teammates. Spectator Diane Carlson was quoted in Hy Zimmerman's *Seattle Times* column for that day as saying she'd, "Never seen a soccer game before. I don't know what's going on, but I'm having a good time watching others. I can't wait to see baseball and football in the Dome. I just came to see the building."

Pelé neatly book-ended the game with a goal three minutes from the start and the winner three minutes from the end. Matt Pentz of the *Seattle Times* recalled the game on its 40th anniversary in 2016.

"The Sounders-Cosmos attendance figure was all the more impressive given that the Sonics [basketball team] were hosting the defending champion Golden State Warriors at Seattle Center Coliseum across town that same day. Yet to focus on only that particular number is to underrate just how formative the Kingdome opener was to soccer's development in Seattle. To a certain generation of local soccer fans, it was a touchstone called upon when describing how they fell for the sport.

"Future Sounders owner, Adrian Hanauer, was in the crowd that day, and even if most of the curious had turned out to catch a first glimpse of the gleaming new dome, it's not difficult to draw a zig-zagging line between Pelé's visit and the 40,000-plus that regularly pack CenturyLink Field for MLS games. 'Within a decade, soccer will be the No.1 sport in this country,' Zimmerman wrote breathlessly, and furthering the theory that time is a flat circle. The NASL would actually fold within the decade, and the current MLS would happily settle for equalling the popularity of baseball (MLB), basketball (NBA) let alone facing the challenge of [American] football (NFL). At that time, however, it's hard to criticise the columnist for getting sucked in by the hype of Pelé's visit, looking into the gracefully arching new dome and imagining a bright future."

That bright future did involve Huddy just a couple of years later and he too was amazed by the Kingdome, a behemoth of a stadium. Playing in it, in front of thousands of eager, committed and supportive fans gave him focus on the pitch, as did being handed the captaincy by Gabriel. It was a master stroke by someone who understood that to give Huddy responsibility – something he thrived on – would see the very best from him. The role of 'guvnor' goes some way to explaining why the period Alan spent in the USA was one of the happiest of his career, alongside his Stoke days. Gabriel truly believed in Huddy, and in what he would bring to the team, and that belief was reciprocated.

"My new life in Seattle was something quite different, a great city with fabulous people. Only Waddington was missing and a few players I'd left behind in England, but I found a new gem in Steve Buttle, a limping nine stone inside forward of sheer class. Mike England of Spurs and Wales was there when I arrived –

they called him Bungalow because he had 'nothing upstairs'. He was a 6"3' centre-half who had plenty of run-ins with Osgood in my days at Chelsea. Mike was okay as a man, but as an athlete, wow, he was like the Boeing planes that tuned up their vast engines next to our Renton Training Ground. I remember watching him run around the track one day with his sunglasses on! One of the main reasons I admired and loved Jimmy Gabriel is one day in training he stopped a session and had an argument with Mike about hitting the ball long. 'Do you think we paid all that money for Alan, only for you to kick it over his head?' Now, as someone who loathes coaching and most coaches at that, this was music to my ears.

"He told Mike in no uncertain terms, 'If a player can't pass the ball across his box to a teammate 15 yards away, he shouldn't be a professional footballer. Pass the ball into Alan's feet – that's why he's here.' Brilliant! Jimmy proved to me that he was my kind of football manager, and we got on like a house on fire, on the training field, in the bar of both of our homes and also at FX McCrory's – the bar underneath the offices at the Kingdome. FX was famous for having the largest selection of spirits in the world, and was where I found Crown Royal. When I first walked in there I was gobsmacked ... the backdrop of the bar was immense – about 25 feet tall – with a ladder behind it that moved along the bar so the barman could reach the top shelf."

Although he waltzed through matches like a footballing Fred Astaire, Huddy developed a short-tempered and frankly quite nasty attitude toward those who weren't consistently at the same level, something that began to upset the equilibrium of the side. In fairness, Seattle were never going to be the best team in the NASL because their recruitment policy and budget weren't on par with the other sides, particularly the Cosmos, so some understanding from the captain wouldn't have gone amiss. His sharp tongue didn't win him friends amongst those on the receiving end, but he was allowed free rein by Gabriel, who turned a blind eye to the outbursts.

After all, it was just the captain doing the captain's job wasn't it? Bringing everyone into line when they weren't pulling their weight. Huddy spared no one and pulled no punches when he was in full flow, and less well known staff such as Mike Ivanow, Mark Peterson, Al Trost and Eddie Krueger must've wondered what had hit them at times. Even the 'star' names on the roster; Harry Redknapp, Jimmy Neighbour and Bobby Howe, to name just three, didn't escape Huddy's ire.

Yet, for all of the problems created by his attitude, Alan was always respected as a player, as Cliff Brown remembered. "One of my memories of Alan when I was part of the Sounders team – and later with the Cleveland Force – was seeing him injected before the game, and then him sitting with his feet in an ice bucket after the match: beer in one hand, cigarette in the other. I always respected his willingness to play in pain. He was not only the most talented player I had the pleasure of calling a teammate, but he was a warrior who set the ultimate example to all of us younger players. It was a different time for sure!"

As far as Huddy was concerned, it was an all-for-one and one-for-all mentality and clearly some didn't show the requisite work ethic. Won 13, lost 17 in his first season was nowhere near good enough in the player's eyes, nor was it for the Sounders' hierarchy who dispensed with Gabriel's services.

"Jimmy made me captain when I signed from Arsenal – because he saw it as a massive move in the right direction for the Sounders. I was their biggest signing. All the other players would only come at the end-of-season from England, whereas I was signed lock, stock and barrel. Jimmy thought we'd have a long, successful relationship – but the team simply weren't good enough and he was punching above his weight. Mind you, I nearly walked out when he was sacked. I loved the fella, truly, but he told me, 'Please Alan, you have a good contract and you have a great life here. I know you love it here so give Alan Hinton the opportunity to manage you.' It was great advice from a truly great man – over the telephone on the night of his sacking. If he was bitter, he didn't show it. I mean, he could quite easily have said, 'Forget Seattle, get out now'."

After a few weeks back in England post-season, Huddy joined the Major Indoor Soccer League (MISL) for the remainder of the summer.

"Seattle loaned us all out to help with the bills and we got well paid. I went to play for my old Chelsea sidekick Eddie McCreadie in Cleveland, Ohio, for the Cleveland Force. It was yet another wonderful experience – he was one of my best friends! Those moves were necessary from a financial perspective because the NASL clubs, unlike their MLS counterparts today, didn't have sponsorship opportunities that are commonplace now.

"Nor were there billionaire businessmen willing to gamble their fortunes on what was, and in many respects still is, a minority sport. The Sounders are now run and advised by those who oversee the very successful Seattle Seahawks. When I joined, it was run more like an amateur club in England and I don't just mean at a playing level either. Everyone was still learning about how to play the game, and how the team played as a unit.

"Adaptation didn't, and still doesn't, happen overnight of course. Pirlo struggled initially in New York yet, just a few years ago, beat England on his own when playing for Italy. Frank Lampard and Steve Gerrard only went overseas for the salary whereas I went there for completely different reasons, being at my peak. I wanted to end my career like I began it – in style. I'm proud that my contribution to the Seattle

SEATTLE SOUNDERS

Sounders was great. For me, it was about so much more than just performing to the gallery week-in and week-out. I gave my all to my teammates, worked extra hard in training and really helped make a difference to those young Americans."

Alan Hinton had been laying the groundwork for the new season in Huddy's absence, and so here was yet another manager to size up. How would he compare to Waddington? Was he a cad like Neill? As it happened Hinton was neither, but he got the results that Gabriel was unable to. Tommy Hutchison had joined on loan from Coventry City, Roy Greaves signed from Bolton and David Nish, Roger Davies, Jeff Bourne and Bruce Rioch all moved from Derby County – Hinton's old side. At the drop of a hat, the upgrade in staff was significant but Huddy's enthusiasm at what the Sounders were going to be about was tempered by Rioch's capture. Four years previously he'd had been on the receiving end of what can only be described as thuggery from Rioch, a crunching tackle carrying more than a hint of malice about it and which ended up breaking Alan's leg.

The pair were never going to get on at Seattle once Huddy overheard Rioch boasting to the youngsters in the side that he'd intended to hurt him in that challenge. Something about wanting to "Bring him down a peg or two". There was no love lost – off of the pitch at any rate. "I tolerated Rioch in Seattle for the good of the team. It must have bruised his ego, having to walk out behind me on match days, because he was captain at Derby, Everton and for Scotland a couple of times."

Such animosity didn't affect the success of the team because the Sounders were virtually unstoppable. Hinton had brought more urgency and tactical *nous* to the managerial position and every player in the team was thriving: 25 wins and only seven losses was the best in the NASL, but even that wasn't enough for success. Despite waltzing the Western Division of the National Conference and having the most wins of any team across the entire six divisions of the NASL, Seattle would lose out on the title to the Cosmos by virtue of the bonus points awarded for goals scored. It was cruel on a team that had done everything possible to break their title duck but even worse was to follow for Huddy.

The play-offs for Soccer Bowl '80 gave the Sounders the perfect chance to make up for the disappointment of losing the title and after comprehensively beating Vancouver Whitecaps in the first round, then being drawn against Los Angeles Aztecs – who they'd already beaten that season – a place in the final at the very least was there for the taking. A 3-0 first-leg defeat certainly wasn't what Hinton had in mind and he tore into his players on the way home from the Rose Bowl. Only 13,466 had watched the first game but buoyed by 35,254 at the Kingdome, Seattle miraculously took the game 4-0. Unlike in England where the aggregate winner then progresses, NASL had also introduced a rule – applicable only in 1979 and 1980 – that if the games were tied at one win each, a 30-minute 'mini-game' would be played. If the aggregate scores from this and the previous two fixtures were level, then a shootout would determine the victor and the vanquished. A 2-1 win for the Aztecs meant a 5-5 aggregate, and so to penalties – where Seattle failed dismally and went out 2-0.

Alan Hinton was deservedly awarded Coach of the Year and Huddy would be delighted for his colleague Roger Davies, who won the Most Valuable Player (MVP) accolade, and also for Jack Brand who took home the North American Player of the Year. Those honours never really bothered Alan because, for him, Steve Buttle was as good as any player in the league on his day yet was consistently overlooked. His intelligence and execution clearly meant nothing to those in charge, so as far as Alan was concerned, their opinions couldn't really be taken seriously. Especially as Rioch had also made the All Star team one season too!

Although it meant nothing in the grand scheme of things, the Sounders emerged victorious in the second Trans-Atlantic Challenge Cup. Alongside the Cosmos, Seattle were the NASL's representatives against two strong sides in Glasgow Celtic and Southampton. Huddy was imperious in both games and was Man of the Match in the final against the Cosmos, which Seattle drew 2-2 but edged 8-7 on penalties. To get there, the Sounders had beaten Celtic 3-1 and Southampton 2-1.

"I had played against Charlie Nicholas in the Trans-Atlantic Challenge where we had also beaten Southampton. They had Alan Ball, Charlie George, Steve Williams, Mick Channon ... a really strong side. Although Bally couldn't resist a little dig saying 'We were on holiday,' he was never on holiday when there was a match on because he was the supreme competitor. Alan Hinton agreed that I was Player of the Tournament and I even recall Charlie talking about my performance against Celtic on Sky's *Soccer Saturday* a couple of years ago. It was *that* good. After that first season under Hinton I was even more convinced Seattle would be my final destination, I truly believed that.

"My most fantastic playing experience there began with me shaking hands in the centre-circle with the great Giorgio Chinaglia, the Cosmos captain who'd started his career in 1964 at Swansea Town, as they were then known. We played them in a friendly at Memorial Stadium and as we met in the centre, he handed me the usual NY Cosmos banner of pure silk. I had nothing and was embarrassed, which told the story about the difference between these two clubs. I apologised and he said, 'Alan, it's not your fault. Have you any children?' I told him that my son Allen was 'over there' pointing to the side line, and he said 'Call him over,' which I did. When young Allen got there, and remember he was only eight at the time, Chinaglia greeted him, shook his hand and handed him the banner. 'That's for you son,' he said. Pure class. That was Giorgio, who I would've loved to have known better, the same applies to Bobby Moore: two giants of our game. Anyhow, I scored the winning shoot-out goal in New York – the first time the Sounders had ever won there.

"In the dressing room afterwards, you'd have thought we had won the World Cup, and before I knew it a camera was shoved in my face. 'Congratulations, you won the match and have been named our Man of the Match,' came the cry from the TV announcer. Straight away and without a moment's hesitation, I said, 'I don't think so, see him over there [Stevie Buttle], he was magnificent and was without doubt the best player on the field.' I was our captain and as usual, honesty was my policy.

"Buttle had Dutch World Cup star Johan Neeskens on his knees at one stage. I stood there in awe of the little fella teasing Neeskens in the centre-circle, like a ringmaster in a circus clowning with a tiger: or a Matador in Spain. 'Ole! Ole! Ole!' Buttle was irresistible both on and off the field. Some might call him a 'cheeky chappy' but he was one who knew exactly what was going on around him. He was the first player I saw chip the goalkeeper from the penalty spot. He did it in training but he would have done it at Wembley, trust me!"

So, doubtless, might Alan, even if the iconic north west London stadium left him cold when he played there in the in the 1972 League Cup final and the 1978 FA Cup final. Perhaps that was as much to do with the manner of the defeat and what went on surrounding it, as the actual defeat itself. Highbury, White Hart Lane, Anfield, the Victoria Ground – they all meant more to him than that soulless bowl, regardless of his performance there against Germany for England. Even the

SEATTLE SOUNDERS

Giants Stadium in New York sent more shivers down his spine than Wembley.

"When I played at Wembley I did not have the feelings I had when playing at other, 'proper' football grounds. Playing against the Cosmos, against Giorgio, Franz Beckenbauer, Johan Neeskens ... that was what playing football was all about. And then the piano bars until five in the morning imagining Frank Sinatra and Tony Bennett walking in. Where Billy Joel met Christie Brinkley and sat at the piano wooing her – it was something else. Which brings me onto Maureen."

Three days before Huddy flew out to Seattle to sign his first contract, Maureen still hadn't made up her mind whether to go with him. Fed up with the nomadic lifestyle that follows any professional footballer around, the thought of dragging their son Allen halfway round the world certainly wasn't one that initially appealed. Huddy had been tearing his hair out for days trying to persuade her to come with him. Allen was still young enough not to be too bothered by it all, and in any event, despite his age, he was already streetwise and could fit in anywhere. At least that's what his dad thought. Allen takes up the story.

"I went to 16 schools as a kid! Moving all around the world, I could never put my roots down in one place so it was one of those situations where I just had to get on with it. I don't expect my dad and my mum to look back and say, 'What did we do to him?' I mean, they wonder why I get the hump sometimes ... I don't get the hump with them, I just had to learn to stand up for myself quicker and grew up so differently from other kids. Even me and my brother are so different."

Talking to Allen there's an obvious sense of resentment at certain aspects of his upbringing, yet surrounding that he still has that unbreakable, unconditional love for both of his parents. In many respects he remains philosophical about the whole experience. It wasn't anyone else's reality – so how could they be expected to understand – but it was his reality. A reality that included being picked on because of who his dad was and, when settling in Seattle, dealing with the taunts because of his accent.

Maureen loved Seattle as it turned out, this really was her kind of place, but she was prepared to go back home at a moment's notice if things didn't improve for Allen at school. Away trips would mean that Huddy was often absent for three or four days at a time, and then – of course – there'd be the socialising. Although it was a marriage in name only by this point, Maureen was at least able to extricate herself from the bubble by going to the shopping malls that were commonplace in the States but something of a novelty in England. There wasn't a week that went by without a new outfit in the wardrobe.

Part of her shopping obsession was to cope with a couple of elements of family life that weren't as fabulous as the rest. For all of their money, Maureen might just as well have been a single parent for the amount of time that Huddy was at home and *compos mentis* enough to be able to deal with things as a father and husband should. Too many nights out for the man of the house often meant that Maureen alone would have to deal with Allen's education and upbringing, which must have been stressful.

"Allen found it very difficult in the early days, going to school and getting picked on and laughed at because of his English clothing and accent. We had to take him out and re-dress him as an American boy: baseball cap and all that jazz. Once he was settled though, he was like Arthur Daley in those parts – having a garage sale selling my boots and even putting a price on Maureen's washing machine! I came home from training one lunchtime, jumped out of my Camaro and saw all of these tiny stickers on my Nike boots – five bucks here, ten bucks there – I wondered what the hell was going on? Nike used to send me boxes and boxes of boots of all types because of playing on grass and Astroturf, and there were literally hundreds of orange boxes lining the walls of the garage.

"I walked through the side door and into the kitchen where Maureen was furious and said to me, 'Have you seen that in the garage?' Holding onto the sink I bent over and began laughing. 'He's selling our stuff and you're laughing, aren't you going to hammer him?' I just looked at her and said, 'He's arrived. He's finally arrived.' She was still livid and said 'I'll need to contact all of their parents and ask for the boots back and refund their money.' Now if you knew Maureen and how she was about money, that was really quite something. She would never give anything to anyone, bringing 'careful' to a whole new level. I was still laughing, almost proud, of my son, but she couldn't see that he'd adapted to a life light years from London. Even his new school friends began to admire him."

Part of their eventual 'admiration' may just have stemmed from the fact that Alan Hudson, Sounders captain, was his father. With that came kudos which would reflect well on Allen – that and the fact that anyone would be allowed in the house. The Hudsons' door was very definitely always open. That too would become a burden at times, but it allowed the family to develop a rapport with their neighbours and locals much more quickly than they might otherwise have done. The scenery had changed, and so had the standard of football, but some aspects of Huddy's family life very much stayed the same.

"When we went out to the States, Dad was still only 27, not when he was 'finished' as a player," Allen said. "He enjoyed himself. We had a big house, great for entertaining and we always had the other players or friends round, or Dad went out. He loved a bird too and he was a good looking boy ... he never had to tell me when I was with him – even at eight, nine, 10 years of age – not to say anything to my mum. I knew what was happening."

If Allen knew the score, then it goes without saying that Maureen did too and when she fell pregnant in June 1980, Huddy certainly wasn't expecting to become a father again. That's not to say that when young Anthony Patrick Hudson was born on March 11, 1981, that he wasn't anything other than ecstatic.

"Anthony was born in Seattle and therefore has dual citizenship. There's a funny story behind his birth. Maureen was due to have him on the day the Sounders were going to Santa Anita for a five-day pre-season tour. It was a dream place that I'd always wanted to go to: *The Rockford Files* and all that. I'd organised for Maureen to be looked after by Roy Greaves' wife Barbara, which worked a treat. On the day of departure, I got to SeaTac Airport around 7am and on boarding I walked up the aisle to tell Alan Hinton of the impending birth. 'Al, that's great, I can understand you staying behind,' he said, to which I replied 'You're joking mate, do you think I'm going to miss this trip?!'

"He laughed his head off. Alan and I had a great relationship and were very close friends, so he understood me. Off we went and Anthony was born two days later. I remember wetting his head – almost drowning him – in a club in Santa Barbara. As it turned out I was right to not be there because he was born with a hernia which was frightening and I wouldn't have been good in that situation. I remember inviting the surgeon to dinner to thank him, as if he'd saved Anthony's life. Not long after, he invited Maureen and me to his home for a dinner party when he showed us a movie of him climbing mountains. I suppose surgeons like danger, don't they? Life and death. It's what they deal with on a daily basis."

SEATTLE SOUNDERS

For a time, the arrival of Anthony lifted the gloom that surrounded the marriage, but it was never going to last. For that to happen, there had to be a change in Huddy's mentality. When he was at home, he would prefer to find solace in the company of anyone but his wife, so friends and colleagues were constantly invited round. Dutiful as she was, Maureen was at breaking point and the rows between the pair became ever more vicious. Playing away from the Kingdome gave him the perfect excuse to 'get away from it all,' but Maureen was still left holding the baby in every sense.

The move to Seattle was just what Alan and Maureen needed, but just not with each other it seems, as the fault lines in their marriage cracked open again and Alan got the feeling that Maureen was going to leave him, taking the boys with her. "Maureen's love for Seattle grew as her affection for me withered. I may have been a bad husband, but I still believe I was a good father."

It's true that Allen looked up to his dad more than his mum, and still retains enormous love and respect for him. Equally, scratch the surface and there's an awful lot of heartache and pain that has given rise to Allen's anger later in life. In any event, one of the fondest memories that the entire family have of their time in Seattle was when Bill and Bub made the trip over in 1981 to see their newborn grandson, and to take in all that Seattle had to offer.

"They came over and although there was still much friction with Maureen, they coped. Well, Mum did. Bill absolutely loved Seattle and I made sure that he did. Dad was never a boozer but I got him to love champagne and orange, and he had a ball in our or Roy Greaves' home until the early hours. Seattle changed all of our lives and Bill didn't want to go back to the UK. I told him that he could stay forever.

"Bill loved that summer because he got so close to Allen.

Seattle really did bring us Hudson boys together and even Maureen could see how happy we were."

I still have an outstanding memory of Dad from when I first took him to the Kingdome. He was completely in awe and the look on his face brought a lump to my throat. As we turned and walked back through a nearby square where all the down-and-outs were sitting, drinking their cans of beer, Bill casually remarked, 'Even their tramps are smarter than ours!' That was him all over – a great sense of humour without knowing it. We went to see the Seahawks playing at the Kingdome one night but unlike with English football, the NFL players warm up for nearly an hour, so we both got bored and left. Fortunately he also got to see me play and he was knocked sideways by how good we were. Considering he'd seen me at my peak at Stoke, that meant a great deal to me. Had we not left, I think Bill would've eventually joined us permanently in Seattle."

The 1980-81 indoor season saw a win-loss record of 9-9, whilst the 1981 regular season wasn't much better with 15 wins and 17 losses. No goals from their captain for the second regular season in a row was a huge surprise. Hinton's crown was beginning to slip but Huddy was still enjoying the ride even if from a scoring perspective, he'd not contributed. His influence was still much more far-reaching. Another indoor campaign – in which he flourished – again finished with nine wins and nine losses. Questions were coming thick and fast for Hinton but many stars had left without being replaced, so one didn't have to look too far to understand where the issues were.

Sooner or later the bubble was going to burst unless there was a serious injection of cash. It began to leave a stain on what was a fabulous experience for Huddy, who knew the end was nigh long before it actually happened – in September 1983. Members of the Collucio family, the club's owners, were still losing money, even though gates remained healthy. Purse strings would inevitably have to be tightened and with Alan one of the main earners – despite being captain and integral to the Sounders' way of playing – he understood what that meant more than most. He didn't dare tell Maureen. Their union had long since been an unhappy one, but he wanted to keep her onside because there were now their two boys to think about.

Aside from young Allen's initial troubles, Maureen enjoyed being a lady of leisure, spending days in the gym making friends and trading off of the fact that she was Huddy's girl. It meant she was incredibly popular in the locale. Unbeknown to her husband, she had long been planning her own career in Seattle and making preparations to make it a reality for her when the time was right, and to give Allen and Anthony the best life she possibly could. Alan's inevitable departure from Seattle brought his matrimonial matters to a head and another upheaval in his life beckoned.

"Seattle were going to fold and after getting my marching orders from the Sounders by a rat named Bruce Anderson, I tried to get another club. I almost went to Tampa Bay and Fort Lauderdale, but wages were a problem for them. To be honest, I would've taken a drop in money to move there, because my love for the USA was monumental, but when it was clear things weren't going to happen, I had to face the unpalatable fact that, if I wanted to continue my career, then it would have to be back home in England.

"I thought Maureen was following me home but she had other ideas. She had been working out at the gym a lot and looking back it should've rung alarm bells with me, but I was too preoccupied with enjoying myself and of course concerned about my future in the game. The new regime at the Sounders were quite adamant that it was a time for change, and that meant I was no longer wanted (or affordable, more like). They had sacked Alan Hinton and foolishly I had gone public and attacked them, a situation that I should've kept quiet about. But, being captain of the most successful team in their history, I felt that these new faces needed reminding."

The loss of what had been a perfect professional life hit Huddy harder than ever and a period of adjustment was required before he could even begin to contemplate kicking a football for a living again.

9

Chelsea and Stoke ... Again

"It might've even been the first ever time a chairman had signed a player over the wishes of his manager."

For the first few months after returning from his Seattle sacking, Huddy was numb. He'd lost his captaincy, his job and his way of life. On top of that he'd also temporarily lost contact with his two sons because of Maureen's initial refusal to move back to Blighty. There's no doubt that April to July of 1983 was an incredibly low point in his life and there was a genuine concern for Alan from those closest to him. However, he'd been far down that road before, and had ended up using it as a positive lever to catapult himself out of the early onset of depression.

It was Waddington that had once told him, "you're doing everything right, just in the wrong order. Don't waste your God-given talent, put your football first and get your priorities right," and those words resonated with Huddy now more than ever. His ability to keep bouncing back was laudable, but you might say he was used to it after the early career disappointment of missing both the FA Cup final and World Cup finals in 1970 – both before he was 20 years of age. That, and a marriage he clearly wasn't ready for. It could have broken him, but he was resolute enough to keep ploughing on.

On returning to England, Huddy stayed with his friend, Tony Davis, in south London for a few weeks, before moving back in with Bub. He had nowhere else to live as the Southfields home was being rented, and there was no way his mum was going to see one of her boys out on the street – however bad things got. Even though he was out of work again and living like a second-rate playboy, he still took time to keep himself in shape. Waddington's words still rang true though, because the old haunts in Chelsea and Fleet Street were regularly frequented.

Alcohol-induced fogs were nothing new of course, but this time it was different, for along the way he even dabbled with the odd line of cocaine. He'd once smoked a joint whilst out in Seattle but found it had absolutely no effect whatsoever. Taking coke most certainly did and it scared him knowing that it was nothing like the booze, which he had a handle on most of the time. He had always been a social drinker but now, similar to when he was depressed at Chelsea from loss of form and injury, he was drinking to forget – something he knew was wrong.

There were moments during that summer when darkness and despair engulfed him and suicide seemed the best option. Only eight years since he had the footballing world at his feet after that monumental performance against Germany at Wembley, life itself had lost its appeal. Within a decade, Huddy's life was as far removed from the glitz and kudos of that night as it was possible to be, for his depression was now all-consuming. Mind you, however terrible he was feeling, Huddy never ignored his training regime because he knew that if a club did come in for him, he had something to prove yet again.

So what changed? How was he able to drag himself up to something anywhere close to his old self? In the end, the answer was a simple one. Although training was his greatest ally, he would've been lost without family and friends who had refused to give up on him. It was hard for them at times, especially when the offers of help were refused and met with a barrage of abuse hurled in every direction. Fortunately for Huddy, his pals were of the long-standing variety and were able to cut through that nonsense and still see the man they knew, somewhere deep inside the wall he had built around himself.

With enough care, attention and patience, they were convinced that sooner or later something had to change – but it was touch and go at one stage. Not in the sense of living or dying, but whether there was a genuine willingness on Alan's part to get better or to continue to wallow in his own self-pity. His love for the beautiful game kept gnawing away and eventually a switch flicked and a decision was made to try and resurrect a fading career once again. Tentative enquiries were made at various clubs to see if they'd be willing to sign him on a free transfer.

"I wanted to go to Fulham to finish my career, for old time's sake, but as in my youth when they said I was too small, it wasn't to be. I even applied for the vacant manager's job but Jimmy Hill blanked me and never even gave me an interview. I tried to get in at Port Vale but their manager, John McGrath also turned me down. Ditto Richie Barker at Stoke City. I was close to hanging up my boots for good when I decided to walk into Stamford Bridge and offer my services to John Neal.

"He handed me a trial but, although I was training incredibly well, after a few weeks he still wouldn't commit. I could tell it was more likely to be a 'No' because he'd even invited me to leave at one point. Chelsea then went on a pre-season camp to Aberystwyth, where only Paul Canoville kept up with me on the gruelling runs on North Beach that Neal sent us on. Ken Bates watched us training on that trip and upon returning to

HUDDY

London, he took any decision out of Neal's hands. He called me into the boardroom and had a contract waiting for me – without a doubt because he thought it was good publicity. It might've even been one of the first times a chairman had signed a player against the wishes of his manager."

It was the lifeline that Huddy needed, but it wouldn't be long before the fickle finger of fate would intervene yet again. Being nowhere close to his previous form, he was destined to never make a first-team appearance in his second spell at the club. Illness and injury would also conspire against him. Playing in the reserves might not have been contemplated before but, given his situation at the time, Huddy grabbed it with both hands.

"I had nothing to do with the Chelsea first-team, as I think they looked at me as a 'has-been' from the '70s. It didn't bother me and, to be honest, after that I thought I'd never play any first-team football again. This may sound strange but I absolutely loved being involved in reserve football, playing in front of a handful of people on freezing cold nights at places like Crystal Palace and Oxford.

"After playing in front of 100,000 at Wembley against West Germany, it should've been a soul destroying experience for me, but it was enriching. We had some great lads and had a good laugh. Mickey Droy, Dale Jasper, Peter Rhodes-Brown, Chris Hutchings were all decent players and the daily training routine kept me going. I remember when we played the first-team in a Friday practice match before they had a big game. We'd keep the ball from them and after about 20 to 30 passes John Hollins – now assistant coach to Neal – would blow his whistle and ask for the ball back.

"We used to laugh because it was so similar to the old 'Can we have our ball back Mister' routine we'd used so often as young boys. It was hilarious. I grew up and played with Hollins, but

CHELSEA AND STOKE ... AGAIN

training under him was difficult as we had different football philosophies. The only two first-teamers I got on with were Colin Pates and John Bumstead. As for Kerry Dixon, Pat Nevin and the rest, let's just say that we didn't get on."

Despite playing reserve-team football under a manager and coach who probably didn't want him there, a thirst for the game had at least returned, even if – by the end of 1983 – Huddy couldn't see a future for himself at the top level. A winding down of a career unfulfilled and a potential early retirement were on the cards. Despite his obvious flaws, Huddy remained a realist and took a 'what will be, will be' approach to his life in general.

It was also around this time that Alan rekindled a friendship with Ann Roberts, who would eventually become his second wife. Ann worked in The Cartoonist, a pub just off Fetter Lane run by his old friend, Tommy Nicholson. Several months previously, whilst on a break from duty with the Sounders, Alan had met Ann – or 'Robbo' as she was affectionately known by certain customers, ex-CID John Mullally in particular – and it was obvious that she'd taken a fancy to the still-married Mr Hudson. She also worked in Vagabonds club in the same area of town, and that's where the pair first met properly. The club was owned by Mullally and there were reasons why Huddy initially kept a distance between himself and Ann.

"John was the boss in Vagabonds and he frequently let everyone know it with his brash, loud characteristics. Although Ann was the girl with stunning good looks behind the bar, because of Mullally's past and his contacts, I ignored her. I used to live on the edge with this particular copper and although I liked him, I was very wary of him – and he loved Ann. My friend Brian Madley of the *Sunday People*, was also very friendly with Ann, who was the centre of attention because of her looks and her immaculate dress sense. She was a real beauty, but to be perfectly honest I behaved myself in there, and simply enjoyed the company of my friends, Leslie May and Tony Davis. However, my first meeting with Ann was to become a turning point in my life, for several reasons.

"Here I was, the captain of Seattle Sounders, in a night club in London, introducing them to music popular on the west coast of America. One particular song – *Even The Nights Are Better* by Air Supply – really moved Ann. It was a song to fall in love to and, before heading back to Seattle, Ann's Aunt Mimi told me that Ann had fallen for me. It must have been the music! Though I was very flattered I still kept my distance, knowing Maureen was waiting for me at home and that Ann was also still married. Both Leslie and Tony remarked that Ann was flirting with me and, had we both not been attached, I would have invited her to go back to America with me. My feelings towards Ann were not of the 'one night stand' variety. I had really made a connection and was happy just to be in her company, nothing more."

After returning to Seattle. it wasn't long before Huddy and Maureen had the mother of all bust-ups. Rows between the pair were a common occurrence because both were as stubborn as each other, but this one was different and, as it turned out, terminal to their relationship. That it happened at the beginning of 1983 was just an odd coincidence, given that he would soon lose everything. The details of that particular argument will always remain private but it's safe to assume that words were exchanged on either side that could never be taken back. Enough was enough. The news – from the Sounders – that Huddy had feared followed a couple of months later, as did Maureen's decision to stay in Seattle despite knowing that going back to England was the only realistic option open to her soon-to-be ex-husband.

Alan had already written to Ann before leaving Seattle,

CHELSEA AND STOKE ... AGAIN

telling her that the next time he came back he would take her out, and he was as good as his word. As Maureen and the two boys continued to enjoy the north American lifestyle they'd grown accustomed to, Huddy had no alternative but to try and hold his depression in check, re-focus on his playing career and get back to business, London-style. In a matter of weeks the spark he'd found with Ann was re-ignited and he quickly made up for lost time, letting her know his true feelings from the off. He already knew just how much Ann thought of him thanks to the tip-off from Mimi, so it was no wonder playing for Chelsea's reserves didn't bother him too much.

"We had the strangest fling, like two teenagers, and it was quite clear we would become an item. I quickly moved in with Ann, who'd now left her husband and it was clear that my marriage was over too. It came as a great relief to us both. I only had eyes for Ann and was very happy. I was certain 'this was it' and that we'd stay together."

Alan and Ann enjoyed Christmas 1983. Whilst booze-filled, it was a continuous round of parties and fun, and Alan was back on top form, enjoying life to the fullest. He was happy and content and in the company of real friends. So what if the first-team boat had long since sailed for him at the Bridge.

As luck would have it, not long after the New Year, his fairy godfather, Tony Waddington, unexpectedly got in touch. Stoke were eight points adrift of safety in the old First Division and they needed a miracle. Would the darling of the Boothen End try and provide it? Damn right he would. Waddington masterminded Huddy's return to Stoke, although it was initially only a month on loan. Huddy was delighted and the formalities were quickly completed.

After being so close to the brink, Alan was back in business but the question on everyone's lips was, 'Could one of Stoke's most celebrated players bring the team back from the brink too?' Richie Barker had been sacked as manager, and his assistant Bill Asprey and Waddington had floated the idea of bringing Huddy 'home'. Having Waddington make the call was a master stroke because there was simply no chance whatsoever of the maestro getting turned down.

Waddington told the *Stoke Sentinel* at the time: "Make no mistake, he has a harder job here than Stan Matthews had when I brought him back. I was able to bring in players to play around Stan, but Stoke have no money." The *Sentinel* also noted Alan's words after his 'second debut' against Arsenal, a match that had his name all over it. "I had an early night on Friday, confident that everything would turn out right, but I had a couple of 'sleepers' to make sure I was fully rested. On Saturday morning the coffee cup shook in my hands as I contemplated what I was asking of myself. Deep down I am a born pessimist. I knew that if I didn't turn it on and Arsenal won, I would pack it in there and then."

He needn't have worried because his impact was immediate. Stoke won three of their next four games, having only won three in the entire season to that point. It was enough for Huddy to be offered a three-year deal, which gave him a new lease of life professionally, but would shatter his new and happy relationship with Ann who steadfastly refused to move from London. Tension grew between them but Alan knew he couldn't miss this particular boat. It was an opportunity too good to turn down. New teammate, Brendan O'Callaghan, a no-nonsense individual, recalled in 2016 the difference in the dressing room after Huddy had arrived.

"I had met Alan a couple of years before and, to be honest, I didn't think he was the type of player we needed to get us out of the mess we were in. Alan's reputation as a maverick was well known and we all had our reservations. In the previous season, 1982-83, we had played really well and had some very good players, especially in midfield. The manager was a guy called Richie Barker who, if truth be known, didn't have a clue. He went to Lilleshall for the summer of 1983 and came back convinced that the long ball game was the way forward.

"This didn't bode well with the players, and our midfield quartet of Mark Chamberlain, Robbie James, Sammy McIlroy and Micky Thomas were in mutiny over the new tactics, because they were made virtually redundant. Barker was eventually sacked before Christmas but the hangover of his regime led to players being disillusioned and downbeat. I think we had about six or seven full internationals but it was Alan's arrival and insistent demands for a better style of football that led to a resurgence of form. That was definitely down to him.

"Alan instilled a belief and hope into the players that had been missing since Alan Durban had left in 1981, and we won seven of the next ten games, hauling us out of the relegation zone at the same time. He also persuaded Bill Asprey to take us on tours to encourage team bonding and Bill, who was a seasoned traveller, needed no prompting! In the first six months of 1984 we went to Spain, Abu Dhabi, Qatar, Tampa Bay, Trinidad & Tobago, Zimbabwe and Zambia – perhaps a bit too much bonding! On these trips there were very few rules, regulations or curfews and our long trips on the plane were one long party. Everyone enjoyed themselves and all the lads were drinking, taking the mickey and laughing. It obviously worked as team spirit was very high and totally different from the puritanical Barker years.

"Our fortunes had changed and we picked up 33 points before the end of the season – more than the League and European champions, Liverpool, who we beat 2-0 at the Victoria Ground. It was a superb win prompted by a masterful performance by Huddy, who simply ran the game from start to finish. Graham Souness tried to kick him at every opportunity but never got within a yard of the maestro, whose link play with Maguire, McIlroy, Painter and Chamberlain was a joy to watch from my position in defence. When we went 2-0 up, I knew we had them beaten and a well deserved pay-back for their arrogant antics against us in previous years."

Though this late career bonus had been entirely unexpected, it did come at a cost, although Huddy didn't miss Ann as much as he expected. Perhaps that had something to do with the terrace adulation being more than enough love for him to handle at the time. It could've been because they'd only been together for a few months prior to his move, or maybe it was the knowledge that Maureen had finally returned to England. To Stoke in fact.

That meant that Allen and Anthony could see their father for the first time in a while, but there did appear to be an ulterior motive. Maureen had heard that the Southfields house was now up for sale and made it crystal clear that she wanted her share of the proceeds.

With Ann in London, Alan now fell for Laurel, an articulate and successful accountant from the Longton district of Stoke-on-Trent. He also reluctantly agreed to Maureen's financial demands. Soon after, Maureen invested her share of the house sale to open her own gym, and then moved in with Huddy's old teammate Ian Bridge.

For Stoke, relegation was a certainty on the day Huddy joined in January 1984, but securing their status via a last-day-of-the-season-win against Wolves, meant it was time to let his hair down again. Football could take a back seat. Against Laurel's advice, he invested in a nightclub with a business partner, a venture that was to later prove his undoing. 'Hudson's Nightclub' would be the place to go for a while. George Best came to the opening and Alan Hudson was big business in the locale again. The 18-hour days spent training, boozing and

CHELSEA AND STOKE ... AGAIN

partying until the early hours were commonplace, but that was not a situation which appealed to Laurel. Her advice had been to invest in a care home for the elderly which provided a stable and long-term income, but that was far too sensible an idea to be seriously considered by someone who enjoyed the nightclub life. However, sensible was exactly what Huddy needed to be at this point, because his continued love of the bright lights and all manner of shenanigans meant that business decisions weren't soundly made.

Returning for the 1984-85 pre-season, it was obvious that a little too much of the good life over the summer had taken its toll and, as Huddy fought to get fit again, frequent injuries were the result. With their talisman not around to save them for long periods, it was a shocking season and one in which the Potters were relegated. Asprey was sacked but chairman Frank Edwards was prepared to offer Huddy the top job because of his motivational skills. Arriving at Stoke-on-Trent train station during the 1985 close season, he called ahead to the club only to be greeted with the devastating news that Frank had died during the early hours that morning.

Given that the remaining directors were those whom Huddy had fallen out with, there was never a chance he'd get the position and so it proved. Mick Mills was handed the role along with coach Sammy Chung, who Alan couldn't stand. The time was therefore right to announce his retirement. There simply wasn't any coming back but it was the right time to go and from that perspective there were no regrets, even if Stoke would have many.

The club weren't even in a position to honour Huddy's contract but he would be gracious enough to suggest they could pay it to him fortnightly from the gate receipts, to help ease the club's problems as well as his own. Despite agreeing to the same – they could hardly do anything else – Stoke would renege on that agreement, meaning that with the modest income he was earning from his nightclub Huddy was now 'getting by' rather than being financially comfortable.

A lack of disposable income and with bills needing to be paid, Alan had little option but to move into the flat above the club. During this time Allen moved in with his father whilst training with, and hoping for a professional contract with, Coventry. Allen's plan didn't work out, and neither did Huddy's aspirations for the nightclub.

His tenure and hold on the business had been hanging by a thread for what seemed like an age, but somehow the wolf had been kept from the door. As a long-term concern, though, it was untenable. Whether he'd been ripped off by his business partner or not, there really was no one else to blame for his cavalier approach to the commercial side of the business. Huddy's problems deepened when Laurel also announced that their relationship was over.

With Laurel gone, and nothing of value to really sustain him on a day-to-day basis, the nomadic lifestyle that had typified Alan's playing career seemed to be the most attractive option at that point. Spending the next couple of years meandering through various cities in England and the United States, calling in favours from friends and trying to set up various tournaments and soccer schools, wasn't the greatest way to rebuild, but he managed to get by.

Gordon Taylor of the Professional Footballer's Association (the PFA) was just one of many to offer help at the time, despite Huddy's notoriously difficult personality. "Alan was a top quality, gifted player who suffered personal problems that we [PFA] did our best to help with," recalled Taylor. "I have had many spiky characters to deal with and try to treat all of my members with the same respect and courtesy. Our help is as confidential as the member wishes it to be, and I would like us to be the acknowledged first port of call for any member on any matter. We have [and had] a 24-hour confidential helpline for all PFA members offering counselling, therapy, medical treatment, operations, funding for education and legal assistance." The aftercare provided was kept highly confidential, in keeping with Alan's wishes, and it helped keep the demons away.

Having settled back in Stoke in 1987, Huddy resumed his close relationship with his parents with regular visits to their new home, a house on The Embankment, and enjoyed the chats he shared with his father. Bill was delighted when Alan's sister, Julie, announced she was expecting a baby girl and was looking forward to seeing his new granddaughter. Tragically however, Bill never got the chance to dote on the new member of the Hudson family. He'd been suffering from a serious heart complaint yet, thinking he was indestructible, stubbornly refused to take the medication he'd been prescribed and ignored his doctor's advice to 'take it easy' and avoid putting strain on his heart. The day that Georgia was born, Bill's heart gave out and, on what should have been the happiest day of any family's life, he passed away.

"I was on the exercise bike at the Richmond Club in Shelton, Stoke-on-Trent, sweating excessive alcohol out of my body, when one of the staff came through to tell me that the Chelsea and Westminster Hospital were on the phone at the reception. My heart skipped a beat as I walked through to hear a female voice on the other end say, 'Mr Hudson, we've lost your father,' to which I angrily replied, 'Well, you'd better bloody go and find him then, hadn't you.' When the young lady then said 'I don't think you understand,' the penny dropped and I understood, perfectly.

"The reason I remember that day so well, apart from the crushing blow of losing my father, is because I was all over the place, I felt physically sick and I didn't know what to do. I went round to my mate George Byatt – who had an office just across the road – to tell him and then headed straight for Stoke station. I got on the train in a terrible state and after about an hour it broke down. I had a seat in the First Class carriage and there was no way I was getting moved on that day. After what seemed like an age, we got going again and after jumping into a black cab at Euston we were horrendously delayed by road works. By the time I got to Mum's I was in a mess. We did nothing but hug each other and cry for what seemed like hours. Completely exhausted, I went into the spare bedroom and just lay there, with the lights off, totally numb.

"My friend, Danny Gillen, had heard I was back and popped around. He told me that Phil Collins was recording in Fulham and we should go and see him. Danny was just trying to help me take my mind off my father's death but couldn't have misjudged my mood more and I told him to leave.

"Danny was back the next day and, feeling a bit better after a good night's sleep I agreed to visit Phil in the studio nearby. I'm so glad I did because, despite still being totally numb, sitting there whilst Phil recorded *A Groovy Kind of Love* was a wonderful and soothing experience. The three of us then had a few drinks before I headed back to Bub's and the grim reality of Bill's totally unnecessary death.

"I have to say that I'm still annoyed at my father for dying because it could have been avoided. He never followed doctor's orders. Although I listen to nobody in authority, I was a brilliant patient whilst going through my ordeal. Strangely enough, being annoyed at Bill must have focussed my grief into a frustrated anger against him and helped me get over his death quicker than other members of the family. It helped me cope. I still love him dearly and miss him madly but I still swear at the photograph of him on the wall in my flat."

CHELSEA AND STOKE ... AGAIN

When the time was right, Huddy went back up to Stoke but his old friend, disaster, was never too far away. In 1990 for example, he and his friend, Terry Bate, were put under house arrest whilst in Bermuda. This had followed an abortive attempt to arrange a football tournament, this time with Rodney Marsh, to be played at Tampa Bay, Florida.

Nottingham Forest, Celtic, Manchester City and Sheffield Wednesday had all signed up, but without going through the proper channels it was always destined to fail. Marsh recalls that: "It was during the Tampa Bay Rowdies season and we held the exclusive rights to Tampa Stadium. Alan contacted the Tampa Sports Authority (TSA), without my knowledge, attempting to lease the stadium for four dates in the middle of our season. Per the Rowdies contract with the TSA, they informed me immediately and asked if I felt it was appropriate. I said 'No'. Alan subsequently flew out to Tampa to ask me if we could make a deal 'together,' to co-promote these games with a revenue sharing agreement.

"I told him it was impossible – a) It would confuse our season ticket holders, sponsors, advertisers and interfere with our exclusive TV, radio and media packages and b) there were not four open dates, and it would mean playing an international game on a Thursday or Friday with a Rowdies game on Saturday – clearly a nonsensical proposition. It was a non-starter but Alan didn't seem to grasp the concept, was angry at my rejection and has apparently been so ever since."

Huddy was livid indeed, and so Bermuda was the next port of call.

"Terry and I got a one-way ticket and took 'Plan B' to Bermuda where Clyde Best was living. He helped us put together one match which turned out to be the Bermuda XI v Aberdeen but it failed miserably. We had set it all up with the help of Goslings, the local brewery, but on the day of the match when we opened the bars, the police came along and said, 'You don't have a licence' – a key fact that Goslings didn't tell us that we, as the organisers, needed to sort out. I mean, you'd think the brewery would know the lie of the land in this regard wouldn't you? As a result, we were all over the papers as a company that were trying to rip everyone off."

It would take almost a month for Alan and Terry to prove their innocence and by now funds had disappeared via legal costs and refunds – including Aberdeen's costs – for 'the match that never was'. Returning to Blighty after his failed money-making ventures, Huddy began living out of a small guest house-cum-hotel in Uttoxeter – where the owner quickly became besotted with him. With no driving licence to get about and dependent on the dole for money, if Huddy wanted to go anywhere, he would have to ask the owner Pam to assist. That she did, and quite enthusiastically as it turned out. Alan recalls something which happened some time after he'd moved in which still sends shivers down his spine.

"I lived at the hotel for quite a while, probably about four and a half years, and I came down one morning to find a letter on the side addressed to a Mrs Pamela Hudson. When I confronted her she said, 'Well, when we are out you treat me like your wife.' I had to leave once that 'Fatal Attraction' moment had happened and so I gathered my gear and returned to London. Before moving back in with my mother – again – I called one of my favourite haunts, The Cartoonist, to talk to my old mate Tommy Nicholson. To my surprise Ann answered the phone and sounded bubbly and really pleased to hear from me. Despite not having seen or heard from me in years, she came to Euston to meet me off the train and looked gorgeous. I had a slightly unsettling feeling that we might get back together, however daft it seemed. To be perfectly honest, she was still irresistible and it wasn't long before Mum was clipping my wings at home again

CHELSEA AND STOKE ... AGAIN

so I had to leave. I needed to feel free and I ended up moving in with Ann across town."

Annie Besant Close, just off of the famous Roman Road market in London's East End, was to be Huddy's manor for the next couple of years. He continued to live a relatively nondescript lifestyle there if truth be told. Not in keeping with what he had been used to back in the day but it was the hand he'd been dealt. Claiming dole may have meant he continued to swallow his pride, but it also allowed him to eventually move forward. And at least he retained Ann's support so it wasn't all bad. In fact, despite him not being able to offer much more than companionship and a few laughs here and there, Ann still stood by him resolutely. She was his rock and though she could've had practically any man she wanted, she didn't look twice at anyone else once Huddy was back on the scene. That said plenty. Such an unbreakable bond often kept spirits high, despite extended low periods from the man of the house.

What can't be ignored either is the sense of community that existed in this part of the world and which had a galvanizing effect on Huddy's mental health. Although prefabs were long gone from London by now, the camaraderie and attitude in the area spoke of that era. Living there really appealed because it was full of genuine folk that he could relate to. They were his type of people.

Although different ethnic minorities were also moving in, all had the same core values at heart and, in the main, relations were cordial at the very least. There was never a problem with making friends because Huddy was able to put roots down wherever and whenever with little problem. That was largely to do with his existence as a professional footballer, which was a double-edged sword of course. No sooner would he feel at home than a move elsewhere could be on the cards.

London *was* home, though, and there was no better feeling

for Alan than knowing he was close to most of his family again. By now Allen was in his 20s and had other things going on in his own life, which meant visits to the old man were sporadic. Anthony was still a teenager and under Maureen's influence so he rarely paid a visit either. The continued absence of both boys and the lack of any significant length of time spent with them largely authored Alan's mood swings. Ann was regularly caught in that crossfire but if it bothered her, she made no mention of it. In hindsight and though it's hard for him to admit, Maureen probably made the best decision at that time, for everyone. On his 'up' days he was very, very good company, engaging, warm and witty. You couldn't wish for better. Maureen, however, couldn't be sure that Huddy wouldn't go completely off of the rails when on a downer, so it was wise, if harsh, when Maureen decided to keep Anthony away from Alan completely.

With the paltry dole handout continuing to be paid on a fortnightly basis, and most spent on booze and betting, it's debatable that Huddy would've been able to do anything worthwhile with his boys in any event, so there really was little point in making a volatile situation ten times worse.

Lack of funds would, eventually, lead to blazing rows with Ann who, despite her loyalty, wanted to be taken care of every now and then. It wasn't too much to ask from a dutiful partner who never had any questions for her man when he went missing for a day or two, now and then.

For all of his charm and effervescence, and the innate ability to be the life and soul, there was no controlling Huddy at times: it was his life on his terms and to hell with everyone else, if that happened to be the mood he was in. As the months went by, with little or no change to the daily grind, the routine of drinking and rowing became more frequent but, no matter what, he was still up at 7am and training every day, just

CHELSEA AND STOKE ... AGAIN

around the corner at the health club whilst Ann was still fast asleep.

It would take a while for things to get anywhere close to the even keel that Ann desired, but her perseverance did pay off. Call it an eureka moment perhaps, but Alan had just about had enough of being a nobody. The road to, even occasional, sobriety wasn't the easiest of paths to follow but to his credit, he managed it regularly enough to start picking up punditry work with *The Sporting Life*.

"I got the paper every day because I not only loved my racing but also the football fixed odds. About two weeks before the Everton and Manchester United FA Cup final [May 20, 1995], I wrote to the editor, Tom Clarke, not realising that I knew him from when I was regularly in the Fleet Street papers. I wrote to him, saying that I could do better than his columnists and with my football experiences and stories, I think it would make good reading. Out of the blue I received a telephone call from him inviting me to his office, which was only 30 minutes from our home, and I was delighted by his warm welcome a couple of days later.

"After 20 minutes of him grilling me about my views, capabilities and aptitude he said, 'Go home and write about the FA Cup final. Tell me what you think the outcome will be, and why, and who are the likely goal scorers. Then send it back to me and we'll take it from there.' I put it all together, suggesting that 'With my old mate Joe Royle now in charge at Everton, I think they'll beat red hot favourites Manchester United 1-0.' I might have even mentioned the goal scorer. I sent it to him and he replied with thanks and told me that it would be his piece for the Saturday morning. I was extremely excited by this, telling Ann to make some food and I'll get the drinks in.

"We invited some friends round for the match and to celebrate my new job – before a ball was even kicked. Luckily, it couldn't have gone any sweeter as Everton won 1-0 thanks to Paul Rideout's goal, and I was in a great new job. The following Monday, Tom called me into his office, took me to lunch and congratulated me on the job, which would be writing each Friday, giving selections and other tips. He really was a lovely, lovely man. Old school, like Waddington. He knew my past, but he still thought that I would be a good addition to his paper."

Although the new job gave him some welcome 'pocket money', it wasn't anywhere close to being enough and Alan's awful mood swings continued to test Ann's resolve. He managed to scrimp together a few quid for them to go on holiday in early 1996, feeling that the break would do them good and calm the waters in an increasingly rocky relationship. The night before they were due to go however, another blazing row saw Huddy walk out and Ann taking a friend in his place.

"Whilst she was away I tried to work out where it was all going wrong and why Ann wasn't happy. I was getting my life back together and slowly we were working it out. I wanted us to eventually buy her house together but I'm sure her family were thinking that I was trying to rip her off. The day she got back from holiday, I met her at Liverpool Street and took her to a wine bar opposite the station.

"I ordered a bottle of champagne – it was only 11.30am – held her hand, looked her in the eye and said, 'Look Ann, something's wrong here, all I want to do is make you happy, let's get married.' I thought that would get rid of her insecurity, because I never looked at another woman, and although she smiled as if to say yes, she came out with something quite bizarre. 'I'd love to marry you, but I don't think I can go through another divorce.' Talk about negative! I repeated myself. 'All I want to do is make you happy, I truly love you and missed you so much this week. Let's try and make this work.'

"The one huge problem was money. It was always money.

CHELSEA AND STOKE ... AGAIN

How could we get married and have a big Roberts family wedding with no expense spared? I couldn't compete with that. In my incredible wisdom, I quickly devised a plan whilst drinking our champagne. 'Let's go abroad and get married – just you and me. Then, in a year or two when we've saved a few quid, we'll renew our vows and have a big family get together.'

"It seemed to work and we headed off to Aunt Mimi's club in Chambers Street. We ordered more champagne and I sat with her twin aunts promising them that I'd make Ann happy and look after her, which I fully intended to do. The wedding was planned for the early summer of 1997, and having already been to Bermuda, as romantic a place as one could wish for to get married, that's where we decided to tie the knot. I knew people there who would organise a small yacht so we could get married on the water."

Finally, things were looking up again.

10

The Accident

"We were faced with a very difficult decision which would be to either leave him alone to take his chances, or an operation that would very likely be fatal."
Dr David Goodier

A confident, articulate and entertaining speaker, Huddy had been in demand on the corporate and after-dinner speaking circuit and did some work for Terry Shepherd at Wembley for Euro '96. It was a financial godsend, and involved talking to around 1,000 people in a corporate tent – before, during and after each game – for £500 a match. He'd give it all to Ann to save for the wedding, and she'd also get the money earned when he worked at Peter Osgood's soccer school on the mornings of those games too. Things appeared to be going in the right direction in general terms, yet Huddy still couldn't escape the feeling that something continued to be missing from their relationship. There was something 'not quite right' between them. The money was as good as it had ever been during the relationship so that couldn't be the problem and although their love life wasn't as lively as when they'd first met, there were no complaints from the man of the house.

THE ACCIDENT

Huddy was wary of asking Ann what really was wrong for fear of getting told something he didn't want to hear. After all, he was an old romantic at heart and couldn't contemplate losing someone who was, at that moment, the love of his life – especially when knee-deep in wedding arrangements. Maybe it was down to an incident from some months before. Ann had seemed unconcerned, which was odd given that it might have tested anyone else's union to the limit. It didn't stop them staying together, though, or getting married.

Ironically, it involved Pam, the hotel landlady from Uttoxeter. Her friend Peter Dare – who was known to Huddy – had come down to The Cartoonist specifically to see him about a 'business proposition'. Although no actual business was concluded during the first meeting, Dare would call back to arrange another at the Tower Hotel on Tower Bridge. On that particular day, Ann was coming along for the ride, but at the last minute decided to go to her aunt's club just across the River Thames rather than playing gooseberry at the meeting. It was, in hindsight, the best decision she could've made.

"It was a Thursday afternoon," recalls Alan, "when I met Peter and we had our first drink in the hotel bar before he said, 'Let's go to my room and sort this deal out.' I should've sussed what might be happening then and there, but I went along with it because [at that time] I was in need of the money. The deal appeared to be a simple one. I was to get three other former players and put on an 'Evening with The Mavericks' in Manchester. Peter said, 'You'll go on stage and chat for a couple of hours for £1,000 each plus expenses. After you come off stage the girls go on.'

"I wasn't bothered about the ladies and made it clear that once we had finished our stint, we'd get our money and go, something Peter agreed to. We continued with small talk and after he ordered some champagne to celebrate, he got straight on the phone to talk to this bloke in Manchester and confirm that the deal had been done, but I'm certain there was nobody on the other end. After saying, 'Okay, I think he'll do it,' Peter put the phone down, turned to me and told me that this other person was delighted but wanted to have a photograph done with a couple of the girls 'for the publicity posters'."

"About 20 minutes later there was a knock on the door and two black girls came in. They were girls I had seen before with Peter in Derby where he lived, and I think they were hookers. I didn't care because I was getting my money and only doing a bloody photo. They sat on the king size bed and started fondling – and I mean fondling – to make it look real. At that stage for all I knew, it *was* real, even though it was a little weird. I poured myself some more fizz, happy in the knowledge that I'd get decent money for a night out with my mates including Frank Worthington and Peter Osgood.

"Champagne in hand, shirt half undone with a girl on each knee, I gave the broadest grin. I must've looked like the cat who got the cream as the camera flashed. As soon as the shot was taken, the girls got up like lightning and walked across the room to sit with Peter. Within a few minutes and after another call had been made, there was a second knock on the door. I looked to see who else was coming in but only a hand reached out and Peter passed the camera over before the door instantly closed.

"I'd had a few glasses of bubbly by now, but I knew that something fishy had happened. I left shortly after and met Ann in her aunt's club. She asked what had happened and I told her that I had done the deal – but I neglected to mention the photograph for obvious reasons. On the Friday morning, I was in the car with my mate Tony going up the motorway to Coventry for an overnight function, and can still hear his voice after about 60 miles: 'Hud, are you okay, I've never known you

THE ACCIDENT

so quiet?' I recounted the story from the day before and told him that I thought I'd been stitched up.

"I got back to London on Saturday and was in my local with Ann and a friend, an Arsenal supporter who owned the furniture shop opposite. I was still uneasy when the phone rang and the barmaid shouted out my name so I went behind the bar to take the call. The caller was the editor of *The News of the World*. 'It's our policy to tell you that you will be front page on Sunday.' It took a moment or two for the message to sink in, and I slammed the phone down.

"Making an excuse that I needed to use the phone in the furniture shop as it was quieter and I could hear the caller easier, I popped over the road. When I called back I went berserk having a screaming match with the editor, but I knew I had been well and truly set-up. Going back into the local to explain everything to my wife was the toughest thing I had ever had to do but there was no sugar coating this one. 'I'm on the front page tomorrow with two black girls,' was pretty much all I could muster because, the truth be told, I was bricking it.

"To my absolute astonishment, Ann took it incredibly well, not going nuts like I thought she might have done. I explained what had happened in the hotel room, and it appeared that she believed me. I walked into the local newsagent on Sunday and bought every copy of the paper – before the string had even been taken off of them. Once home, Ann was sitting up in bed having a cuppa and I threw the pile of papers on the bed. 'You might as well have the lot,' I said before walking out. The next step was having to tell Bub about it.

"Mum was devastated but when she said that she couldn't go to the bingo anymore because of it, it cracked me up. The paper called me a pimp and a drug dealer, and it made for pretty grisly reading let me tell you. Apparently I was involved in a hostess ring and the like according to the paper, and for anyone close to me to be reading that, the natural reaction would've been for them to stick one on me. I couldn't have blamed them either.

"What didn't really add up was that Ann and her family never really mentioned it again or asked for other details. If it were me, I would've at least confronted the issue and asked for an explanation. But no, nothing. Not even an argument about it. However, from then on, Ann's family just blanked me. Perhaps they thought that I was belittling her, and rather than get involved in conversation they'd just stay in the background. That might appeal to some but not me. I found it hard to not have any sort of relationship with them, it remained very disconcerting for me."

Fortunately, the episode hadn't hindered Alan's work with *The Sporting Life*. Tom Clarke continued to employ him on the same deal, and never even mentioned the entire episode. He was at least one friend who could still be counted on. With the money from the column and various corporate functions that Huddy was now being invited to, the pennies kept the couple ticking over. Only close friends knew how rocky the relationship was at times because, to the outside world, they still seemed very much a couple.

Months passed without any hint of further scandal, and social life was back to almost becoming the whirlwind it had been years before. Yet the day-to-day monotony of the relationship behind closed doors kept eating away at Huddy. He needed some excitement again. The spark had gone from their relationship and he couldn't abide being bored. It could be described as just the normality of the situation – something that every couple experience at various stages in their relationship – which was at the core of his brooding. Nevertheless, and despite their troubles, the marriage went ahead.

THE ACCIDENT

"It only turned out to be a disaster didn't it. I mean, how can you go to this beautiful island and endure not one, but two nightmares! House arrest first time and Ann in a trance all through the ceremony on my second visit. I ended up spending the night on the balcony drinking pink champagne all alone, whilst she was at our wedding reception downstairs. The following morning Ann, Aunt Mimi – who'd flown in just for the wedding – and I watched the ceremony on DVD. Ann barely looked at me through the whole thing, something Mimi later picked up on. It was one of the worst social experiences of my life, because what I thought was going to be a fantastic event went like a damp squib. I'm 66 now and if I've a 'last request,' it'd be to go back there and hope it's third time lucky!"

Both continued to put a brave face on things, and were actually looking forward to the Christmas of 1997, when something happened to completely shatter his world, and that of his entire family.

Monday, December 15, began as normally as any other day. Huddy was up with the lark and after putting on his training gear, took a 10-minute walk to the gymnasium off Roman Road. Two hours cycling on the bike followed by 2,000 sit ups and a steam bath were the order of the morning before dealing with a day full of functions, both in a corporate and personal capacity. His best blue suit had been dusted down and his gold tie, black crocodile shoes and light brown Crombie complemented the look.

After showering, Huddy popped home to put his training kit in the wash and kiss Ann goodbye. He'd then make his way over to a hotel in Kensington for the Sports Writers' Association's annual awards luncheon, as a guest of his *Sporting Life* employer, Tom Clarke. Whilst travelling there on the District Line, Huddy would bump into old pal Dean Powell, who'd worked with Frank (Kellie) Maloney and Frank Warren.

HUDDY

The pair shared a drink and a brief chat at the hotel bar before the bell sounded, calling the guests to take their seats, where Alan found himself sat next to jump jockey (now trainer) Jamie Osborne. Despite the difference in their backgrounds, both personal and sporting, he was fabulous company and as always when one happens to be enjoying themselves, the time disappeared.

Alan could have chatted all night but unfortunately there was somewhere else he had to be that day, and so just after 4pm he made his way over to the Connaught Rooms in Covent Garden to meet Mel Tame and celebrate his friend's 60th birthday. Mel worked for Sun Chemicals, a company that Huddy had done occasional work for in West Ham's hospitality boxes at Upton Park. They'd lunch regularly and it was a pleasure to be able to spend part of Mel's big day with him. As was usual at such parties, most wanted to reminisce with Alan about the old days, and he was only too happy to oblige, regaling the party-goers with tales and anecdotes from yesteryear. At 7pm, as the celebrations drew to a close and guests began to head home, Alan put on his Crombie and was preparing to leave when he was recognised by an Arsenal supporter by the name of Henry Tumbridge.

"The party was upstairs but as we got to the bottom stair a voice called out to Henry. I followed him into the bar area where a few of his friends were. They all loved their football, and we chatted for a few minutes. As we did so, the manager of the venue approached me and we spoke about the upcoming World Cup in France. I told him that I'd be working there for David Brown in a corporate capacity, mingling with the paying customers. I had been over to watch the draw for the competition and was with David in the Stade de France when I saw Pelé and also spoke to my old mate Bogićević from the New York Cosmos."

THE ACCIDENT

Alan and Henry left and made their way towards Holborn station. Jamie's Bar was lit up and as it was a bar that Huddy knew well, he offered to buy Henry a quick drink to wish him a Merry Christmas and a Happy New Year. Talk turned to home life and Henry was clearly never happier than at that moment. Quite the opposite to his drinking partner who, by his own admission, was "going down a cul-de-sac with Ann," having tried everything to understand her and what issues were getting between them. Nevertheless, the time which the pair had spent together – no more than an hour and a half in total – was a good way to end the day and Huddy hopped on the Central Line to Mile End, a journey of some 15 to 20 minutes.

Alighting at the station, his normal routine would be to walk across the platform and take the District Line to Bow Road, one stop further along. On this particularly beautiful December night, however, Huddy decided to take a walk to reflect on the day's events, and wonder what reception he might get when he walked through the door. Whenever taking this specific route home, he would call Ann to ask if she wanted anything from the local supermarket and on this occasion she didn't. He'd always cross the road at *exactly* the same point each time, without exception, and as he did so that night his life changed forever.

A car being driven at high speed slammed into his back as he stepped onto the pavement after crossing the road, sending him 15 feet into the night sky. Knocked unconscious on impact, his limp body came to rest at the foot of the tree which Huddy had hit in mid-air. The driver hadn't hung around to see the carnage, and there were apparently no witnesses to the accident. Not one. Well, none willing to come forward that is. To put Huddy's injuries into perspective and what happened in the days and weeks following the accident, the report of his Consultant Orthopaedic Surgeon, Dr David Goodier FRCS (Orth), makes grim reading:

'Alan Hudson was brought to The Royal London Hospital by ambulance on 15th December 1997 arriving at 9.25pm. The London Ambulance Service had brought him in, he was a pedestrian that had been bit by a car in a 'hit and run' type road traffic accident. The Royal London Hospital has a 'trauma team' who rushed down to A&E. He had an obvious head injury and was confused and thrashing about, so it was required to immediately anaesthetise him and put a tube down to take over his breathing. He was severely unwell with massive blood loss and with a lot of local bruising visible around the pelvis and groin.

'The CT scan of the head showed that he had a large brain bleed (extradural haematoma) which was underneath a fracture of the skull where the bones had been pushed inwards. He also had various injuries to the bones of his face including the left eye socket, cheek bones and nose bones. He had broken the sternum and had multiple rib fractures affecting both sides. His left kidney was ruptured and there were severe fractures of the pelvis with complete separation of the right half of the pelvis, confirmed on x-rays and CT scans. The bladder and urethra were both lacerated and damaged.

'He was taken by the on-call emergency team to theatre, where attempts were made to reduce the blood loss. Since most of the blood was being lost by the laceration of blood vessels around his pelvis, these attempts included applying an external fixator to the front of the pelvis. This involves driving pins into the prominent bone of the pelvis (iliac wing) and attaching bars running from one side of the pelvis to the other. Unfortunately, due to the severity of the injury at the back of the pelvis, he continued to bleed. He had immediate neurosurgery whereby the blood clots were removed from the

THE ACCIDENT

brain, but overnight he ended up with more than 30 units of blood being transfused. Attempts were made to try and see if the bleeding could be stopped by angiography but the team were running out of options and Alan was dying.

'I myself was not on duty that night. I arrived at 8am for the morning trauma meeting where his case was discussed. The problem with the type of fracture that he had was that it was very rare, and involved both the front and the back of the pelvis. The classic external fixators that were used to try and control the bleeding only really worked at the front, and a special type of external fixation clamp was necessary to use around the back. These were quite rare, but by bizarre coincidence a company rep had been showing me one only a few days before and left it in my office. This was however just a trial instrument with 'sample only, not for medical use' written on it! I had been trying to persuade our managers to buy one, but they were not convinced by the fact that I would probably end up using this three times a year, and the mortality rate even with it is two out of three.

'I went up to the operating theatre. The anaesthetists were desperately trying to pour more blood into him, but as he had not only lost blood but also all the clotting factors that go with it, he was continuing to bleed and was close to death. The demonstration model of the clamp was fully functioning so I asked the theatre sisters to sterilise the pins, and applied it to his pelvis. Fortunately, this was successful and I was able to compress together the back of the pelvis which allowed a blood clot to form and his bleeding rapidly slowed down. By midday he was well enough to be transferred to the intensive care unit from theatre. Because of the blood he had lost, the legs swelled up and he developed bilateral deep venous thrombosis. The pressures in the compartments of the leg rose dramatically jeopardising his circulation further, and he had to go back to theatre urgently for decompression of both legs by a procedure known as 'fasciotomy'.

'This is where the entire length of the upper thigh, inner calf and outer calf are slit open allowing the muscles to swell. We were still not sure what the prognosis was from his head injury, but permanent brain damage was likely. Given that he had had a massive transfusion of over 32 units of blood by this point, there was also the likelihood of developing a condition of adult respiratory distress syndrome i.e. the lungs stopping working, particularly as he had had significant chest trauma. He had also had kidney damage and might need dialysis, so everybody involved in his care felt at this point it was highly likely he would die.

'The only positive side was that the neurosurgeons had inserted a pressure monitoring bolt into his brain to keep an eye on the brain pressure and this remained satisfactory. He went to theatre for the fasciotomies, but the lungs got worse, presumably due to blood clot flying off from the legs to the lungs. Dr Otto Chan had to position a filter into the main blood vessels in the back of the abdomen (inferior vena cava), which again was politically difficult as the management felt the particular type of filter he needed was too expensive to keep in stock. Nevertheless, Dr Chan proceeded and this did seem to stop the blood clots flying off to his lung.

'All the way through Christmas there were problems with sepsis of the chest. It was so overwhelming and it had affected his heart and lungs so severely that he was on copious doses of drugs to maintain his blood pressure ('inotropes'). He was so ill that on 27th December the blood clot perforated through his rectum and infection was spreading from his rectum into the massive amount of clotted blood behind his abdomen. We were faced with a very difficult decision which would be to either leave him alone to take his chances, or an operation that

THE ACCIDENT

would very likely be fatal – to perform a colostomy to divert the faecal contents away from the blood clot.

'The general surgeons eventually agreed to doing the colostomy. He had further operative procedures to drain haematoma and to deal with the fasciotomies and he remained on ITU [Intensive Therapy Unit], but due to the length of time he had been unconscious a formal tracheostomy had to be performed. This was done on 7th January in ITU as he was too sick to be transferred back to the theatre. Alan continued on the supporting drugs with dialysis for the kidney, catheters for the bladder and massive doses of antibiotics. Infections continued to be a problem, and he went for multiple operations to deal with recurrent focuses of sepsis.

'By the middle of January 1998, the pelvis had stabilised sufficiently to allow removal of the external fixator frame, and the blood clot filter was removed from the vena cava. There were multiple surgical visits, mainly for clearing out septic and dead tissue from the pelvis, scrotum, thigh wounds, calf wounds etc., and by 4th February 1998 he had recovered enough to start waking him up. On 12th February 1998 after 59 days on the intensive care unit he was transferred out to a regular ward. He still needed regular input from the speech therapist, dietician, renal team, orthopaedic surgeons and neurologists, but from my point of view the pelvis had healed sufficiently that he would not require any further surgery here.

'Investigations showed that the fractures had caused significant damage to the plexes of nerves that supply the legs and pelvis. We felt that this would cause problems with him walking and that he might never have walked properly. He was transferred to the special urology unit at St Bartholomew's Hospital on 3rd April 1998 where his rehabilitation continued. Due to the severity of the other injuries, the actual pelvic fracture which was the major threat to life was dealt with while he was predominantly unconscious so I never actually spoke to Alan during the entirety of his treatment! It was actually not until November 1998 that he came back for a follow-up appointment.

'He had, as expected, got some weakness due to the loss of nerve function in the right foot but did manage to walk into clinic. He had numbness affecting the calf and the big toe, the left side also had some nerve damage but was recovering. Due to the slashing open of the wounds on his thigh and calves to relieve pressure, he had extensive numb patches and required extensive further surgery to his urethra and bladder. My role therefore was confined to wandering in the morning after Alan had been injured and finding him still bleeding to death but by luck had a piece of kit in my office that was able to stop the bleeding. Unfortunately, it was not licensed for patient use, and I had extensive conversations with the hospital solicitors about using this piece of kit, but it did stop further bleeding.

'He had horrendous complications from the injury and the aftermath but overall his recovery was excellent. In terms of specifics relating to my relationship with Alan therefore, my treatment was all done and dusted while he was unconscious and he in fact knew nothing about the illegal use of the external fixation clamp until sometime later. He has always been an exemplary patient since then, even at our most recent meeting when he came to see me having had problems with an ankle fusion that had failed.

'The only other thing to say is that the pattern of injuries were compatible with being hit by a car, I have absolutely no idea whether this would be accidental or deliberate but it is the pattern of injury we see commonly in pedestrians struck by motor vehicles. Alan may have of course been inebriated, but I have no idea whether this was indeed a causative factor or not, this is merely guesswork. Blood samples for alcohol levels

THE ACCIDENT

were not taken at the time, and there were no witnesses of the evening.'

Harking bark to the immediate aftermath, the entire family were devastated. Son Allen told *The Independent* at the time: "I had a phone call at one in the morning and have been at the hospital since. At five or six o'clock we were told it didn't look like he was going to pull through. Me and my family sat in the chapel praying and he's turned it around somehow." Ann was also bereft, despite their issues. "According to the police, Alan had apparently stepped off the pavement and was hit by a car. I can't believe it. We were only just getting ready for Christmas together – and now this."

First wife Maureen was warned that her ex-husband might not pull through, and that she would have to face up to telling their sons that they wouldn't see their dad again. Fortunately, it was a message that she never had to relay to them. "It's awful," she told *The Independent* a couple of days after Huddy was admitted. "When I first rang the surgeon, he said it was touch and go, but now he has a 50-50 chance of pulling through. Alan's a fighter." Glenn Hoddle, England coach at the time was one of many from the football fraternity to voice their devastation at this turn of events.

Alan's close friend, Martin Knight, also recalls the aftermath with great clarity. "Jenny, one of the girls in my office at work, approached my desk and without saying anything placed the lunchtime *Evening Standard* in my line of vision. 'He's your friend isn't he?' she said gently as my eyes fell onto the news item that said Alan Hudson, the former Chelsea, Stoke City, Arsenal and England footballer had been knocked down by a car the previous night, and was fighting for his life in a London hospital. Doctors were quoted as saying that he had a 50-50 chance of survival.

"Alan had been at my firm's Christmas party only a few nights before and had been on sparkling form. I read the article over and over again looking blankly at the '70s image of Alan the paper had dragged out of the cuttings library to accompany the article. The phone rang and it was Anthony, my longstanding friend and Alan's cousin. I struggled to think what to say if he was ringing me to tell me that Alan had died. 'He's still alive Martin, just about. It's not looking good though, they're pouring blood into him and it's just pouring straight back out again.' Anthony didn't say much more, or if he did I cannot remember. I knew the next few hours were going to be critical, so I jumped into a cab and headed for the Royal London Hospital.

"There were four or five armchairs in the ward waiting room, donated many years ago by the looks of them. Foam oozed out one of the arms like pus from boils. George, Alan's uncle, sat forward with his eyes staring at the floor, as Bub, Alan's mother, sat back in another chair dabbing her eyes with a tissue. Ann's bag was on one chair – she was with Alan and the doctors. Anthony paced up and down this tiny room. They all looked frightened. That look of fear when things had got out of control and you couldn't influence events. In the corner of the small room was a payphone and the wall surrounding it was a mosaic of biro-drawn doodles and useful phone numbers – minicabs, prostitutes and the Samaritans.

"Anthony was on phone duty taking calls from family members and friends and the main hospital switchboard had been parrying calls from the media all day. The room had an air. It was an air of imminent bereavement. I showed my face, spoke for a few minutes to Anthony and quietly left. This was a time for only Alan's very closest family and friends. When I went to bed that evening I checked the teletext and Alan was still hanging on. I fully expected that the next morning when I awoke I would be reading about the death of my childhood hero and recent friend.

THE ACCIDENT

"But he clung on over the next couple of days and, bolstered by the fact he hadn't died, I rang the waiting room payphone. Anthony answered, his voice sounding much stronger. 'Come over,' he said. 'Something's happening.' The temporary home of the Hudson family was slightly happier when I turned out of the lift and walked to the waiting room. George stood up and shook my hand as I walked in and even Al's mum and Ann raised a smile. I thought there must have been a breakthrough. 'How is he?' I asked. 'Still the same, replied Ann quietly. 'The doctors have said that his heart can pack up at any moment but the blood loss is under control. It's too early to say whether he has brain damage.'

"The prognosis sounded pretty dire to me. 'Something's happened at Julie's home,' Anthony began to explain. A cross had appeared on the wall. 'When Alan nearly died the other night it shone brightly in the room and has now faded back a bit. As long as the cross is there, we think Alan's going to be alright.' They all nodded as Anthony recounted the details. The family were in deep emotional trauma and had not slept properly for days. I tried not to raise an eyebrow at this because if this was helping them get through, then that was fine with me.

"Anthony must have seen my automatic scepticism. 'It's true Mart. Most of the family have been around to see it,' George nodded. I couldn't imagine someone less likely to succumb to any spiritual or religious suggestion. He likes his horses, his music and his pint. He's a sharp bloke with a good sense of humour, not given to fantasy or exaggeration. The same goes for the rest of the family. A more down to earth bunch you could not meet. 'Does Alan wear a cross?' I asked. Apparently he didn't. 'Best go out and get him one then,' I said."

At this time, the family were also introduced to the renowned psychic and medium, Betty Shine. A popular author in her own right and a respected healer, she was mired in controversy in the early 1990s after she had been visited a few times by former Coventry City goalkeeper David Icke. It's alleged that she was the one who told Icke he was the Son of the Godhead – amongst other things – during their meetings, and this would form the basis of Icke's 'new age' beliefs that he was so keen to espouse to the world on the *Terry Wogan Show* in 1991. It was an interview that would prove devastating to Icke's credibility and, to an extent, Shine's. However, by the time of Huddy's accident, any negativity that had existed toward her had all but disappeared.

It's important to note firstly that Betty Shine had no idea who Huddy was. Not a clue. Yet, as she recounted in her book *The Infinite Mind*, she was drawn to a small photograph of a man in the *Daily Mail* one morning in January 1998, and only the small words underneath told her it was a photo of 'Alan Hudson, ex-footballer'. Odd as it may seem to those who are still hugely cynical toward psychics, their beliefs and practices, Shine felt his presence as she read about the details of his accident. 'A very strong male voice said to me, "Please help me." Then he said, "I want you to contact my wife and tell her not to give up on me, that I'm still here." He then went on to give me more details of his private life.'

Shine turned to Kevin Keegan for some guidance because of her lack of understanding of the football world. She had been friends with the Keegan family for some time, particularly with wife Jean, and an offer of help was duly given. David Connolly, one of Huddy's friends, was then contacted and was left dumbstruck by what Shine would tell him. She recalled in *The Infinite Mind* that 'I was able to have a conversation with David Connolly [...], he told me that he had always been a sceptic where psychic matters were concerned, but that he was conscious that something very extraordinary was taking place,

THE ACCIDENT

especially once I was able to pass on to him private information that Alan had given me about his family. David and I talked for some time, and I was able to help him with some problems of his own, which made it easier for him to pass on Alan's messages to his wife, Ann.

'I was naturally concerned about whether the messages I had received from Alan would be welcome to Ann, as one never really knows how such communications will be received by the family. After all, they didn't know me, and although they could check me out through my books, they might want to dismiss the whole thing as fantasy. Who could blame them? The evidence Ann was going to receive from David was very specific. All that mattered was that she could accept it was correct. The following day I received a call from David who told me that although Ann had been shocked, to say the least, she had confirmed everything that Alan had said about his family. She asked David to tell me that she would be contacting me.'

Shine would then pass on daily messages to Ann via David and due to their unerring accuracy, Ann and the wider family couldn't be anything other than convinced that they were indeed hearing from Huddy, despite their rational selves questioning the absurdity of the situation. Ann also wrote in Betty's book; 'He [Alan] had asked her to contact me with the message that he was going to recover despite his terrible injuries. In fact, he was giving us his own diagnosis. This seemed incredible as his injuries were so bad that the medical team looking after him had said that he was unlikely to pull through, and he was in a coma. Although I had always been very sceptical about such matters, I listened to everything that David had to say, as Betty appeared to be extremely accurate, even when detailing the very delicate issues of his injuries. [...] Alan's condition was touch and go but Betty was always there, giving me an exact diagnosis and the outcome, which was always positive. Each time she was proved right. I began to get a great deal of comfort from her calls throughout the ordeal of the ICU [Intensive Care Unit]. [...] Betty Shine is a very special lady who has helped me immensely.'

The cross-on-the-wall episode also found its way into Betty's book and by way of explanation she recounted that; 'When his [Huddy's] sister Julie was told about the accident she became desperately upset, screaming for her father. As she did so, a gold cross appeared on the wall behind her. It stayed for two days and was seen by five other people. I believe that when she screamed for her dead father, who was helping Alan, he activated this symbol to give his daughter peace of mind. Julie told Ann that the cross had no shadow – this is quite normal with such phenomena. Spirits do not have shadows either, they *are* the shadows! Some time later, Julie redecorated the room, but the incredible energy impact needed to form the cross in the first place had left an indelible mark. The cross remains on the wall.'

The agonising wait to see if Huddy would pull through took an inevitable toll on everyone. All of their lives would need to be put on hold and all of their energies focused on the same thing. How would they all cope if he didn't make it? Fortunately, that was a question that never needed asking. In early February 1998, and after the great skill, care and attention of the doctors, nurses and medical teams had paid off, Huddy was well enough to be woken from his coma. It was a slow, careful process and one which had the entire staff and family in floods of tears.

On February 12, after 59 days, he was transferred to another ward. Huddy was skin and bone, weighing no more than six and a half stone. Weak beyond belief, he would still manage a smile a couple of days later, showing everyone that the old boy was still alive and kicking inside the shell that he'd become.

11

A Third Life

"It was an incredibly tough time but because of my experiences throughout my career, it stood me in good stead whereas others might have caved in."

One might have expected Ann to be all over her husband, fussing and attending to his every need, especially given that – for a while – he was paralysed from the waist down. Although that's true in part, Huddy remembers that almost the complete opposite was the case at times. The distance between them at home before the accident was now beginning to manifest itself in the hospital. Huddy was battered, bruised and broken, but his other half often wouldn't even sit close enough to hold hands on occasions. None of her family had paid him a visit either, something that his own family had noticed and thought somewhat strange.

As he began recollecting certain things about the accident, as well as having others fill in some of the gaps in his memory, Huddy wanted to know if the driver of the car had been apprehended – the driver was never identified – but the line of questioning appeared to unnerve Ann. With more operations necessary before he could even think about leaving the hospital, and the frostiness between them ever more palpable, there was a sense in Alan's mind that she was going to leave him. She wasn't going to spend her life pushing around an invalid in a wheelchair. It was something he mentioned at the time to his Uncle George but it was brushed off as the effect of the drugs he was on.

Huddy was moved to Bart's and by the late summer of 1998, the police had announced to the press that they believed the circumstances surrounding the 'hit' were an accident. That Alan had apparently walked out in front of a car whilst on his mobile phone and was, to add insult to injury, drunk – which would be a natural conclusion to draw because of his reputation. That conclusion wasn't shared by Huddy at the time, and he will never agree with the police's findings. But the Met had spoken and 'Fleet Street' relayed that version of events to the public.

A number of newspaper headlines had his whole family seething. George Best called it incredibly indecent and insensitive and some of the worst headlines he'd ever seen. Suspicions surrounding the whole episode were heightened when Alan received regular visits from a solicitor, called in by Ann's family.

"This peculiar man came regularly, at a time when I couldn't get out of bed and couldn't walk. He said things like, 'When you walked in front of the car,' to which I'd respond 'You're not listening to me, I walked through the side street where I would call my wife to see if she wanted anything from the supermarket and crossed the road at the same place I always do. Why would this time be any different?' Then he'd keep trying to suggest that maybe I'd crossed back over to the paper stand. I told him the self same thing umpteen times but every day for a couple of weeks, he'd come in and continue with the same line of questioning hoping I'd crack and confirm the police's version of events.

"I got bloody annoyed and eventually asked him to leave. With him sacked, it really began to grate on me that he had been trying to railroad me into saying something that didn't happen. They just needed my testimony to say it was accidental and then it's 'all's well that ends well'. Why was that? It led to me thinking that the hit-and-run was a deliberate act rather than an accident, but the police steadfastly refused to interview me. Indeed, before I'd even left hospital [11 months on from the accident], they'd closed the case file. Apparently a 'lack of witnesses and CCTV evidence' meant there was no chance of apprehending the culprits and taking the matter further. I found that unbelievable.

John Westwood, a friend of Huddy's, had come forward to say he would testify to hearing a car revving up further down the road where the accident took place [and seconds before the actual accident], but once the police starting delving into his background and asking personal questions, he backed out.

The longer Alan's hospital stay continued, the less Ann was there for him in terms of support and care. Maybe that was partly to do with him not wanting to wash, shave or look at his gaunt reflection in the mirror. This was his, and therefore her, reality but clearly one she hadn't signed up for. He'd completely lost his appetite too, and Bub had to plead with him just to try the drinks that acted as a meal substitute. Uncle George at least remained a rock, bringing in clean, fresh clothes as often as possible.

On one particular day in the late autumn of 1998, Ann came into the room, which was akin to a school gymnasium, whilst Huddy was having his numb feet manipulated by a young American nurse named Rosie. Through Alan's experiences in the USA, he found that many of the young girls from that part of the world were not worldly-wise and quite naïve, and Rosie dropped right into that category. She was clearly struck by how beautiful Ann was, and told him so once she had left the room. "Don't be fooled by her beauty, she is the reason I am here," he said to an open-mouthed Rosie who gasped in disbelief. He meant it though. Uncle George, who still thought Alan was both illogical and delusional through the drugs, was also aghast. It was the same day that he'd asked his wife to sit with him on the bed and she'd refused. The fact that she was still beautiful was completely incidental to him thereafter. Beauty, after all, is only skin-deep.

Huddy was eventually well enough to get up and walk around. He'd have his physio in the mornings followed by a trip to the White Hart pub opposite to watch the horses or the football. His visitors would sometime even visit him in the bar rather than by his bedside! Eventually discharged after being told he was using the hospital 'like a hotel', one of the last things Huddy did before leaving Barts was to see a marriage guidance counsellor. It was kept quiet from both families because it was, after all, a private matter.

With him, in all respects, laid bare, Alan opened himself up to the point where he had to make a quick decision. Did he let Ann explain her strange behaviour, or put the pressure on by coming straight to the point? If you know Huddy, you'll understand that he would plump for the latter, so he just came right out and said it. "I think you're wasting everybody's time dear, she's made up her mind." Ann said almost nothing for the entire time and if there was one single moment when he absolutely knew his marriage was definitely coming to an end, that was it. Looking back, it's one of the few regrets he still has today, that he should've at least let Ann say her piece and speak her mind. It would've stopped all of the 'what if' moments that he's had since.

A THIRD LIFE

Finally back home in November 1998, Ann asked Huddy to sleep in their small spare room, which caused another almighty row. Within a few weeks, and two specific incidents, Alan finally concluded that his second marriage was effectively over. The first occasion was when he and Ann were out with Tony Davis and his wife. Tony remembers that day with complete clarity and recalled how he'd noticed how embarrassed and uncomfortable Ann appeared, because of Alan's colostomy bag, and thought to himself that the end of his friend's marriage would not be too long in coming. The very next week, Alan was shocked when seeing Ann jotting down what she'd be buying her family and friends for Christmas, and noticed his name wasn't on her list. She offered up no explanation when asked and that was the cue for him to move on again. Living back with Bub would provide the solitude and time he needed to get himself back on track.

"I was at my lowest ebb, absolutely devastated that Ann had given up on me, so I left and went back to Chelsea to start again. I was on crutches and my Uncle George was with me all of the time – as he was for the year I was in hospital. It was an incredibly tough time but because of my experiences throughout my career, it stood me in good stead whereas others might have caved in. Ann had become my toughest opponent."

Re-learning even the most basic of functions was now part of the daily grind. Walking was laborious and extremely painful, even though there was numbness in his toes. Now a frail, elderly looking man, he shuffled his way about and those who'd known him pre-accident but hadn't seen him for a while were shocked at his gaunt appearance. Using the crutches did bring one unexpected benefit though – before too long Huddy's upper body strength was returning. The sheer effort required to get from A to B saw him put his old training head back on, grit his teeth, and just get on with it. On the occasions when the pain and exhaustion got too much, George would be on hand to help Alan get about by pushing his wheelchair.

"Every day now is a chore," he told Reuters in an interview some time later. "I look at my crutches standing there by the wall and I realise that day in December 1997 has put a completely new complexion on my life. Whereas most people are ill maybe once or twice a year, it's every day for me. Getting out of bed is hard, I don't wear socks any more because I can't put them on my feet and I struggle to stand up in the shower. People don't really understand what I've been through. This is a new life of being disabled and I have had to come to terms with that and live with it. I'm not dramatising things, but my playing and training saved my life. I trained every day right up to the day when the car hit me."

By spring of 1999, Huddy felt well enough to make a pilgrimage back to the Resuscitation Room of the Royal London Hospital, something he'd been keen to do as soon as he had understood the lengths to which the doctors and nurses had gone to save his life. A genuine and heartfelt 'thank you' was the very least that he could do, but Alan was determined to do 'the right thing' and deliver his message in person.

"One of the most outstanding moments in my life was going back to the Royal London, where Dr Frank Cross showed me and Uncle George around. It was daunting, because I had read my medical report and knew this was the place where they'd wheeled me in and cut the blood-soaked clothes from my body. There was one young nurse, Rosie, in the Resuscitation Room on the day we visited, who'd been there that night and could remember the mess I was in back on December 15, 1997. Oddly enough, although I've returned to Wembley several times since that amazing performance against West Germany, it felt nothing like my return to the hospital that day. Visiting the hospital and meeting the staff was much more important to me because it was the scene of my greatest triumph: when I refused to die and fought for my life. The years of pain and mental anguish I'd suffered after missing that FA Cup final and the World Cup back in 1970 were finally extinguished and laid to rest. Thanks to the brilliant medical staff and my own resilience, I was alive and that's all that counted now. Winning that battle was truly more special and rewarding than my greatest 90 minutes on a football pitch.

"I had words with this young lady and asked if she could get hold of the ambulance crew who'd scooped me off the pavement in Mile End and taken me to the place where my life was saved. I then walked around in a daze, reliving the experience in my mind, with the young nurse looking me up and down in disbelief – which seemed to be the order of the day. Frank Cross talked me through what went on from the moment they wheeled me in. We visited the Intensive Trauma Unit – the place where I spent 59 days – and it was eerie in there. If only because of knowing the amount of people that had been so poorly whilst being treated by the amazing doctors and nurses. Rosie was absolutely delighted to see me, and she made it very clear after questioning me about my visit that 'nobody ever comes back.' I replied that I had come back to thank her, and that I was going to write a book. I had wanted to get the feel for the place, which I most certainly did.

"However, I made it very clear I was also there to thank everyone else who helped me and my family through such a difficult time. As I stood there on my crutches talking to her, a crowd was slowly gathering along the corridor as word had spread. They were looking me up and down like I was a ghost, something I definitely resembled back when I was in there, going down to six stone from my post-football weight of thirteen and a half. Before I left, I asked her about the machine that Dr Goodier used to save my legs, an unused sample left by a medical rep. 'Can I buy one and donate it to the ITU?' I asked but she said, without any hesitation, 'Alan, after what you have been through you should enjoy every penny you have because you should not be here.' It was lovely to hear, but a little disappointing because I was hoping that The Alan Hudson C-Clamp Machine might save another poor soul."

Part of Huddy's routine in the earliest days after his hospital stay would be to go back to Bart's for regular treatment, designed to keep him as well as could be expected, given the extent of his problems. The monotony was necessary, but soul destroying at times. So in order to keep his spirits up and help him get back on his feet again, metaphorically speaking, his friend Terry Shepherd organised a function to raise some much-needed funds. It was a fitting tribute to the high regard in which Alan was held, as the function was a sell-out. In actual fact, it could've been sold out three or four times over. Those that didn't manage to get tickets, still made a donation into the kitty, swelling the coffers nicely.

As so often happens at such events, the booze flowed as well as the conversation but when David Goodier, Huddy's surgeon, got up to speak later in the evening, there was a respectful and immediate silence. In great detail, Dr Goodier recounted his memories of the time that Huddy had spent under his care. You could hear a pin drop, and the only noise came from the sniffles of those that had been reduced to tears by the oration. It brought into sharp focus to all those present, the lengths that the hospital staff had gone to, to keep him alive, and the true extent of Alan's own personal survival battle. It seemed inconceivable he could still be of this world after taking such a physical battering.

After 20 silent minutes, save for that one lone, authoritative voice that filled the room, everyone rose in unison to give a well-deserved and extended standing ovation and round of applause. The auction planned for later could only be a success after hearing such a speech, and so it proved. By that time, Dr Goodier had already slipped away, keen not to take any focus away from the recipient of the benefit. Huddy remains eternally grateful that, despite his incredibly busy schedule, Dr Goodier still made time to attend and speak so eloquently.

"It was after that speech that I was approached by Bernard Clarke, Terry's brief, and he asked if he could represent me. We were at the QC's office at the back of Blackfriars, where all the bigwigs work, and a certain Mr Badenoch, a relation to David Badenoch my urologist, asked me, 'What have you done to upset the police so much? I have never seen a case where the victim has been so victimised.' I replied that I'd had a falling out in Bow Police Station one evening over a domestic, when Ann locked me out of our house. She told the police that I didn't live there and they locked me up in for the night. I called them every name under the sun and that was where the rift with the Old Bill began. I asked Badenoch if I could take a case against the police and, at the very least, get them to open a hit-and-run case file, but he told me that I didn't have a cat in hell's chance.

"This led to the most crucial part of my recovery, as I knew that I had one hell of a fight on my hands. I used the decision of not being able to get justice – as I saw it – as my target. I fought every day, training as hard as ever before, even though I was in my wheelchair a lot of the time. I used the hurt that I felt at the police, and what I saw as Ann's betrayal of me, as my inspiration. What they say about triumph over adversity definitely works with me, and it helped me get through this period. George was throwing medicine balls at me a couple of thousand times a day as I did my sit-ups, which led to my colostomy bag getting completely out of order. After a call to the hospital, Frank Cross arrived at my side and he gave me an almighty bollocking saying, 'Alan, how long has it been like this, why didn't you let me know?' He got on the phone immediately to Professor Williams, the brains behind the reversal called The Gracilis Neosphincter Operation. This was a four-part operation over 18 months which was, although daunting, quite phenomenal.

"Frank put down the phone and said, 'I've got you an appointment to see the professor at the Royal London, he is fantastic.' Within a few weeks, George, my physiotherapist Claire and I were in Professor Williams' office, surrounded by several young doctors and nurses. He asked if it was okay if they stayed which of course was fine by me.

"Swinging from side-to-side in his chair, he said 'Alan, I hear you're pretty gung-ho about this operation,' to which I replied, 'If you ask my uncle George and Claire they'll tell you that I'm pretty gung-ho about life itself.' We locked eyes, and it was then that I knew he was my man. He reminded me so much of Tony Waddington, quietly efficient with such amazing confidence. That was what impressed me and he did not let me down."

Although this new life was far from enjoyable, Huddy had, after much soul searching and the support of his close family, got around to accepting his lot. Being wheelchair bound or on crutches and dealing with leaking colostomy bags took a heavy mental toll though. Legs that had previously been the tools of his profession were now nothing more than a painful inconvenience. As a result, many was the time when, for no apparent reason, his manner would be brusque at best. Those who didn't know him well enough rightly took exception to his sharp tongue, even if his ire was somewhat understandable. Surviving as opposed to living was another kick in the teeth for him without doubt, but he needed to move forward.

Although he had several serious medical problems, Alan's drop foot became his greatest adversary. Out cold for eight-

and-a-half-weeks in ITU, with no movement in his feet and toes, eventually both his feet 'dropped'. It led to him clipping the floor on his travels, especially if there was an uneven paving stone. He'd go flying and, predictably, many passers-by assumed it was an alcohol-related problem, yet the truth was that Alan couldn't get up due a lack of strength and balance. All the things he had as a player had now gone missing.

"The one outstanding memory I have of being in my wheelchair was one Sunday lunchtime when I was a patient at Barts and my cousin Anthony [Uncle George's son] and I went to the pub across the road. As I sat there I said to myself, 'Today's the day to get out of this chair,' and waited for Anthony to go to the gents. Once he did, I held onto the rim of the bar and pulled myself out of that contraption. I called the barman who looked at me in amazement. 'Give me a large Jack Daniels and ginger ale, please mate,' I said, and the people on a table in the corner all gave me a round of applause. I didn't know that they were there otherwise I'd have got a round of drinks in, but it was uplifting! Anthony came back out and his face was a picture. Times like that were few and far between but it gave me the impetus to keep going."

Some 18 months after leaving hospital, in mid-2000, he was hit for six again, although this time it wouldn't be a car that would do the damage. Bub had begun to feel unwell with an illness that just wouldn't pass. Having been invited by Eddie McCreadie for a break in the US, Huddy knew this was just what he needed but, at the same time was unhappy to leave Bub when she was so under the weather. With Julie and others around to convince him that they'd be able to look after her, he took some much-needed leave but would be devastated upon his return.

"I had a fantastic break with Eddie in Tennessee. He's a very, very dear friend, and a man I'd loved since my days as a schoolboy at the Bridge. The best left-back in the world at the time, he looked after me in those days. I spent a fortnight with him and his wife Linda, which was wonderful after my hospital experience, but when I arrived back at my mum's there were a few people in the flat, and it was clear that all wasn't well.

"I was still upbeat and on such a high that I never fully appreciated the gravitas of the situation at the time. Even when Julie called me into the corridor outside the flat and told me in a roundabout way that Bub had cancer, it really didn't sink in at that moment. I didn't want to believe it."

The blow of Bub's cancer affected the whole family and despite their natural closeness, the Hudsons were often at odds with each other, unable to deal with seeing Bub wasting away before their eyes. Her refusal of any treatment, coupled with Alan's own medical concerns, made a difficult situation almost unbearable. His last words to his mum were, "You have to fight this thing," but even in her – by now, gravely ill – state, she wouldn't buckle. "Alan, I'm not as strong as you. What you went through in hospital was extraordinary, but I'm just not like you." The words are as crystal clear in his mind now as they were when Bub spoke them back in 2003.

Huddy was still living with his mum when she died and, as part of the healing process, he redecorated her flat shortly afterwards, with Allen helping to lay wooden floors. Although still distraught at losing his mother, the process certainly helped, but a phone call from the council, informing Alan that he was required to vacate the flat, soon changed the mood completely. One might have expected that the family would be allowed to grieve in peace and quiet and Huddy allowed to get on with his life, but that notion was shattered when he was advised that because his name wasn't on the rent book, he was for all intents and purposes living there illegally. Even his perfectly reasonable argument that he couldn't possibly ask his mum to have changed the details while she was dying fell on deaf ears. Needless to say, he was livid and went berserk at the head of the council's housing department.

The manner in which he'd taken the council to task may have contributed to their refusing to allow him to stay there, with Allen as his carer. Allen had been technically homeless for some while too, calling in favours from friends or family and moving from one room to another, so living in Bub's flat not only meant that it could potentially be kept in the family but that father and son could spend time in each other's company – even if the reason for doing so was tragic and not what they would have wanted. Huddy was in pretty dire need of a carer at that time too, but the council wouldn't budge. With very few realistic options open to him, Alan moved back to Stoke and over the next couple of years he endured a pitiful existence of a series of short-term lodgings with friends, acquaintances and, if truth be known, anyone who'd take him in.

"Bub's funeral and the weeks after went by in something of a blur, because I was having to face up to life without my mum and then without our home. My head was spinning and I was all over the place. Although I thought I could cope like I always did, this was, like the accident, one of the most painful and trying times of my life. I had to get away – and stay away."

However difficult things had become for him on a day-to-day basis, at least he had a life. Long-time friend George Best wouldn't be so lucky because in 2005, he would lose his own personal battle with the booze, something that affected Alan deeply, perhaps because there were many parallels that could be drawn between his life and Best's.

"I was back in London for a bit, and in a bar in Knightsbridge with Tommy Nicholson when a newspaper was handed to us with the headline that George had been rushed into the Cromwell Hospital, which was just a mile away. I'd seen George a few weeks before in the Phene Arms and, with a glass of wine in his hand, he'd asked me, 'Huddy, do I look alright? Everyone keeps telling me I look off colour, I'm looking yellow, but I feel great.' Although he did look a bit off colour, he said he felt fine so I just told him to look after himself. Now that he was in hospital, however, I knew I had to go and see him.

"Tom, I'm going first thing in the morning," I said and even though he suggested that Bestie had never visited me once whilst I was in hospital, I knew I'd regret it if I didn't go. Anyway, 'two wrongs don't make a right'. The following day, I arrived at the hospital with my friend Malcolm and we were advised by the receptionist that George wasn't up to seeing any visitors. I asked that a message be passed to him saying I'd come to wish him well. Shortly afterwards, George's consultant, Dr Hughes appeared. 'Alan, George will give you a couple of minutes, come on,' and we walked through to his room.

"His girlfriend, Alex was there and he was sitting in the corner chair, wearing a pair of pyjamas and looking petrified. What hit me was the thought that I'd been on the field with his genius and out in his night clubs in Manchester, and now he looked like any ordinary 'lost soul'. 'George,' I said, 'I'll only be five minutes, but I must tell you two things. Firstly, this is going to be a long-haul so write a book, not like the rest of your books which were ghost-written but the true story about George Best – your true feelings, pulling no punches. And secondly, I come here today not just for myself, but for everyone in Chelsea who loves you.' I hugged him goodbye with a tear in my eye. The best player I'd ever played against, and one of the best men I'd ever known, had been reduced to a pitiful sight.

"George and I had a very special relationship. We never had each other's number and never invaded each other's privacy but would always find a way to get in contact with the other when needed. He once turned up at a book launch of mine in

A THIRD LIFE

Knightsbridge and was sitting on our table with my son Allen and his son Calum, when the television cameras approached us. In a flash I moved his glass next to mine, out of the way. Later Calum said to Allen, 'Did you see what your father's just done?' and Al replied. 'Yeah, because he loves your dad and won't have the cameras take liberties.' That was something I would never let happen – Best was the best! To be close friends with the greatest player on the planet was quite something."

When George finally passed, it gave Huddy a chance to reflect some more. Though he was often melancholic, there was never a thought of the drink being tossed aside. It was then, as it had always been, a crutch to help him through and his way of dealing with the trials and tribulations of life. If Best's death did anything at all, it perhaps made him occasionally more cautious, but nothing more than that.

Alan eventually received an insurance pay-out from the hit-and-run and wanted to use the funds to buy a place in Tampa Bay but, having been let down on that deal and knowing that Alan wanted to invest in a business in a country with a warm climate, his friend Tony Davis put Alan in contact with Dogan Arif, part of the Arif criminal family which terrorised south London with their drug trafficking business in the 1980s but known to Huddy through his involvement with Fisher Athletic. Arif owned a hotel in Famagusta in the Turkish controlled northern part of Cyprus, which Alan knew well from Stoke's tour to the island in 1975-76. Excited by the prospect of earning a living through investing his £100,000 pay-out in a hotel project, Alan moved to Cyprus in 2005, expecting a large return on his money at a later date.

"After three years spent on the island, he wanted to return home and the expectation was that he would do so with a decent wedge in his pocket. However, the collapse of the Cypriot property market and the world financial crisis, meant it was yet another disastrous piece of business for Alan, and he ended up losing virtually all of what he'd put in. He now had no choice but to go back to his old friends, cap-in-hand, in and around the Stoke area.

The next few years in Stoke were a breath of fresh air with no real drama to speak of. Occasional troubles aside, that period was amongst the most normal of his life. On May 14, 2010, he received a call from Allen to tell him he was a grandad and the feeling of holding his granddaughter, Stevie-Marie, in his arms for the first time is something that will never leave him.

"It was just like any other day in the Potteries as I stood in the Staff of Life pub, run by my friend Terry Bate, with my then girlfriend Diane, who we knew as Dusty, Terry and Alan Connolly. I was having a drink whilst waiting for Allen's call before boarding the train to London when *I Gotta Feeling* by the Black Eyed Peas started playing. The words still make me tingle whenever I hear that song because as it played in Terry's pub, my mobile rang and it was Allen to tell me that little Stevie-Marie had arrived safe and well, and it was still playing when Terry handed me a bottle of Jack Daniels to celebrate!

"Twelve months later, I remember Allen bringing Stevie-Marie up to Stoke to celebrate her first birthday and it coinciding with Stoke's first ever FA Cup final appearance, against Manchester City. We were at The Grapes pub, where I was living at the time, and there was a big Stoke-themed party. In my speech before the game I had a huge smile on my face when I said, looking at my granddaughter who was wearing a red and white striped shirt, 'It's taken Stoke 100 years to reach their first final but Stevie-Marie's made it after just 12 months – a typical Hudson!"

Whilst being thrilled with the birth of his granddaughter, Alan experienced a totally opposite emotion on an earlier jaunt down to London to see his friends and celebrate the opening of

A THIRD LIFE

Tommy Nicholson's new pub in the Barbican. Huddy bowled in with Tommy Wisbey, one of the Great Train Robbers, and was really enjoying the party when, up at the bar, something had clearly caught 'Tommy Nick's' attention – his gaze averting from the conversation he was sharing with Alan. As Alan turned around, his expression changed, as if he'd seen a ghost, because sitting by the bar with a friend was Ann. She began to say 'Hello' but Alan was already out of the door, with Wisbey mouthing his apologies to the host as he followed Huddy to a nearby pub. Clearly shaken, Alan explained to his bemused friend why he'd made such a sharp exit and it proved to be the last time he saw or heard from Ann, who he understands is now living overseas.

Alan's life changed again in 2012 when he fell out with the owners of The Grapes in Stoke and, having exhausted the goodwill of those he knew in the area, decided to move back down to London and in with Allen and Stevie-Marie. The three of them in a Wood Green studio flat was a recipe for disaster, and a big falling-out was inevitable. Things came to a head after a few months when Allen, who'd been struggling with his own depression and various mental health issues, flipped out. It meant that Dad was on his travels again.

"I had to leave and so went looking for other premises, but Kensington and Chelsea Council told me I would have to stay in a hostel. Great, eh?! I was still broke but getting my disability allowance and my pension from my Stoke City days helped me get by."

Despite many reservations, there wasn't a whole lot Alan could do to remedy his circumstances. So a £9-a-week hostel would, like it or not, become his new home. It was whilst here too that he was regularly 'papped' by the tabloid press when struggling up the stairs to the front door on his crutches. The sensationalist headlines appeared to glorify and take some satisfaction in the fact that Huddy was now at 'rock bottom'. One thing was certain – it was an almighty comedown for someone who was once a darling of Fleet Street.

The *Daily Mail* gave him the time of day in a 2013 interview which began by describing his surroundings. 'It's less than a four-minute walk from Notting Hill Gate station, down Pembridge Gardens with its oak trees and Georgian Terraces. It's a nice street lined with expensive cars. But there are six steps out front with no handrail. For Hudson, it's a prison. "I can't complain too much about it because it's only £9 a week, but it's tough," he says. "When I got there, I was given all these rules. I can't bring anyone back, not even my son. You wouldn't want to bring anyone back. It's a small room. It has a toilet that I can't really sit on because of my legs, a shower and a single bed. It feels like a prison sometimes. It can take me five minutes to get up and down them [steps] and I have to – because I can't stay in there all day.' Usually that means trips to the pub. Hudson isn't sure if he's dependant on alcohol or not, but he has a drink most days. "I need a drink and a sleeping tablet if I'm going to get any sleep," he says.'

It was around the time of that interview – and another for the *Daily Mirror* – that Alan had an operation to deal with his one remaining dropped foot, which he'd struggled with for years. Getting up and down those stairs was far too problematic, as was walking for anything other than a short distance up the road. Perhaps most galling of all was that he wasn't even able to dress himself properly because of the problem and so, by inserting two pins into the foot and 'pulling it up,' the hope was that it would alleviate his symptoms to some degree.

Huddy was moved on to Hesketh Place, Holland Park, where he stayed for a short time before a chap at the council called Alan Erikson eventually persuaded his colleagues to accept Huddy's pleas of disability and of wanting to be near his

A THIRD LIFE

family. Within a few weeks, he was back in the World's End estate, a stone's throw from his sister Julie. He's still there today living what he often refers to as his 'third life'. Childhood and Chelsea was his first, with Stoke manager Tony Waddington 'resurrecting' him professionally for his second. Post-accident is his third.

"My previous lives have gone now. I have to forget what I used to do. I can't put my tracksuit on and go running any more. When I have a party with my friends every year on December 15, they say 'Why are you celebrating the anniversary of your accident,' and I reply, 'I'm celebrating still being here.'"

12

Keep Moving Forward

"He's never changed. Not a bit. Not since the very first day I met him. Given his story, that's very rare and makes him all the more special in my eyes."
Bobby McDonald

In many respects, things have turned full circle for Huddy. In 2017 he still lives on the World's End estate in Chelsea, no more than 10 minutes walk from the prefab where he was born in Elm Park Gardens, and close to the house on The Embankment where he'd lived with his mum, post-accident, until her death in 2003. Seven red brick tower blocks, with smaller interconnecting low-rise flats, remain an imposing and antiquated vista from the River Thames. Situated at the fag-end of the King's Road, the area is very different to Huddy's formative years. Back then, almost all of the families were locals but now the damp-stained rooms are mostly filled with a mixture of immigrants from all around the world.

There's no issue at all concerning the multi-cultural nature of the place, but as many of his neighbours don't speak fluent English, and have differing cultural norms, it's a challenge to build close relationships with them beyond a nod and the occasional 'hello'. Furthermore, World's End is home to many with serious personal issues, such as drug addiction, mental health issues and long-term unemployment. It's a town within a town, if you will, where those that appear to struggle with everyday life are thrown together and left to get on with it.

Broken glass is scattered on the floor and a pungent whiff of marijuana greets you as you make your way in and through the estate. Stereos play anything from reggae and roots to hard-core techno, mostly to drown out the raised voices from one of the many troubled tenants who live here. The concentration of people in this relatively small area is as high as anywhere for miles around and where once the area was somewhere you could leave your doors unlocked, knowing every soul who passed by your door, now it's a place where kids – and even some adults – can't be left alone.

You can see the Thames from Huddy's window. Open his front door, look left, and there is Edith Grove, where the Rolling Stones were thrown out of their digs in the '60s. Turn your head a little more and 100 yards away at 488 King's Road is where the famous 'Granny Takes a Trip' boutique once existed. It's now home to Rocco Borghese and its bespoke Italian chandeliers, which is more than a little out of place being in such close proximity to an estate where it's not just granny taking a trip. They are reminders of happier times which Alan occasionally visits as he allows his mind to wander.

He has the advantage of being something of a local 'celebrity' – if such a thing exists – and that goes some way to explaining why he's left alone to go about his daily business. That and the fact that he still knows enough characters who've 'got his back'. Tony Millard, who went to Seattle with him two and a half years ago, Peter May, brother of his best mate Leslie who died so tragically young, and Huddy are the three most successful people to come out of World's End, so it stands to reason why the trio would still be popular.

HUDDY

His first school, Park Walk, is a corner kick away from his flat, and despite the changing face of the current populace, this is still very definitely his manor: his home. Stoke may have been a welcoming and warm bolthole for some time, but this is the area that he knows like the back of his hand, having grown up in this part of London. Although there have been considerable architectural changes, it's still possible to appreciate certain parts, and the Victorian-era Park Walk itself rises beautifully in between the rows of bland and unkempt terraced houses.

At the other end of the spectrum, just half a mile away, is the Chelsea known to the world, with its 'high net worth' business-leaders, media and entertainment stars, influential politicians, and the families of the fabulously rich – many from dubious means – from around the world, who've made London their home. This totally different part of the local population can be found towards Sloane Square, and the contrast between the 'haves' and the 'have nots' is far more stark now than when Alan Hudson was born in 1951, and would shock many who see Chelsea as the epitome of affluence and excess. They may share the same borough, and the postcodes of World's End and Sloane Square may be similar, but the standard of living, life chances and social mobility of the two parts of Chelsea most certainly aren't.

Huddy has no desire to mix with the Russian oligarchs and the other *nouveaux riche* who throng to the juice bars, exclusive jewellers, artisan delis and antique shops. No, they're not his cup of tea – or his vodka and orange – at all. He'd rather be amongst 'his own'. That's why he enjoys spending his days in Riley's, a local pub a few minutes from his front door. Full of fiercely proud working-class patrons, most of whom have known each other for years, it's true that the pub has seen better days, but a lick of paint and some new furniture couldn't make the place any more welcoming. Huddy feels at ease there and, safe and valued in his 'home from home', his mind often wanders to memories of old friends who meant so much to him.

"I used to regularly visit Ilene May, Leslie's mother, after he'd passed away. She lived right above Riley's and was devastated when she lost her son, who was in his early 30s when he died. She broke down one morning, telling me about the day she realised that Leslie was terminally ill and was most definitely dying. She said, 'I'd look up the stairs every morning and didn't recognise him, Alan, he'd turned green.' I knew Leslie's illness and death had killed her too. She simply couldn't live without her Leslie. I sometimes sit in Riley's, looking up towards her old flat and I can feel the tears in my eyes."

If one should happen to be in there on a Chelsea match day, it's wall-to-wall with Blues fans of all ages – proper football folk who know their stuff. Huddy's photo adorns the left-hand side of the bar and as you walk in you can't miss it. There he is in his '70s pomp, decked out in the royal blue and smiling broadly, alongside his friend Peter Osgood. Many is the time that new customers have entered and pointed in reverence at the picture, only to later scan the room and find one half of the duo propping up the bar. Suffice to say that Alan is never short of a drink or two in there, nor a drinking partner. Complete strangers still want to talk about the 'good old days', and regale to anyone who cares to listen just what a player he was. Even if the narrative has been heard hundreds of times before, he respectfully doesn't show any sign of boredom. In any event, such complimentary verbosity can never get old, and the sentiments – plus the alcohol – have always been appreciated.

But, these people are not his friends. They haven't drunk with him for years. They haven't seen him at his very worst. They haven't been there to 'cock-a-deaf-un' at his vicious tirades. They don't really know him at all. Those that do are held very dear indeed. Close pals that keep their own counsel, rather than rushing to make a quick pound or two from the press when Huddy goes off the rails again. Like many pubs, the customers at Riley's are made up of a random cross-section of society. They may be those on the way home from work, or men and women for whom employment is just a pipe-dream, those who like a tipple whilst studying the racing form, or hard-core boozers mixing with a few of life's oddballs.

In Riley's, they tell it exactly as it is, and that's something Alan can not only relate to, but also appreciates, because it's the same straight bat he's always played himself. It's a venue where the landlord and regulars look after their own, and it goes some way to explaining why he feels comfortable there. The convenience factor of Riley's being almost on his doorstep has to be taken into account too. There are other boozers he could frequent but, unless there's a chaperone that can drive him there, there's little point. Vodka and orange is still vodka and orange wherever it's served, after all.

"Riley's is run by Liam, a very decent man, who took over from Richard 'The Irishman' – who now runs the Pride of Pimlico – and like me, going to Stoke City from the bright lights of London, Liam has had to adapt to the whims of all of the regulars. The resident barman is Kevin, who is a bit close to the mark sometimes with the customers but, again, is thoroughly honourable and decent at heart. My young niece, Georgia, works behind the bar. She's the star of the Hudson family, the girl who was born on the day of Bill's death, never being able to know a man who'd have adored her. Georgia is smart, attractive and has that trademark Hudson smile: genuine and warm. She's the shining light in the pub, but I'm biased of course, aren't I?

"One of the regulars here is 'Bubbles'. He's a Chelsea fanatic and was a big part of the 'Chelsea Revolution' in The Shed.

KEEP MOVING FORWARD

His love for the club continues and that's why he and I have such good banter in Riley's – because we're both equally as passionate about the club, but our views are the polar opposite of each other. Possibly the most knowledgeable football man in the pub is Gary Condon, brother of Billy, Riley's window cleaner. David Nava is a well-known character in the area and when we're all in full flow, strangers beware! It's great fun though and the banter is relentless and unforgiving.

"Riley's is a focal point for Chelsea fans on match days. I've got all the time in the world for the fans, but not the club and can't bring myself to watch if the game's on the TV in there. I still feel they 'turned me over' in 1974 – and that goes for Peter Osgood too – but I have to find a way to deal with that anger and use it positively, like I did after the accident. The anger drove me hard and helped me to fight death and recover from my injuries.

"Up the road is another pub, The Chelsea Potter, which could have been named after me! My move to Stoke had more effect on me than any other, because of my admiration for Tony Waddington and for the honesty of the area ... believe it or not, I have more close friends there than here in Chelsea. They've supported me, and still do. I'm treated like royalty there. I don't play on it, I simply embrace it because I earned the respect by playing consistently well for my boss and those fans, who certainly knew their football. My time there these days is limited, but I always look forward to seeing those lovely people who lived what was so nearly a 'dream come true', until that roof blew off!"

Bobby McDonald, an old friend of Huddy's and a regular in Riley's, comments that if there's one thing guaranteed to annoy Alan's friends in the pub, it's the way the general public are conned into believing the bile regularly spewed out by the tabloids, even if Alan has become indifferent to it by now. The stories printed about him are as far removed from the man they know as it's possible to get. Alan's no angel of course, but the side of him that only his inner circle get to see isn't going to sell paper's is it?

"I've known Alan since he was 12 years old, when he lived in the prefab. He's a good man, from a good family and he's a very kind bloke who takes care of his friends – even now. People come in here and get a pint for him and then they lurk around him. Al's very popular and we still get people coming down from Stoke to come and see him. Nice people. He always buys them a drink because they've taken the trouble to come and see him, and because that's what he does. He's a very generous man and he always has been.

"My favourite memory of him goes way back to when we were playing football in 'the cage'. It was like a bomb site but the way that he and his brother John stroked the ball around was amazing. When he went to Chelsea it was just like watching him playing against us on the broken, pot-holed concrete – he was that good. If he was playing today he'd be on £250,000 a week, no danger. Playing against Best and with Osgood, Charlie Cooke and all of that era ... with the talent he had, it was very sad what happened.

"He's always drank in here – and a few other locals! – but he's never changed. Not a bit. Not since the very first day I met him. Given his story, that's very rare and makes him all the more special in my eyes. He's had a chequered history and I thought he was going to snuff it back in 1997, I really did. I visited him in hospital at lot ... it was terrible. How he's still alive today, seriously, I've got no idea. After everything he's been through, it baffles me. But I'm delighted he's still here. He's so resilient and is such a lovely man with a heart of gold."

If you knew Bobby McDonald, a 'face' back in his day and not a chap to be messed with, you'll understand that he's not given to speaking with such genuine warmth. But he means every word of his eulogy of Alan, and it isn't rose-tinted in any way. Another from the school of hard knocks who gives it to you straight with no flannel, Bobby's recollection is honest and endearing.

It's not really a surprise either, to hear that he isn't alone when it comes to describing the character of someone who many still believe is one of football's 'bad boys'. For all of Huddy's faults, he remains someone that can look at himself in the mirror at the end of each day, and that's incredibly important to him.

His sister Julie won't have a bad word said about him. "I love Alan to bits but I could be a better sister. I don't see him enough – even though we only live two minutes from each other – because I've got an autistic son and look after loads of other kids in the area. But if I need anyone, Alan would do anything for me, absolutely. About two weeks before the accident, Alan and I had a big falling out. He was with his friend Malcolm, talking about footballers and how much they earn nowadays. Because I'm so much like him and love putting my two bob's worth in, I said – whilst looking directly at Alan; 'Footballers! You're all tossers. But doctors and nurses, now they're worth every ...' but before I could finish, he'd cut me dead.

"How ironic that two weeks later, the very people I'd been praising would be saving his life! He must have remembered that row because when he first came out of the coma, his first words to me were, 'I don't want to speak to you, you've got too much to say for yourself.' That situation didn't last long of course! When he came home after the accident he was a totally different person, and even more straightforward than before. He doesn't give a monkey's and won't suffer fools gladly. He just says it as he sees it and a lot of people can't deal with that. Obviously the media like to portray Al in a certain light, of course they do – and they'll always do that to him. Even if he just minds his own business it doesn't matter because, like George Best, they think he's out on the piss all the time. He does like a tipple – who doesn't? – and he might have a lot of things going on, but he just gets on with his life. I've been to lovely places with him, met people I would never have met otherwise, and we've got closer as we've got older. I just love him."

Allen has had his fair share of ups and downs with his dad too, but they remain as close as a father and son could be. That not only says a lot about the Hudsons as a family, but also about a side of his personality that almost everyone outside his close friends and family has no idea about. You can have a stand-up row with him but 10 minutes later he'll have shaken your hand and moved on. It's a trait that has enabled him to regularly patch up his relationship with Allen when, frankly, their paths should have separated long ago. Their love for each other remains strong and obvious, even if Allen still harbours regret as to how their lives panned out.

"I live with my mum [Maureen] now, renting a room from her whilst trying to build a house in her garden. We're a strange old family alright, but a strong family. I know every family is odd in their own way but we seem to tip the scales! I'm exactly like my dad and we're like best mates. He rings me every day – about 10 times! Dad's very honest and so am I, but some of his traits aren't the greatest. People don't like straight talkers and he's never had a problem with telling the truth – as he sees it – and what he thinks.

"I also think he played football honestly. The old man had a great career and though many in the game knew what sort of person he was, they also knew what a genius he was on the pitch. A captain and a leader of his teams without wearing the armband. What a shame that England football supporters never really saw the best of him, apart from that Germany game at Wembley. Imagine if 24-hour sports channels were around then, they'd be talking about him across the world. George Best and I got quite close, and he would never leave without saying what a great man my dad was, and that he was the best midfielder he'd ever played against. He didn't need to do that.

"His close friends still like him because he is authentic, but then you've got the other 99% of people who don't want him in their company, because they're worried he'll say something that will totally embarrass them. I love the fact that he's not – and never has been – worried by what people think of him or been led by money or fame. He is still real and true to himself.

"If I've one regret, it's that people don't talk to me unless they've known me for years. People don't see me as me, they only see me as Alan's son. No one ever says, 'How are you?' It's always, 'How's your dad?' I sometimes wonder if anyone is ever going to ask how I am. I'm not really that self-centred but it grates. A few years back, Dean Moore [Bobby Moore's son], Calum Best and I started writing a book from the sons' point of view - because I don't believe people know what it's like – but it didn't work out. Dean couldn't open up about his experiences and became an alcoholic – as did I – but he sadly died in 2011, and I was the last person he spoke to. Having a famous old man can cause a lot of problems.

"I definitely felt under pressure every day, football-wise too. I was always going to be compared to Dad but was never going to be as good as him. I was decent, don't get me wrong. I had some of his genes and I could play, but I could also lash out a bit, and my granddad didn't like it at all. It was the frustration of never being good enough and even if I'd proved myself, playing-wise, I still had to prove that I wasn't like him, personality-wise.

"As for the press, it's like they've got no one else to write about sometimes. Out in the US, they celebrate their best but in the UK they're all villains. The media aren't happy unless they're slagging someone off. When that picture of Dad came out, with him on crutches, he was homeless and living with me and was wearing a pair of white tracksuit bottoms I'd given him. It really hurt me."

After all he's been though, it's clear that Huddy is now able to live his life without regrets. Bitterness? Yes, there's plenty of that, and the way certain things eat away at him will never leave him. But regrets? Never in a million years: *My Way* could have been written just for Huddy.

Close family, good friends, his integrity and the fire of injustice are the key elements of Alan's life these days. Strip away some of that cantankerous façade, and let go of those things that he's still bitter about – and held onto for nigh on 40 years now – and he might enjoy a more peaceful existence, it's true. But he'd lose some of his identity in the process and no one wants that. They just want the Huddy they know, love and respect. After all, his is a life that has *always* been defined by rallying against adversity in all of its forms, and so he's hardly likely to stop fighting now.

Though the pain will never leave him, Alan now uses it as a positive force that will guide him for the rest of his life because, for the time he has left – however long that may be – Alan Hudson has made a promise to himself: to keep moving forward and to never look back.